THE LYRIC VOICE IN ENGLISH THEOLOGY

T&T Clark Studies in English Theology

Series editors
Karen Kilby
Mike Higton
Stephen R. Holmes

THE LYRIC VOICE IN ENGLISH THEOLOGY

Elizabeth S. Dodd

LONDON • NEW YORK • OXFORD • NEW DELHI • SYDNEY

T&T CLARK
Bloomsbury Publishing Plc
50 Bedford Square, London, WC1B 3DP, UK
1385 Broadway, New York, NY 10018, USA
29 Earlsfort Terrace, Dublin 2, Ireland

BLOOMSBURY, T&T CLARK and the T&T Clark logo are trademarks
of Bloomsbury Publishing Plc

First published in Great Britain 2023
Paperback edition published 2025

Copyright © Elizabeth S. Dodd, 2023

Elizabeth S. Dodd has asserted her right under the Copyright, Designs and
Patents Act, 1988, to be identified as Author of this work.

For legal purposes the Acknowledgements on pp. viii–ix constitute
an extension of this copyright page.

Cover image: clairevis/iStock

All rights reserved. No part of this publication may be reproduced or
transmitted in any form or by any means, electronic or mechanical,
including photocopying, recording, or any information storage or retrieval system,
without prior permission in writing from the publishers.

Bloomsbury Publishing Plc does not have any control over, or responsibility for,
any third-party websites referred to or in this book. All internet addresses
given in this book were correct at the time of going to press. The author and publisher
regret any inconvenience caused if addresses have changed or sites have ceased
to exist, but can accept no responsibility for any such changes.

A catalogue record for this book is available from the British Library.

A catalog record for this book is available from the Library of Congress.

ISBN:	HB:	978-0-5676-7030-4
	PB:	978-0-5677-1313-1
	ePDF:	978-0-5676-7031-1
	eBook:	978-0-5676-7032-8

Series: T&T Clark Studies in English Theology

Typeset by Integra Software Services Pvt. Ltd.

To find out more about our authors and books visit www.bloomsbury.com
and sign up for our newsletters.

For George, Nathaniel, Jonah and Grace

CONTENTS

Acknowledgements	viii
List of Abbreviations	x
INTRODUCTION: LYRIC THEOLOGY, LYRIC THEORY AND ENGLISH LYRIC TRADITION	1
Chapter 1 MELOS OR BABBLE – LYRIC BEAUTY AND THE SPIRIT OF PENTECOST	31
Chapter 2 'O!' LYRIC ADDRESS AND PRAYER IN THE SPIRIT	65
Chapter 3 THE VOICE OF THE LORD – THE PROPHETIC SPIRIT IN THE LYRIC 'I'	95
Chapter 4 THE SOUND OF THE WIND – FRAGMENTATION AND ABUNDANCE IN THE POETIC LINE	125
EPILOGUE: THE LYRIC VOICE IN ENGLISH THEOLOGY	155
Works Cited	163
Index	180
Index of Bible Verses	184

ACKNOWLEDGEMENTS

Thanks are due to colleagues and students in the learning community at Sarum College, especially in the Centre for Formation in Ministry and the MA in Theology, Imagination and Culture, to colleagues in the wider South Central TEI and Winchester University, and to participants in the study days on Poetry and Spiritual Practice. Also to colleagues in the Oxford Centre for Religion and Culture, especially its directors during my time, Nicholas Wood and Anthony Reddie, and all the participants in the lecture series on Theology, Poetry and Theopoetics, and Poetry and Culture in Crisis. I have benefited immensely from the wisdom of compatriots in the Society for the Study of Theology and in the Grove Doctrine group, and from stimulating conversations at the American Academy of Religion, the George Herbert Society, the International Society for Religion, Literature and Culture, the Thomas Traherne Society and the Vaughan Association.

Deep apologies go to anyone who has been missed from the following list, which is far from exhaustive. I am grateful to conversations with many people over the years, including, among others: Nicholas Adams, Robert Beckford, Naoma Billingsley, Jacob Blevins, David Brown, Paul Burden, Mark S. Burrows, David Clough, Ash Cocksworth, Hilary Davies, Sean Oliver Dee, Paul Fiddes, David Ford, Thomas Gardner, Colin Greene, Malcolm Guite, Simon Jackson, David Jasper, L. Callid Keefe-Perry, David Mahan, Rachel Mann, Eleanor McClauchlan, Brother Patrick Moore, Louise Nelstrop, Karen O'Donnell, Barnabas Palfrey, Ben Quash, Christopher Southgate, James Steven, Joseph Sterrett, Michael Symmons Roberts, Andrew Taylor, Susannah Ticciati, Carol Tomlin, Phillip Tovey, Pádraig Ó Tuama, Giles Waller, Heather Walton, Helen Wilcox, James Woodward and Simeon Zahl.

Some prior and related reflections on lyric and some of the poets addressed in this book have been previously published in the journals *Scintilla* and *Literature and Theology*, in the *T&T Clark Handbook of Christian Prayer* (2021), edited by Ashley Cocksworth and John C. McDowell, and *The Power of the Word*, volume 5 (2020), edited by Mark S. Burrows, Hilary Davies and Josephine von Zitzewitz. Material from the latter has been gratefully reproduced with permission from the publisher. Lines from the poem 'Grace' from *A Portable Paradise* (2019) © Roger Robinson, reproduced by permission of Peepal Tree Press. All Bible references unless otherwise stated are taken from the NRSV. A short introduction to lyric theology is also being published in the T&T Clark Handbook of Theology and the Arts (2024), edited by Imogen Adkins and Stephen M. Garrett.

No project like this can be completed without sacrifice. In this case the main casualties were the husband and the housework. Deep thanks go to George for his long-standing forbearance and his knowledge of sea shanties, to both sets of grandparents, to Anne next door and the staff at York House Busy Bees, Salisbury. Thanks to Nathaniel and Grace, who inspired the reflections on babble and umbilical breath, and to Jonah, who inspired the reflections on memory and gratitude.

ABBREVIATIONS

BBT	Black British Talk
BCP	*Book of Common Prayer* (1662)
CCW	Geoffrey Hill, *Collected Critical Writings*, ed. Kenneth Haynes (Oxford: Oxford University Press, 2009)
ELH	*English Literary History*
GSS	Sarah Coakley, *God, Sexuality and the Self: An Essay 'on the Trinity'* (Cambridge: Cambridge University Press, 2013)
MLE	Multicultural London English
OED	*The Oxford English Dictionary* (Oxford: Oxford University Press, 2021). Online. https://www.oed.com
PEPP	Roland Greene, ed., *The Princeton Encyclopedia of Poetry and Poetics* (4th edition, Princeton, NJ: Princeton University Press, 2017). Oxford Reference
SE	Standard English

INTRODUCTION: LYRIC THEOLOGY, LYRIC THEORY AND ENGLISH LYRIC TRADITION

Spring, the sweet Spring, is the year's pleasant king;
Then blooms each thing, then maids dance in a ring[1]

So begins the first volume of Francis Turner Palgrave's *Golden Treasury*, a classic anthology of the 'best' lyric poetry.[2] If such jolly insouciance is taken to be exemplary of lyricism, then this book has set itself a difficult task in advocating the significance of lyric for theological discourse. Over the last century, lyric in Anglo-American poetry and criticism has gone from representing the height of Western creativity and civilization to, for some, a quaint feature of English poetics whose persistence is met with perplexity or embarrassment. Lyric is key to a threefold aesthetic taxonomy comprising epic, drama and lyric that is rooted in Romanticism.[3] This taxonomy has proved highly valuable for postliberal accounts of the different voices of theology and for Western theological aesthetics influenced by the work of Hans Urs von Balthasar. Yet within these discussions there remain significant misgivings about the virtues of the lyric voice, particularly where the association between lyric and personal expression leaves it open to charges of solipsism or monism. The theological turn to spirituality has cultivated theologies which often draw on lyric texts such as devotional or mystical poetry, hymns

---

For a brief introduction to theology and lyric, see Elizabeth S. Dodd, 'Why Lyric? A Theological Perspective', *T&T Clark Handbook of Theology and the Arts*, ed. Imogen Adkins and Stephen M. Garrett (London: T&T Clark, forthcoming).

1. Thomas Nashe, 'Spring, the Sweet Spring', in *The Golden Treasury of the Best Songs and Lyrical Poems in the English Language*, ed. Francis Turner Palgrave (London: Macmillan, 1861), 1. http://dbooks.bodleian.ox.ac.uk/books/PDFs/590750102.pdf.

2. Ibid., Preface.

3. On the three poetic genres, see *e.g* T. S. Eliot, 'The Three Voices of Poetry' (1953), in *The Lyric Theory Reader: A Critical Anthology*, ed. Virginia Jackson and Yopie Prins (Baltimore, MA: Johns Hopkins University Press, 2014), 192–200; W. E. Rogers, *The Three Genres and the Interpretation of Lyric* (Princeton, NJ: Princeton University Press, 1983); Frederick J. Ruf, *Entangled Voices: Genre and the Religious Construction of the Self* (Oxford: Oxford University Press, 1997).

and spiritual writings. However, there is still much to be done to examine the implications of lyricism for theological discourse. This book seeks to contribute to a rebalancing of theological perspectives on lyric by uncovering the outline of a lyric theology. Its reflections are structured according to a standard definition of the lyric poem as short, musical, emotionally expressive and written in the first-person singular.

While previous theological accounts of narrative and drama have often been rooted in classical poetics and theory, this book approaches lyric through the lens of the English lyric tradition. There are three main reasons for this. Firstly, because a theological account of poetry ought not rely on theory alone but engage directly with poetic texts and their reception, as located in historical context and part of a living tradition.[4] Modern theological aesthetics owes much to the later work of Martin Heidegger and, through him, to German Romantic poets such as Novalis and Friedrich Schiller, but the English lyric has proved an equally fruitful medium for theological reflection. From Anglo-Saxon hymns to medieval carols, early-modern metaphysical poetry and high Romanticism, the history of the English lyric sees poetry functioning not only as an aid to spiritual practice but as a theological voice in its own right.

Secondly, the decision to focus on English lyric tradition here makes a case for the significance of lyric in the field of English theology. Claims have been made for the dramatic as a particularly English mode of theology (and by 'English' read 'Anglican'), but lyric has held an important status in the history of English poetry and of English theology.[5] Consider, for example, the significant contribution of lyric poets whose voices remain a part of theological discussion to this day, from George Herbert to John Donne, William Blake, S. T. Coleridge, Gerard Manley Hopkins and W. H. Auden, to name a few. One might also think of the role played by lyric poetry and practice in the work of key contemporary theologians working in the British Isles: from Sarah Coakley to Gavin D'Costa, David F. Ford, Michael Jagessar, Christopher Rowland, Nicola Slee, Christopher Southgate, Heather Walton and Rowan Williams, again far from an exhaustive list. The common characterization of British theology as anti-systematic, concerned with the particular, occasional or the fragmentary, might also be viewed through a lyric lens. This perspective turns the focus from

---

4. My thanks to David Jasper for a conversation on this subject.

5. Ben Quash has described his theodramatics as reflecting distinctively Anglican ways of thinking: provisional, layered, communal/traditioned and resisting both systematization and individualism, in *Theology and the Drama of History* (Cambridge: Cambridge University Press, 2005), 8–9. Consider also the influential work of David Ford and Samuel Wells on dramatic theology, equally rooted in Anglican tradition: David Ford, *The Drama of Living: Becoming Wise in the Spirit* (Grand Rapids, MI: Brazos Press, 2014); Samuel Wells, *Improvisation: The Drama of Christian Ethics*, 2nd edn (Grand Rapids, MI: Baker Academic, 2018).

a concern with lyric texts alone to a consideration of what theology looks like when conducted in a lyric mode.[6]

Thirdly, this study is informed by developments in Anglo-American lyric theory, which address some of the reservations that theologians have expressed about lyric. Contributions to lyric theory in recent decades have returned to its classical roots in music and performance, seeing it as a public and epideictic discourse. The grammar of the performed and performative lyric – a corporeal, musical and culturally embedded form – might prove crucial to a theological account of lyric for the twenty-first century.

There are good reasons to approach a book on lyric theology through the English lyric tradition, but this method also carries risks and challenges. On the one hand, it is impossible to silo English poetry and theology away from the important British and global contexts of which they form a part. The previous paragraphs alone have already hinted at the crucial role of voices of Irish, Scottish, Welsh, Caribbean and Indian heritage in this conversation, as well as the ongoing interconnections of Anglo-American scholarship. On the other hand, it would also be a grave error to elide all this rich cultural diversity under the banner of the 'English' lyric, even if by 'English' one simply meant 'Anglophone'.[7] While centred on English poetic and theological contexts for reasons of scope, this book seeks to include a range of voices where relevant. Apologies must be made in advance for any inelegancies of expression that might appear to subsume or ignore cultural diversity and difference. These are not merely difficulties of classification but relate to broader issues of history, tradition and the canon. This book addresses texts that have long been key touchstones of the English devotional, religious or spiritual lyric, but also looks for how this canon might be reassessed and expanded, by highlighting confessional diversity and by drawing on female and non-binary voices, Black British poetry and the spoken word.[8]

This book's reflections on the implications of lyric for theological discourse are grounded in pneumatology. Again, there are a number of reasons for this.

---

6. Following Alastair Fowler, a 'genre' is defined as a historical body of literature that develops over time, while a 'mode' is transhistorical, *Kinds of Literature: An Introduction to the Theory of Genres and Modes* (Oxford: Clarendon, 1982), 108.

7. For a discussion of this issue, see K. Davis *et al*, 'England, Poetry Of', in *The Princeton Encyclopedia of Poetry and Poetics*, ed. Roland Greene and Stephen Cushman (Princeton: Princeton University Press, 2017). Oxford Reference. [hereafter *PEPP*].

8. Although there may be a rough consensus around the canon of 'religious', 'devotional' or 'spiritual' English lyrics, none of these terms is entirely satisfactory. The first two suggest a degree of orthodoxy or religious commitment that might be considered detrimental to the creative freedom required for good poetry, while the latter is arguably too broad to be a useful category. In the absence of a better, more overarching term for lyrics of theological significance or interest, this book generally uses the term most immediately appropriate, while allowing a degree of ambiguity to challenge received ideas about what constitutes a theologically significant lyric.

To adopt a crude Trinitarian taxonomy, if epic theology might be considered to imagine a Father's-eye-view of the great narrative of salvation history, and dramatic theology finds itself focussed on the events of Christ's life and the tragedy of the cross, then lyric must occupy the space of the Spirit.[9] The Spirit – *ruach*, *pneuma* or *spiritus* – is encountered in the scriptures as a breath or wind that inspires, disrupts and brings new life. Lyric as performed speech, either literally or in the imagination, is governed by breath and so, this book will suggest, provides a medium for reflection on the mystery of the Spirit, who inspires human beings with life and eloquence, who inhabits human speech and through whom humanity is drawn into the conversation of the Trinity.

Defining lyric

The rest of this Introduction focusses on outlining in more depth issues of lyric theory, lyric theology and English lyric tradition that are foundational for the main chapters. The working definition of lyric introduced above – short, musical, emotionally expressive and using a first-person perspective – is by no means universal or comprehensive but broadly summarizes the major features of lyric in post-Romantic criticism.[10] More than poetic devices, these features are indicative of the ways in which lyric *makes sense*, which means not just its interpretive perspective but the ways in which it constructs meaning.

Musicality provides the most straightforward definition of lyric, coming from its etymological roots in poetry sung or chanted to the music of the lyre.[11]

---

9. On Christ's life as a drama, see Hans Urs von Balthasar, *Theo-Drama: Theological Dramatic Theory*, 5 vols (San Francisco: Ignatius Press, 1989–98), vol. 2, 77–84. In dramatic terms the Father might be imagined as the director of the great play of creation, with Christ its main character. From an epic perspective the Father might be described as the author of the narrative, although there are important distinctions between epic and narrative theology. For a discussion of the theological implications of changing critical perspectives on the author, see Hans W. Frei, *The Eclipse of Biblical Narrative: A Study in Eighteenth and Nineteenth Century Hermeneutics* (New Haven: Yale University Press, 1974), 310–13.

10. See, *e.g.*, M. H. Abrams, 'Lyric', *A Glossary of Literary Terms*, 4th edn (New York: Holt, Rinehart & Winston, 1981): 'Greek writers identified the lyric as a song rendered to the accompaniment of a lyre. The term is now used for any fairly short, non-narrative poem presenting a single speaker who expresses a state of mind or a process of thought and feeling.' Virginia Jackson describes a similar shift in definitions of lyric 'from adjective to noun', with the modern lyric defined by 'brevity, subjectivity, passion, and sensuality', 'Lyric', in *PEPP*.

11. This innovation has been traditionally attributed to the Greek poet Archilocus of the seventh century BCE.

This is by and large a lost music, since the music of these ancient lyrics was never transcribed, while modern poetry of the page has found a self-sufficiency in the music of the words alone. There remains a silent echo of music in the rhyme, rhythm and metre of the textual poem, which gesture towards lyric's oral roots. The resurgence of orality through the spoken word scene has seen the re-integration of words and music in poetry, as will be seen in the work of Kae Tempest and Warsan Shire.

In re-orienting the central characteristic of lyric away from the lyric 'I' and towards the music of words, contemporary lyric theory has returned to its Aristotelian roots.[12] Aristotle's *Poetics* was not primarily concerned with lyric but with dramatic poetry. Its tangential discussion of the *melic* has nevertheless been determinative for Western lyric poetics, both in its account of the human aptitude for rhythm and harmony and in its classification of this as secondary to the instinct for imitation.[13] The priority of *mimesis* over music can be seen in S. T. Coleridge's critique of the 'mere mechanism of [inferior] verse' which, echoing Aristotle, describes rhyme and rhythm as mere versification, while true poetry is the representation of universal truths.[14]

The subordination of meter to *mimesis* involves a subordination of music to image that can be detected in a modern theological preoccupation with metaphor.[15] A focus on metaphor owes much to the philosophy of Ludwig Wittgenstein and Heidegger, but also reflects developments in the world of poetry. Specifically, it resonates with the imagistic tendencies of modernist poetics, which emphasized the capacity of a poetic image to 'present[] an intellectual and emotional complex in an instant of time', preferring free verse to the restrictiveness of formal or metrical poetry.[16]

It is a modern truism to say that poetry does not need to rhyme. Indeed, the highly formalized poetic music of previous ages can be received as not merely

---

12. For a nuanced discussion of lyricality as musicality, see Susan Stewart, 'Letter on Sound', in *Close Listening: Poetry and the Performed Word*, ed. Charles Bernstein (Oxford: Oxford University Press, 1998), 28–52.

13. See Aristotle, *Poetics* 4.9.

14. Samuel Taylor Coleridge, *Biographia Literaria*, ed. Adam Roberts (Edinburgh: Edinburgh University Press, 2014), chap. 2, p. 32, https://ebookcentral.proquest.com/lib/oxford/detail.action?docID=4462445.

15. Metaphor has been discussed as integral to religious language, a mechanism for making or finding new meaning and probing the boundaries of silence. See, *e.g.*, Janet M. Soskice, *Metaphor and Religious Language* (Oxford: Clarendon, 1985), 161; Rowan Williams, *The Edge of Words* (London: Bloomsbury, 2014), 6, 129. Consider also David Brown's preoccupation with metaphor and image in his account of poetry as part of his three-volume *magnum opus: God and Mystery in Words: Experience through Metaphor and Drama* (Oxford: Oxford University Press, 2008), Part I. The language of symbol, which owes much to Paul Tillich, is also relevant to the imagistic tendencies of modern theology.

16. See Ezra Pound, 'A Few Don'ts by an Imagiste', *Poetry* (March 1913): 200.

archaic but ridiculous and, when used in modern poetry, a sign of the amateur at work. The embarrassment of *melos* is also its power and its danger. What C. Day Lewis called the 'singing line' is a lyric beauty, described below as a sonic sweetness, that evokes the dangerously persuasive properties of the music of language.[17] The power of rhetoric, like the song of the sirens or the pied piper's music, can charm the hearer and sweep them away from the paths of sense or reason. Chapter 1 addresses head-on the beauty, power and danger in the music of words, through the sweetest of medieval lyrics: the lullaby carol.

Emotional expressivity and the first-person perspective have together provided the dominant model of lyric poetry in the post-Romantic period.[18] These characteristics are epistemologically significant because they are attached to the idea of the lyric poem as the apparently sincere communication of the thoughts and feelings of the poet. They have also proved hermeneutically problematic in the wake of the New Criticism, which questioned the assumption that a single, stable subjectivity lurks 'behind' the poem. Structuralist critics such as Jonathan Culler have instead read the poem as a purely textual construct, in which the figure of the poet is largely irrelevant to the interpretation of the poem.[19] Expressivity may play a cathartic, even therapeutic function for the poet and the reader, but modern criticism is haunted by the suspicion that such ingenuousness is a deception, or worse a form of self-deceit. From a theological perspective, the epistemological significance of affectivity has become a topic that is, if not generally approved, then much discussed.[20] Chapter 2 explores lyric expressivity not as an appeal to the authority of a possibly illusory sincerity but as the inescapable grammar of affectivity and subjectivity that shapes thought and practice, as heard in the intimate mode of lyric address.

It is worth noting that, as lyric identifiers, affectivity and expressivity are applied well beyond the bounds of Western poetry. Earl Miner theorizes the 'affective-expressive' lyric as a foundational global poetic, as applicable to Persian ghazals, the poetry of the Psalms or medieval troubadour ballads as to the great Romantic lyrics of William Wordsworth.[21] Miner describes affective expression not only as a universal feature of poetic language but as a fundamentally religious poetic, as it is in the mode of intimate address to the divine that emotions of desire, woundedness and joy are most potently expressed.[22] A key historical moment that illustrates this point is the early-modern translation of the love lyric into devotional poetry. This tradition is addressed in Chapter 2, through the *Holy Sonnets* of Donne and

---

17. Cecil Day-Lewis, *The Lyric Impulse* (Harvard: UMI, 1965), 3.
18. See Jackson, 'Lyric', *PEPP*.
19. See p. 15.
20. See, *e.g.*, Sarah Coakley, ed., *Faith, Rationality and the Passions* (Oxford: Wiley-Blackwell, 2012).
21. See Earl Roy Miner, *Comparative Poetics: An Intercultural Essay on Theories of Literature* (Princeton, NJ: Princeton University Press, 1990), 8–9, 82, 85, 116, 123–4.
22. Ibid., 86, see 116–17, for a discussion of George Herbert's *The Temple*.

Herbert's *Temple*. The grammar of lyric affectivity is a rhetoric of persuasion, as of lover to beloved. It is also a way of making sense through feeling, a working-out and working-through of what Barbara Lewalski has called 'the various and vacillating spiritual conditions and emotions the soul experiences'.[23]

John Stuart Mill famously defined lyric as 'feeling confessing itself to itself, in moments of solitude'.[24] The apparent monologue of this lyric 'I' is arguably one of the most powerful features of lyric discourse, through which the reader is either invited into another interior world or compelled to examine their own. Romanticism's high view of poetry as a bearer of truth is intimately bound up with the lyric 'I'; in Coleridge's hands, the poetic declaration that 'I am' demonstrates the identity of the 'self' or 'spirit' with 'the great eternal I AM'.[25] Chapter 3 explores the prophetic weight of this lyric voice through an exploration of the capacity of the lyric 'I' to convey the voice of the Lord.

At the same time, this book must contend with the problematizing of the lyric first-person perspective. The historical turn in lyric criticism has highlighted the anachronism of reading all poetry as self-expression. M. H. Abrams' seminal work on Romanticism drew on classical theory to argue against post-Romantic readings of the lyric voice as the expression of an individual mind rather than, according to a Platonic model of lyric, an artistic imitation of one.[26] More recently, and more controversially, Virginia Jackson has gone so far as to see the lyric as an altogether post-Romantic invention, heavily criticizing a post-Romantic misreading of all poetry as, in John Ruskin's terms, 'the expression by the poet of his own feelings'.[27] These historicist arguments have leant weight to more epistemological critiques of lyric subjectivity. What Keats once labelled the 'egotistical sublime', or in Derridean terms might be called the phallic 'I', has been accused of being irredeemably bound up with solipsism and individualism.[28] Mikhail Bakhtin associated lyric with 'monological' discourse that neglects the wisdom of dialogue, while Theodor Adorno described lyric as the individual voice in conflict with or in flight from the collective.[29] In these assessments, the lyric 'I' entails a confidence in the self, as having the capacity to know of and speak for itself, that deconstructionist critiques have exposed as no longer tenable. As will be discussed in Chapter 4, what Gillian

---

23. Barbara Kiefer Lewalski, *Protestant Poetics and the Seventeenth-Century Religious Lyric* (Princeton: Princeton University Press, 1979), 4.

24. John Stuart Mill, 'Thoughts on Poetry and Its Varieties', *The Crayon* 7, no. 4 (April 1860): 95.

25. Coleridge, *Biographia*, chap. 12, p. 188.

26. See M. H. Abrams, 'The Lyric as Poetic Norm' (1953), in *Lyric*, ed. Jackson and Prins, 140–3.

27. Ruskin, *Fors Clavigera* (1873), 3.34.6, cited in Jackson, 'Lyric', *PEPP*.

28. John Keats, 'Letter to Richard Woodhouse, 27 October 1818', in *Life, Letters, and Literary Remains, of John Keats*, ed. Richard Monckton Milnes (London: Edward Moxon, 1848), 1:221–3.

29. See below, pp. 11–12.

White has termed 'lyric shame' has dogged modern poetry, resulting in a range of avant-garde, modernist and postmodern poetics that seek to dismantle the tyranny of the first person.[30] Flawed as it may be, it is the contention of Chapter 3 that the grammar of subjectivity remains inescapable and must be reckoned with.

As T. S. Eliot has pointed out, 'short' is the least precise descriptor for an entire poetic mode, although it may be of some practical use when it comes to the selection of poetry for anthologies.[31] The definition of every short poem as a lyric could be taken as evidence of what Jackson and Yopie Prins have called 'lyricization', the modern process through which the expressive lyric became synonymous with poetry, poetry synonymous with art and art with civilized sensibility.[32] On such a broad definition, lyric loses any usefulness as a descriptive category. Shortness nevertheless carries poetic significance, indicating a restriction in length imposed by the requirements of form. Whether the fourteen lines of a sonnet or the five of the limerick, such restriction is often considered a paradoxical spur to creative freedom. In the ode, elegy or meditative poem, restriction results from consideration of a single event, thought or feeling, reflecting the Romantic aspiration towards discovery of the universal through meditation on the particular. The final chapter looks at how in twentieth-century poetry this ideal disintegrated into fragments, assessing the peculiar forms of fragmentary unity out of which new ways of speaking can emerge.

The previous paragraph raises the question of whether a book on theology and lyric has much to contribute beyond a book on theology and poetry more generally, of which there have been many.[33] Some of the lyric features described above might be said to characterize any poem. A drama or an epic might be metrical, and they might incorporate expressive soliloquys through which a character speaks for themselves. A degree of overlap is not surprising. It not only reflects the difficulties of classifying the diverse and evolving world of poetic form but is also consistent with classic interpretations of lyric as the heart of all poetry. Indeed, G. W. Herder viewed lyric or song as the primal root of all language.[34] Canadian literary critic Northrop Frye took up this unitary theory in his definition of lyric as the musical

---

30. Gillian C. White, *Lyric Shame: The 'Lyric' Subject of Contemporary American Poetry* (Cambridge, MA: Harvard University Press, 2014). See also W. R. Johnson's summary of the historical rise and fall of lyric, which became in the twentieth century 'first ashamed and bewildered, then terrified, by the idea of saying I', *The Idea of Lyric: Lyric Modes in Ancient and Modern Poetry* (Berkeley: University of California Press, 1982), 15.

31. Eliot, 'Three Voices', 824.

32. Jackson and Prins, *Lyric*, 7.

33. For a fuller discussion of this question, see Dodd, 'Why Lyric?'.

34. Johann Gottfried Herder, 'Essay on the Origin of Language', in *Two Essays on the Origin of Language: Jean-Jacques Rousseau and Johann Gottfried Herder*, trans. John H. Moran and Alexander Gode (Chicago: University of Chicago Press, 1966).

pole of poetry that exploits the linguistic formation of sense out of sound to craft new ways of speaking.[35] Frye's perspective is particularly informative for this work, which finds in the music of lyric an opportunity to expand theological engagement with poetry beyond a common emphasis on the imagistic world of metaphor, towards an exploration of breath, sound and performance.

Lyric and theology

Another reason to focus on lyric in particular as opposed to poetry in general is the influence of the aesthetic taxonomy of epic, lyric and drama on modern theology.[36] This model of the three poetic genres claims a classical foundation in the philosophy of Aristotle and Plato, but finds its modern roots in the poetics of J. W. von Goethe and the æsthetics of G. W. F. Hegel. Hegel's *Æsthetics* charted the development of civilization through periods of 'epic' and 'lyric' creativity towards a 'dramatic' era that would finally be superseded by philosophy. As discussed further in Chapter 3, while this great dialectic culminates with drama, Hegel also has much to say about a lyric that is not merely superseded by but incorporated into the dramatic mode.[37] Chapter 2 touches on the vaguely Trinitarian overtones of this tripartite division, which cannot be explored fully in this study. Hegel's taxonomy has been highly influential for modern theological æsthetics, as taken up in von Balthasar's seminal *Theo-Drama*.[38] This work has proved formative for

---

35. See Northrop Frye on 'The Rhythm of Association', in 'Theory of Genres' (1957), in *Lyric*, ed. Jackson and Prins, 33–4.

36. An alternative taxonomy with theological currency would be the binary framework of lyric and narrative, which echoes a more general division between poetry and prose. This framework has proved a useful hermeneutic lens for the lyric passages that intersperse the histories in the Hebrew Bible, such as the songs of Moses and Miriam (Exodus 15.1-21). From a narrative perspective, such lyric passages appear as interruptions to the story, a moment for pause, contemplation, remembrance or celebration. From a perspective that privileges the lyric, such passages may be seen as a window into the heart of the Bible, much as (following Athanasius' *Letter to Marcellinus* 1 (PG 27: 12a), 101-29) the Psalms have often been read as the epitome of the scriptures. For standard accounts of lyric in the Bible, see B. A. Strawn, 'Lyric Poetry', in *Dictionary of the Old Testament: A Compendium of Contemporary Biblical Scholarship*, ed. Tremper Longman III and Peter Enns (Westmont: InterVarsity Press, 2010), 443–6; Tod Linafelt, *The Hebrew Bible as Literature: A Very Short Introduction* (Oxford: Oxford University Press, 2016), 5.

37. See below, pp. 95–6.

38. For a detailed description of how this dialectic plays out in von Balthasar's *Theo-Drama*, see Karen Kilby, *Balthasar: A (Very) Critical Introduction* (Grand Rapids, MI: W.B. Eerdmans, 2012), 44–7. Following Quash, Kilby argues that, in spite of itself, von Balthasar's dramatic theology tends in an epic direction.

interpretations of the implications of lyric for theological discourse in Anglo-American theological aesthetics.

To better understand the contribution this book seeks to make to these debates, it is worth dwelling a little on von Balthasar's account of lyric and its legacy. In foregrounding the dialectical synthesis of epic and lyric in drama, von Balthasar casts both epic and lyric modes in a somewhat undesirable light that has arguably been amplified in subsequent theological assessments of lyric. Compounded by the priorities of narrative theology and the legacy of the Wittgensteinian linguistic turn, von Balthasar's influence on postliberal and analytic Anglo-American theologies has had a dramatic impact on theological perceptions of lyric.

As with Aristotle's *Poetics*, it is salient to note that von Balthasar's influential account of lyric was not concerned with lyric at all but with drama. The lyric of von Balthasar's *Theo-Drama* is cast as the antithesis of 'epic' or systematic theology, both of which provide a foil for the superior mode of dramatic theology. This might explain why a theologian otherwise deeply invested in the theological importance of spirituality makes little of a lyric form that he identifies with prayer: 'the internal motion of the devout subject, his emotion and submission, the creative outpouring of himself'.[39] It is striking how, in order to fit into the scheme of the work, highly lyrical texts such as the Psalms, Augustine's *Confessions* and Boethius' *Consolation of Philosophy* are praised not as lyrics but as dramatic works.[40] Similarly, the relationship of 'I' to 'Thou' is imagined in terms of dramatic dialogue rather than the intimate address of the devotional lyric.[41] Chapter 2 in this book will recover the lyric grammar of the address of 'I' to 'Thou', finding in it not only an expressive but a ritual and rhetorical relationality, with important implications for understandings of prayer.

If the *Theo-Drama* overlooks the value of lyric discourse, this may be attributed not only to the dialectical structure of von Balthasar's project but also to the role lyric plays in a polemic against subjectivist pietism or modern liberalism, which von Balthasar elsewhere calls a 'romanticism remote from reality'.[42] The *Theo-Drama* presents an argument for orthodoxy as orthopraxy, against which stands the threat of the 'I myself' alone.[43] Divorced from action and abstracted from the wider perspective of the community, the 'I' turned in on itself calcifies or decays. Chapters 3 and 4 in this book address reductive perspectives on the lyric 'I' by finding in both Romantic and modernist poetry models of a publicly oriented lyric first person.

---

39. Balthasar, *Theo-Drama*, II, 55–7.
40. Ibid., II, 166; I, 126.
41. Ibid., II, 56.
42. Hans Urs von Balthasar, *Explorations in Theology: The Word Made Flesh*, trans. A. V. Littledale and Alexander Dru, vol. I, 2nd edn (San Francisco: Ignatius Press, 1989), 208. *NB* von Balthasar makes no explicit reference to lyric in this essay.
43. Balthasar, *Theo-Drama*, I, 252.

Elsewhere in von Balthasar's work, greater prominence is given to the lyric voice. For example, *The Glory of the Lord* extols the virtues of Ignatius' affective spirituality, Irenæus' 'poetic' style, the 'great, symphonic, lyrical and rhapsodic music' of Augustine and Denys, and the poetic sincerity of John of the Cross and Gerard Manley Hopkins.[44] Nevertheless, even here the music of lyric is subordinated to an imagistic conceit that governs the work: of the vision of revelation as like the reception of a work of art.[45] When von Balthasar reads John of the Cross, it is vision that is 'the transcendent spring from which the tremendous power of … lyricism flows'.[46] An argument could be made for prioritizing vision over hearing in the reception of revelation. In scriptural accounts of divine encounter which combine the visual and the auditory, the vision is usually described first, accompanied by the voice of the Lord.[47] Nevertheless, while light moves faster than sound that does not make thunder secondary to lightning. Indeed, Canadian critic and theorist Walter Ong has argued that in some respects auditory metaphors for revelation are preferable to the visual from an epistemological and Christological perspective, rooted as they are in a theology of the Word.[48] In Genesis 1.3 the Word heralds the light. Just so, the sight of glory might point back towards the divine lyric speech from whence it springs.

Von Balthasar cannot bear sole responsibility for the neglect or even rejection of lyric in modern theological discourse. His influence has nevertheless been significant, particularly through the development of theological dramatic theory and the advocacy of 'dramatic' theologies by theologians such as Ben Quash, David Ford, Samuel Wells and the American theologian Kevin Vanhoozer. Vanhoozer's dramatic interpretation of Christian doctrine, which sees the Father as the director of the great play of salvation, takes up von Balthasar's implicit critique of liberalism and George Lindbeck's account of 'experiential-expressive' theology, in its attack on 'lyric theology' as a purely internal monologue that 'neither recognizes nor responds to the prior word/act of the triune God'.[49] Quash follows not just von

---

44. Hans Urs von Balthasar, *The Glory of the Lord: A Theological Aesthetics*, trans. John Kenneth Riches, 7 vols (Edinburgh: T&T Clark, 1982–89), vol. II, 24; ibid., 3, 126.

45. Anne M. Carpenter describes von Balthasar's distinctive poetic theological grammar in terms of symbolic language, centred on the beauty of God as described in *The Glory of the Lord*. Anne M. Carpenter, *Theo-Poetics: Hans Urs von Balthasar and the Risk of Art and Being* (Notre Dame, IN: University of Notre Dame Press, 2015), 3.

46. Balthasar, *Glory*, III, 147.

47. Consider, *e.g.*, the calling of the prophet Ezekiel (Ezekiel 1), the Baptism of Christ (Matthew 3.16-17) and Saul's conversion (Acts 9.3-4).

48. For a more detailed discussion of Ong, see below, p. 98.

49. Balthasar, *Theo-Drama*, I, 129, 252-3; Kevin J. Vanhoozer, *The Drama of Doctrine: A Canonical-Linguistic Approach to Christian Theology* (Louisville: Westminster John Knox Press, 2005), 91–3 (92). Lindbeck has in mind Rahnerian transcendental individualism and Schleiermacherian subjectivism, and also cites Bernard Lonergan, Rudolf Otto and Paul Tillich as examples of 'experiential-expressive' theology, George A. Lindbeck, *The Nature of Doctrine: Religion and Theology in a Postliberal Age* (Philadelphia: Westminster Press, 1984), 16, 30–45 (31).

Balthasar but also Bakhtin in defining lyric as the 'genre of the self-contemplating mind', a monological voice that suffers in its egotistical isolation from the community, and against which he proposes the polyglossia of dramatic dialogue as a more historically embedded and communal way of knowing.[50] In different ways, both of these critiques miss the social orientation of a lyric discourse that has an audience and an addressee, which might incorporate a multiplicity of voices and which might thereby demonstrate an engagement with otherness and transcendence.[51] Guided by grammars of love and hope, the intimate address of lyric might provide an equally fruitful ground as drama for consideration of the character of faithful and imaginative theological conversation.

Von Balthasarian theological æsthetics and Wittgensteinian linguistics may lie behind a sometimes-reductive theological anti-lyricism that is centred on the claims of subjectivity attached to the lyric 'I'.[52] Scottish theologian Fergus Kerr explained Wittgenstein's significance for theology in terms of his refutation of the metaphysical concept of the subject: a corrective to what Kerr calls Descartes' 'famous turn to the first-person perspective'.[53] To reject the notion of a self that is distinct from society and its own body appears here to entail rejection of the lyric first person. A suspicion of the first person has become embedded in post-Wittgensteinian reflections on theological method and practice that connect the lyric 'I' not only with epistemological error but with the sin of modern individualism. Rowan Williams has described the supposed sincerity of self-expression as undermining the integrity that begins with self-critique and embraces dialogue.[54] Poet-theologian and Anglican priest Mark Pryce has critiqued the 'uninterpretable and uncommunicative "lyricism"' of self-absorbed expressive poetry, 'starving on the pigswill of inward concerns'.[55] In response to the ironic insincerity of a lyric 'I' that fails to confront the realities of self and world, evil and suffering,

---

50. Quash, *Drama*, 43.

51. For a re-reading of Bakhtin that allows for a social and dialogical interpretation of lyric, see, *e.g.*, Jacob Blevins, ed., *Dialogism and Lyric Self-Fashioning: Bakhtin and the Voices of a Genre* (Selinsgrove, PA: Susquehanna University Press, 2008), 15–16.

52. It is worth noting the more positive perspective on lyric offered by Wells's account of 'the drama of Christian ethics' as 'do[ing] justice to the role of the subject, the way that events arise from the hearts and minds and actions of people, rather than from impersonal external forces', in Wells, *Improvisation*, 27.

53. Fergus Kerr, *Theology after Wittgenstein*, 2nd edn (London: SPCK, 1997), 3.

54. Rowan Williams, *On Christian Theology* (Oxford: Blackwell, 2000), 5.

55. Mark Pryce, 'Taking Form: On Becoming a Christian Poet', in *Making Nothing Happen: Five Poets Explore Faith and Spirituality*, Gavin D'Costa *et al.* (Farnham: Ashgate, 2014), 85–126 (89). Pryce draws on von Balthasar, Quash and Williams to make this point. In the same volume Ruth Shelton also discusses the 'I' in poetry as 'problematic', 'Steady until Sundown: Searching for the Holy', ibid., 49–84 (51, 63).

the theodramatic lens of tragedy advocated by Donald M. MacKinnon has been a particularly potent tool.[56]

As discussed below, a response to these critiques is drawn here from contemporary lyric theory, which shows the lyric 'I' to be a more complex and nuanced phenomenon than sometimes assumed. As a multifaceted, culturally constructed and socially located subjectivity, the modern lyric 'I' provides a means of moving beyond a crude rejection of illusory sincerity towards a consideration of how the inescapable grammars of subjectivity influence doctrine and practice.[57]

Divorced from the rich history of lyric poetry, lyric easily becomes a straw man against which supposedly more mature and responsible modes of theological discourse are to be preferred. Theological critiques of lyric have made it a cipher for affective pietism, Romantic idealism, liberal subjectivism or modern individualism, co-opting it into polemics that risk reinforcing confessional and theological divides. Rather than prolonging these debates, this book's account of lyric builds on some of the assumptions of dramatic theologies, such as the importance of history, culture and society, and some of the principles of postliberal theology that underlie them, such as the belief that revelation is mediated through language and culture and the task of theology is to discern and refine its grammar.[58] It seeks not to replace dramatic theology with lyric but to correct reductive readings of lyricism, to facilitate a better consideration of the three poetic modes of theological discourse. There is much work to be done in this area, but as the epilogue suggests, to give lyric proper consideration might lead ultimately to a more perichoretic, as opposed to dialectical, model of the three voices of theology, one that does better poetic justice to the interdependent interweaving of different ways of speaking about God.

---

56. On the influence of the categories of drama and tragedy, see, *e.g.*, Kevin Taylor and Giles Waller, eds, *Christian Theology and Tragedy: Theologians, Tragic Literature and Tragic Theory* (London: Routledge, 2011).

57. Consider also the contribution of Simeon Zahl, who approaches these issues from the perspective of experience as a source of theology, defending 'the irreducibility of subjectivity in theological reasoning' by arguing that experience is, in the end, always 'experience of God'. Zahl locates modern theological ambivalence towards such subjective 'enthusiasm' not in Cartesianism but in the legacy of Luther and Barth. Zahl's challenge to 'take subjectivity seriously' is salient to a theo-lyric reflection on the first person that seeks to acknowledge the presence of the Spirit in human experience. Simeon Zahl, *The Holy Spirit and Christian Experience* (Oxford: Oxford University Press, 2020), 42, 17, 35.

58. See Lindbeck, *Doctrine*, 33, 36, 120.

Lyric theory

If it wants to be relevant to the wider academy, contemporary theological engagement with lyric should not ignore the modern landscape of lyric theory and criticism. There is much to be learnt from developments in this field from the 1980s onwards. Rooted in modernism, the early twentieth century saw what has been described as an 'anti-lyric' reaction in Western poetry.[59] This had far-reaching implications: from Adorno's socialist critique of poetry after the Holocaust to Paul de Man's deconstructionist theories of lyric reading.[60] The dominant model of lyric reading in the mid-twentieth century came from the New Criticism, which abstracted the text from context, history and even authorial intention, and turned the lyric 'I' into a solitary voice, aloof and alone.[61] Determined to move beyond the New Criticism, lyric studies in the 1980s returned to classical theory to recontextualize lyric as a public, epideictic and rhetorical discourse.[62] As Scott Brewster argues, 'lyric, far from presenting the unmediated thoughts and feelings of an isolated individual, centres on the relationship between the self and others, the self and history, and the self and language'. Brewster adds 'performance' to the standard definition of lyric, identifying it not as a soliloquy but as an address to an audience.[63] The category of performance undergirds much of the discussion that follows, which foregrounds orality and performativity, speech and song, and the roots of lyric in primal poetic forms such as chant, riddle and charm.[64]

Another legacy of the New Criticism has been the development of the New Lyric Studies and the contrasting revival of lyric theory, centred on the epideictic and rhetorical lyric of the Pindaric ode, and its cognates in psalms and hymns. The New

---

59. For a definition of anti-lyricism in modern poetry, see Douglas Barbour, *Lyric, Anti-Lyric: Essays on Contemporary Poetry* (Edmonton, AB: NeWest Publishers, Limited, 2001), 7–8.

60. Theodor Adorno, 'On Lyric Poetry and Society (1957; 1991)' in *Lyric*, ed. Jackson and Prins, 339–49; Paul de Man, 'Lyric and Modernity', and 'Anthropomorphism and Trope in Lyric', in *The Rhetoric of Romanticism* (New York: Columbia University Press, 1984), 239–62.

61. See, *e.g.*, the discussion of I. A. Richards in *Lyric*, ed. Jackson and Prins, 160.

62. See, *e.g.*, Johnson, *Idea of Lyric*, 1–4. For a summary of developments in lyric criticism in the mid-1980s, see Chaviva Hošek and Patricia A. Parker, eds, *Lyric Poetry: Beyond New Criticism* (Ithaca, NY: Cornell University Press, 1985). *Cf.* the continued affirmation of the solitary lyric 'I' by scholars such as Helen Vendler, who describes lyric as 'the *performance* of the mind in *solitary* speech' (my italics), *The Art of Shakespeare's Sonnets* (Harvard: Harvard University Press, 1997), 1–2.

63. Scott Brewster, *Lyric* (London: Routledge, 2009), 14, 1–2, 12.

64. On the primitive roots of lyric in chant and charm, see Andrew Welsh, *Roots of Lyric: Primitive Poetry and Modern Poetics* (Princeton, NJ: Princeton University Press, 1978), vii. See also Daniel Albright, *Lyricality in English Literature* (Lincoln: University of Nebraska Press, 1985), viii, 1, on the association between lyric, incantation and magic.

Lyric Studies, represented by Jackson, entails sometimes controversial historicist critiques of lyric reading that have called into question the very notion of a genre called lyric.[65] This movement has provided a spur to the revival of lyric theory, most notably Jonathan Culler's magisterial *Theory of Lyric* (2015). This work, which has proved formative for this study, offers 'a more ... capacious account' of lyric that is not tied to subjective self-expression alone.[66] Culler's structuralist leanings tend towards an 'anti-theological' stance that focusses on the text and its reception by the community in history, rather than the intentions of a God-like author behind it, but his work nevertheless has significant implications for a theological account of lyric.[67] Contemporary studies of the poetry of the Hebrew Bible, for example, have drawn on Culler.[68] By doing the same, this book acknowledges a seminal figure in lyric theory and makes use of a work that encapsulates key developments in the field. Culler's focus on lyric as epideixis, rhetoric, ritual and performativity opens up important avenues for theological interpretation, which are applied here to the construction of a lyric theology.

Culler defines lyric as epideictic discourse, a public language of praise and blame which, in the words of Jeffrey Walker, 'invites its listener ... to an act of

---

65. For a summary of the New Lyric Studies and its impact on lyric criticism, see Stephen Burt, 'What Is This Thing Called Lyric?', *Modern Philology* 113, no. 3 (February 2016): 422–40. https://doi.org/10.1086/684097.

66. For a potted history of the lyric genre, see Jonathan Culler, *Theory of the Lyric* (Cambridge, MA: Harvard University Press, 2015), 49–77. For a summary of Culler's account of lyric, see pp. 349–53.

67. 'Anti-theological' is a term from Roland Barthes that entails a concern more with poetics than hermeneutics, with the structures of language over its meaning. This can be a critical perspective but also a more explicitly anti-religious polemical stance (a lack of interest in the 'author' behind the text which might signify by extension a rejection of a God-figure behind events or a Spirit who inhabits the poem). On his structuralist stance, see Culler, Lyric, viii; on ritual see ibid., 336; on his anti-religiosity, see Jonathan Culler, 'Comparative Literature and the Pieties', Profession (1986), 30, which takes particular aim at Frye's 'complicity' with religion. For a critique of Culler's position, see Robert Detweiler, 'Vexing the Text: The Politics of Literary-Religious Interpretation', Christianity and Literature 41, no. 1 (1991): 61–7.

68. See, *e.g.*, F. W. Dobbs-Allsopp whose definition of the Hebrew lyric as 'A Sung Word': musical, 'oral' and 'performative' incorporates insights from Culler (alongside a range of other critics). Dobbs-Allsopp defines lyric as '"short, non-narrative poetry"' that is 'non-mimetic' or a ritual event, voiced, characterized by apostrophic address and '"extravagant"' or '"sublime"', 'The Idea of Lyric Poetry in the Bible', in *On Biblical Poetry* (Oxford: Oxford University Press, 2015), 178–232 (179, 181, 185, 195–6, 212). Kate Heffelfinger notes how lyric theory has hitherto been applied scantily to Hebrew poetry due to an understandable desire to distinguish Hebraic poetry from a Hellenistic and westernizing interpretation, in *I Am Large, I Contain Multitudes: Lyric Cohesion and Conflict in Second Isaiah*, Biblical Interpretation 105 (Leiden: Brill, 2011), 22.

contemplation, evaluation, and judgment'.[69] The making of poetic judgements involves delving into questions of meaning and value, issues of intimate concern to the theologian. The epideictic lyric is a rhetorical as opposed to a mimetic art.[70] Lyric as a mimetic art, the imitation of private thoughts and feelings, is associated in Plato's *Republic* with the deceitful power of a poetry that, for all its appearance of reality, is always several steps removed from real life.[71] To read lyric as rhetoric is to acknowledge the power of lyric utterance, sidestepping the question of what the lyric 'I' represents and how faithfully it does so.[72] This book examines the rhetorical power of words, and its dangers, in the light of a modern theological distrust of rhetoric, but also in relation to the power of Word and Spirit, through passages such as Acts 2.1-8 and Ezekiel 37.1-14.

Culler's account of lyric is divorced from any metaphysical claims, but he highlights the ritual and, by extension, religious character of lyric. The religious power of lyric discourse is implicitly acknowledged in Culler's account of academic 'embarrassment' with what he calls lyric 'hyperbole'.[73] This discussion centres on two features of lyric address: apostrophe and prosopopoeia, by which the lyric voice appears to speak to an absent, inanimate or imagined object. What Culler calls the 'extravagance' of the lyric sublime is the claim to make this object present to the reader in a manner that 'hyperbolically risk[s] animating the world, investing mundane objects or occurrence with meaning'.[74] The theological implications are clear in Culler's labelling of this instinct as a self-delusory 'version of the Resurrection of the Body', a breathing of life into the dead which is little more than wishful thinking.[75] The extravagance of lyric hyperbole may, as Culler claims, sit uncomfortably with modern criticism, but is arguably entirely at home as spiritual or theological discourse. Chapter 2 will discuss the Trinitarian implications of Culler's account of lyric address as 'triangulated' address, through the lens of early-modern prayer-poetry, while Chapter 4 discusses the power of Spirit and Word to bring the dead to life.[76]

---

69. Ibid., 3, 307–14; Jeffrey Walker, 'Aristotle's Lyric: Re-Imagining the Rhetoric of Epideictic Song', *College English* 51, no. 1 (January 1989): 8.

70. See Culler, *Lyric*, 50–1.

71. Plato, *Republic* 10 595a-608b. Plato described three kinds of poetic imitation: first-person narrative, narrative through the imitation of a character (drama) or a mixture of the two (*Republic* 3 392d-394). Diomedes in the late fourth century CE turned these three voices into a system of three *genera* or genres, the roots of the modern lyric, drama and epic. See also Aristotle, *Politics* 1340a18-23, 38f, on rhythm and melody as mimetic of emotion.

72. On lyric power, see Mutlu Konuk Blasing, *Lyric Poetry: The Pain and the Pleasure of Words* (Princeton, NJ: Princeton University Press, 2007), 3–4.

73. Culler, *Lyric*, 178–9, 190, 258–63.

74. Ibid., 38.

75. Ibid., 179.

76. Ibid., 8.

The ritual quality of lyric, rooted in its religious origins in psalm, chant and prayer, implies performativity.[77] Not merely a memory of an experience or a judgement upon it, Culler describes lyric as an event in itself, 'conjuring, endowing, acting'.[78] Designed not just for performance but for repeated reperformance, the poetic event has a liturgical quality that enables words to take on new power and new meaning in changing times.[79] The music of rhyme and rhythm is central to this poetic event. Much more than incidental versification, the musical features of the lyric sublime give significance to sounds and authority to the words they make.[80] Chapter 2 explores this aspect of lyric through the 'O' of address to another, drawing on the liturgical theology of Catherine Pickstock.

Culler's lyric theory turns away from an exclusive focus on subjectivity, but this is not to deny the significance of the lyric 'I'. Culler makes the important point that the lyric 'I' is often not singular or stable but multiple. As in Sappho's famous poem to Aphrodite, the lyric poem can include a number of voices or *personæ*.[81] This widened perspective on the lyric 'I' emphasizes its public orientation. Culler describes the lyric 'I' as a collective 'I', drawing on Adorno's essay on 'Lyric and Society' and on Wordsworth's affirmation of lyric as 'a form of social action'.[82] Chapter 3 will turn to the prophetic 'I' to explore Culler's contention, following Adorno, that 'there are other ways to participate in the social than to represent it', while Chapter 2 discusses the collective liturgical 'I' and Chapter 4 the multiple or dissolved 'I' of modernist poetics.[83]

Pneumatology: Breath of life, power of wind, presence of God

At this point, it is worth taking a more explicit theological turn to the other leg of the methodological stool supporting this theo-lyric study of English lyric tradition. Alongside theological aesthetics and lyric theory, the main chapters are undergirded by Christian pneumatology, specifically the scripturally inspired imagination of the Spirit as breath. The Hebrew, Greek and Latin terms *ruach*, *pneuma* and *spiritus* can all be translated as s/Spirit, breath or wind. The poetics of this ambiguity engenders a rich seam of multiple, interlocking, conflated and even contradictory senses of the Spirit as the breath of life, the power of the wind and the presence of God.[84] In Genesis 2.7, for example, God breathes life

---

77. On performativity and performance, see ibid., 125–31.
78. Ibid., 219–20.
79. Ibid., 35, 37.
80. Ibid., 132–85.
81. Ibid., 10–13.
82. Ibid., 296–348 (331–3, 325).
83. Ibid., 330.
84. For further reflections on the layered interpretations facilitated by this semantic ambiguity, see the discussion of Ezekiel 37.1-14 and John 3.8 in Chapter 4.

into Adam, a life that is also spirit.[85] This life is infused with God's power and presence but is also mortal, brief as a breath (*e.g.* Psalm 78.39). The moment of birth can be experienced as an intimate act of in-spiration (Genesis 2.7) or like the powerful wind of Acts 2.2 (the birth of the church). In prophetic literature, God's breath contains the power to create but also to destroy, like a sulphurous volcanic exhalation (*e.g.* Isaiah 30.33, 40.7). The presence of God can also be felt as a gentle breeze: whispered in Elijah's ear (1 Kings 19.12) or breathed upon the disciples (John 20.22). In the following chapters, different dimensions of the Spirit-as-breath are applied to a reflection on the theological significations of lyric discourse through a phenomenology of poetic recitation, centred on the act of breathing.[86]

These reflections on the Spirit as breath are informed by themes in modern pneumatology, particularly a contemporary theological account of the relationship between body and spirit. Luce Irigaray, an important influence on British feminist theology, has challenged the Western dualism of matter and spirit through an account of the partnership of body and air in the breath.[87] Drawing a connection between childbirth and meditative practices such as yoga, Irigaray explores the body's capacity to enrich its relationship with the air that surrounds it through discipline and exercise, and celebrates the more intimate life-giving fusion of breath and body in the mother's blood, which oxygenates the foetus.[88] In the light of these reflections, the partnership of Mary with the Spirit in the conception and birth of Christ, as described in the Nicene Creed, might be interpreted as a poetic act of co-creation. This book applies these themes to a consideration of lyric creativity, taking the partnership of body and air in the act of breathing as a model of human participation in the Spirit and of the presence of the Spirit in the world.[89]

There is a connection between the relationality of body and spirit, and that between word and breath. In Psalm 33.6, God creates the heavens by word and

---

85. Consider also how two Hebrew terms for breath – *ruach* and *neshamah* – work together to craft a parallelism of breath and spirit. *E.g.* Job 33.4 reads, 'The spirit [*ruach*] of God has made me, and the breath [from *neshamah*] of the Almighty gives me life.' See also Isaiah 42.5, where God is described as giving breath (*neshamah*) and spirit (*ruach*) to humanity. In Genesis 7.22 the creatures in the ark are described as 'everything that had the breath [from *neshamah*] of the spirit [*ruach*] of life'.

86. Burt, 'Lyric', 428, notes the importance of breath to lyric poetry throughout its history.

87. Irigaray has inspired theologians such as Tina Beattie, Sarah Coakley, Janet Martin Soskice and Graham Ward. See Rachel Muers, 'Feminism, Gender and Theology', in *The Modern Theologians: An Introduction to Christian Theology since 1918*, 3rd edn, ed. David F. Ford and Rachel Muers (Oxford: Blackwell, 2005), 443–4; Sarah Coakley, *God, Sexuality and the Self: An Essay 'on the Trinity'* (Cambridge: Cambridge University Press, 2013), 98 [hereafter *GSS*].

88. See Luce Irigaray, 'The Age of the Breath', in *Key Writings*, ed. Luce Irigaray (London: Continuum, 2004), 165–70.

89. See especially Chapter 4.

breath.⁹⁰ Irenaeus famously laid the ground for a Trinitarian interpretation of this passage by characterizing Word and Spirit as the two hands of the Father.⁹¹ The parallelistic imagery of the Psalm conveys not so much a categorization of the Godhead as the characterization of creation as a speech act, a metaphor with implications not only for Trinitarian or creation theology but also, as seen in Chapter 4, for a theology of creative participation in the Spirit.⁹²

This book is shaped by an understanding of lyric as poetry made to be spoken or sung, where the printed words are not the poem itself but more like a script or musical score. It is breath that brings the performed poem to life. In the same way that the space around the poem on the page is an expectant space, not without shape, texture or colour, so the breath that surrounds the uttered poem is never static or entirely silent but given substance by the soft movement of air. To consider the space around the poem as a breathing space and not a silent space might mean to meditate on the creative Spirit of Genesis 1.2 as operating through the body, as integral to it as oxygen in the blood but also external to it like wind in the air.

To read the lyric as governed by the breath is perhaps to resist, at least to an extent, the apophatic moves taken by theological reflections on poetry as words that push the boundaries of silence.⁹³ Breath is not an absence of words but a vital component of speech. It not only surrounds the poem but is integral to its structure and form. In pre-modern texts, such as Hebrew scriptures or medieval manuscripts, there was no poetic lineation to indicate rhythm and metre.⁹⁴ The structure of the poem was revealed only by the interchange of breath and word in performance. The lyric intelligibility of iambic pentameter (a signature form of the English lyric since Geoffrey Chaucer) is also shaped by the rhythms of breath and body. The ten-syllable line that structures the thought is a sentence-like length designed to be spoken in a single breath, while the heartbeat rhythm impels the poem forward. As discussed in Chapter 4, this relationality of word and breath in the lyric has important implications for a grammar of participation in the Spirit.

A theo-lyric of the Spirit as breath cannot ignore the theme of inspiration. There has been a close kinship between ideas of poetic and spiritual inspiration throughout the history of the English religious lyric, with poetry described as being given to the poet in much the same way that the Spirit gives the gift of eloquence

---

90. Psalm 33.6 is crucial for notions of the Spirit as proceeding from or 'breathed' by the Father. See Lampe, *God as Spirit*, 222; Basil of Cæsarea, *On the Holy Spirit* chap. 16, cited in Eugene F. Rogers, ed., *The Holy Spirit: Classic and Contemporary Readings* (Chichester: Wiley-Blackwell, 2009), 143–4.

91. Irenæus, *Against Heresies* bk 5 chap. 6.

92. NB *dāḇar* (Psalm 33.4 and 33.6) could be translated as either 'word' or 'speech', while in Tertullian's Latin there is a clearer distinction between *sermo* (speech) and *logos* (word).

93. See, *e.g.*, Mark S. Burrows, '"Raiding the Inarticulate": Mysticism, Poetics, and the Unlanguageable', *Spiritus: A Journal of Christian Spirituality* 4, no. 2 (Autumn 2004): 174.

94. Hebrew texts even omit the vowels, so that the words remain unfinished, even nonsensical, until brought to life through breath.

to apostles and preachers.[95] The earliest known lyric text in the English language was, according to the story recorded by the Venerable Bede, inspired by an angel who commanded the monk Cædmon to 'sing me something', in terms strikingly reminiscent of Homer's story of the muses who 'breathed ... a divine voice' into the poets.[96] There is a similar exchange in the 'Introduction' to William Blake's *Songs of Innocence* between the poet and a Christlike cherub, who also exhorts the poet to 'Sing a song'.[97] Much as in Hebrew prophecy, the call of the poet is not an ecstatic possession but an encounter that requires creative cooperation.[98] Blake spoke of his great poem *Jerusalem* as 'dictated' and yet written in a verse style of his own choosing.[99] According to Bede, Cædmon received his first poem in a dream, but also the *leothcræft* (poetry-craft) to create more.[100] The chapters in this book read inspiration literally as inhalation, addressing the creative partnership of poet and muse as an avenue into reflection on the invocation of the Spirit in prayer, worship and preaching. The in-breathing of the Spirit has also been a powerful motif in mystical accounts of prayer and spiritual transformation, exemplified by John of the Cross's memorable depiction of the Holy Spirit as a 'spiration' who elevates the soul, making it 'capable of breathing in God the same spiration of love that the Father breathes in the Son and the Son in the Father'.[101] Drawing on a phenomenology of the performed lyric, the chapters of this book explore not only

---

95. Peter's sermon in Acts 2 was often considered an exemplar of Spirit-inspired eloquence, while Bede also interpreted the multilingual miracle of Acts 2 as a sign of divine wisdom and eloquence. Kees Dekker connects this with Bede's account of Cædmon's inspiration, in 'Pentecost and Linguistic Self-Consciousness in Anglo-Saxon England: Bede and Ælfric', *The Journal of English and Germanic Philology* 104, no. 3 (July 2005): 354–6; see Bede, *Expositio Actuum Apostolorum* 16–17. Consider also Gregory the Great on the Spirit: 'whomsoever He has filled, He himself at once makes eloquent', *Regulae Pastoralis* bk 2 chap. 4. The eighth-century *Life of St Cuthbert* extends this to poetic eloquence, invoking the Spirit thus: 'you, who are accustomed to grant new eloquence with flame-spouting tongues, grant the gifts of the Word to the tongue singing your gifts', *Life of Cuthbert* lines 37–8, cited in Tristan Major, *Undoing Babel: The Tower of Babel in Anglo-Saxon Literature* (Toronto, Canada: University of Toronto Press, 2018), 115–16.

96. Bede, *Ecclesiastical History* bk 4 chap. 24; Hesiod, *Theogony* line 30.

97. William Blake, 'Introduction', *Songs of Innocence* (1789), 111. *NB* all citations from Blake's works are taken from *Blake: Complete Writings*, ed. Geoffrey Keynes (Oxford: Oxford University Press, 1969).

98. See Coakley, *GSS*, 113n14.

99. William Blake, 'To the Public', *Jerusalem* (1804–20), Plate 3.

100. Bede, *Ecclesiastical History* (Old English version) bk 4 chap. 24, trans. Benjamin Slade (2005), https://heorot.dk/bede-caedmon.html.

101. John of the Cross, *Spiritual Canticle*, commentary on stanza 39.3, in *The Collected Works of St John of the Cross*, trans. Kieran Kavanaugh and Otilio Rodriguez, 3rd edn (Washington, DC: ICS Publications, 2017), 740.

inspiration/inhalation but expiration/exhalation and the turning of the breath as aspects of creative participation in the Spirit.

The interplay of body and air, word and breath, poet and muse are all related to the broader question of the relationship between Spirit and spirit. Modern theologians have found different ways of expressing the closeness of this relationship while preserving a distinction between the Spirit and the human creature. Radical orthodoxy has turned to the Augustinian-Platonic language of participation, a term which gives a sense of the Spirit as all-encompassing and preserves God's primacy in all things. Eugene Rogers and Sarah Coakley also draw on this tradition, using the language of sexuality and desire to stress the intimacy of the relationship between God and humanity. Rogers describes a Trinitarian life that 'dilates … to include human beings within it', while Coakley's 'Spirit-led' theology draws on Romans 8 to describe the Spirit as the one who 'incorporates' human beings into the Trinity.[102] Inspired by the early church, Geoffrey Lampe's *God as Spirit* speaks instead of 'theandric operations', works that are at one and the same time an act of God worked out through humanity and a human act that is divinely inspired.[103] Katherine Sonderegger moves in a similar vein in choosing the term 'mixture', which also echoes Origen's account of the 'mingling' of Spirit and pray-er in *De Oratione*.[104] In Sonderegger's hands, this language emphasizes the extent of the Spirit's incorporation into humanity: 'ingredient down into the very sighs of our ignorance and our faith'.[105] For Sonderegger, the potentially controversial, discomforting term 'mixture' captures the shocking humility of a divine *kenosis* through which humanity can truly know God in the world.[106]

It is one of the contentions of this book that a theo-lyric reflection on word and breath might have an important contribution to make to these pneumatological discussions. As often claimed in modern theological accounts of poetry, one form of language is not reducible to another, and so lyric may have the capacity to say things that simply cannot be spoken in other ways.[107] One of the great scriptural

---

102. Eugene F. Rogers, *After the Spirit: A Constructive Pneumatology from Resources outside the Modern West* (Grand Rapids, MI: Eerdmans, 2005), introduction, Kindle; Coakley, GSS, 86, 111.

103. Geoffrey Lampe, *God as Spirit* (Oxford: Clarendon, 1977), 88, 94.

104. Origen, *De Oratione* 10.2, cited in Coakley, GSS, 127; Katherine Sonderegger, *The Doctrine of God*, Systematic Theology, vol. 1 (Minneapolis: Fortress Press, 2015), 416. Sonderegger echoes Lampe's *God as Spirit* on p. 418: 'The modes and relations of God toward us simply are *God*, God with us.'

105. Ibid., 463.

106. The echo of Romans 8.26 ('groanings too deep for words') is significant here, as discussed in Chapter 3, pp. 78, 81, 87.

107. See, *e.g.*, Amos N. Wilder, *Theopoetic: Theology and the Religious Imagination* (Eugene, OR: Wipf & Stock, 2014), 6, 8, 12.

lyrics, Revelation 22.17, brings the New Testament to a close with an invocation of Christ in which the voices of the Spirit and the church become one:

> The Spirit and the bride say, 'Come.'
> And let everyone who hears say, 'Come.'
> And let everyone who is thirsty come.
> Let anyone who wishes take the water of life as a gift.

The lyric mode here presents another perspective again on the relationship of Spirit and spirit. In these words of invocation, the ultimate optative act which seeks the presence of Christ and the fulfilment of all that has been promised, there is not only a participation, partnership, mingling or mixing but a melding of voices such that they cannot be told apart.

It would be unwise to simply equate poetic creativity with the Spirit of creation, or the poem with the inspired voice of the Lord. Nevertheless, it seems more than reasonable to turn to lyric, so often used as the language of prayer and devotion, to reflect on the timbre and cadence of a discourse that seeks to resonate with the Spirit of beauty and joy, of love and justice, truth and life. Thus, each of the chapters of this book in a different way listens out for the sound of the Spirit heard in and through a lyric poetics, as the One who works in partnership with the Word in the speech act of divine creativity, who breathes in and through our prayers, who inspires human speech, in whom we live and through whom we participate in the creative work of life before God. At issue is not poetry as such but how the lyric voice communicates humanity's creative negotiations with the structures of life: of body, culture and community, conveying the relationship between immanence and transcendence in and beyond human speech.

English lyric tradition(s)

Before moving on to more substantive discussions, it is worth a final note on the category of the 'English lyric tradition', as used in this book. As mentioned above, while there are good reasons for choosing this focus, it is not without its difficulties. Alongside the merits of English lyric tradition outlined above, the author's educational and cultural background and the inclusion of this book in a series on English theology have together influenced the decision to focus on this area in this exploration of theological lyric theory.

If this project is to point towards any more generalizable conclusions, issues surrounding the 'Englishness' of the English lyric must be acknowledged. In its earlier history, the championing of English poetry was cast as a defence of a despised vernacular against the cultural dominance of Latin and other European languages. In praise of English poetry, commentators have typically pointed to distinctive features such as the range of vocabulary available to the English poet, which owes much to the combination of Anglo-Saxon with Norse and Latin in English. In the early seventeenth century, Samuel Daniel praised the 'natural' music of accentual-syllabic metre, often attributed to the irregularity of English grammar which struggles to conform to the quantitative or syllabic metre of Latin and Romance poetry.[108] Iambic pentameter reflects the rhythms of English speech but also lays claim to a more global æsthetic and epistemological value as an echo of the universal rhythms of heartbeat and breath.[109] Herein lies the danger. As English became the language of empire, claims to global significance took on the tone of domination. Through the Romantics of the eighteenth and nineteenth centuries, lyric became an expression of English sensibility, a refinement of thought and feeling that supposedly reflected a refined civilization.[110] Not much later, Palgrave thought that lyric reflected the particularity of 'the English mind' and hoped that his collection would be read wherever English, 'the dominant language of the world', is used.[111] The impact of such linguistic colonialism has been felt up to the present.[112] Seamus Heaney's poem 'Singing School' portrays the peculiar experience of studying English literature in Northern Ireland in the 1950s and 1960s:

> Ulster was British, but with no rights on
> The English lyric: all around us, though
> We hadn't named it, the ministry of fear.[113]

Cultural influence is never unidirectional. Through the legacy of empire, English lyric tradition has incorporated linguistic varieties such as creole, patois, Multicultural London English and dialect poetry. It is therefore important in a study such as this to avoid implicit assumptions about poetic normativity that

---

108. Samuel Daniel, *A Defence of Ryme* (London: Edward Blount, 1603).

109. On English meter, see T. Cable, R. H. Osberg, G. T. Wright and R. McDonald, 'English Prosody', *PEPP*.

110. On the roots of this development, see Thomas Warton, who identified poetry with the national spirit and praised the 'perfection [of poetry] in a polished age' in *The History of English Poetry from the Close of the Eleventh to the Commencement of the Eighteenth Century*, vol. 1, 3 vols (London: J. Dodsley, 1774–81), i–ii; discussed in René Wellek, *The Rise of English Literary History* (Chapel Hill: University of North Carolina Press, 1941), 85–6.

111. Palgrave, *Treasury*, Preface. Moving into the twentieth century, literary criticism around the First and Second World Wars turned to the English lyric as evidence of a national spirit and a distinctive 'English genius'. See, *e.g.*, Laurence Binyon, 'The English Lyric', *Journal of the Royal Society of Arts* 89, no. 4600 (November 1941): 786.

112. On the antagonistic relationship of some Caribbean poetry with iambic pentameter, see Chapter 1, below. See also the discussion of Kae Tempest in Chapter 3.

113. Seamus Heaney, 'The Ministry of Fear', in *North* (London: Faber & Faber, 1992), 57, Faber Poetry Library.

perpetuate Anglocentrism and to draw conclusions conscious of the complex and difficult history of the English lyric.[114]

The chapters of this book are therefore situated in a critical relationship with the canon of theologically significant English poetry. The contributions can make no claim to being representative, but they do seek to be inclusive in terms of culture, confession and gender.[115] Although modern performance poets and UK minority ethnic voices tend to be discussed at the ends of chapters, it will hopefully be clear that these sections are not supplementary but integral to the main argument, casting new light on texts from the historical canon of the devotional lyric.[116] The linguistic multiplicity of medieval poetics, for example, takes on new significance in the light of the multilingual context of postcolonial Britain, while the Romantic emphasis on the individual takes on new forms in the charisma of the performance poet.

Decisions about which texts to address in this study have also been influenced by insights drawn from contemporary lyric theory. Anthologies of English religious poetry have commonly celebrated the lyric as the genre of private devotion, the voice of the solitary individual before God.[117] This study does not reject this widespread and influential expressivist model of the personal devotional

---

114. Such sensitivity is remarkably rare in studies of the devotional lyric hitherto. Consider, e.g., Jay Hopler and Kimberly Johnson, eds, *Before the Door of God: An Anthology of Devotional Poetry* (New Haven, CT: Yale University Press, 2013), which is a collection of global devotional poetry that privileges the English lyric tradition. In Andrew Hass, David Jasper and Elisabeth Jay, eds, *The Oxford Handbook of English Literature and Theology* (Oxford: Oxford University Press, 2009), Oxford Handbooks Online, Jay argues that straying beyond the canon of theologically significant literature, which is predominantly Anglican, male and English, would be 'historically misleading', although in his postscript Hass notes 'globalization' and 'culturality' as key elements of the future of English literature and theology, 'Now and in England', 3–14 (12) and 'The Future of English Literature and Theology', 3–14, 841–58 (841).

115. Several of the anthologies mentioned below highlight George Herbert and seventeenth-century metaphysical poetry as the height of the English religious lyric, but for Peter Levi the apogee of English religious poetry is the radical individual spirit of William Blake (Peter Levi, ed., *The Penguin Book of English Christian Verse* (London: Penguin, 1984), 30), while Donald Davie highlighted Isaac Watts, Charles Wesley and William Cowper as exemplars of a Protestant ascetic æsthetic (Donald Davie, ed., *The New Oxford Book of Christian Verse* (Oxford: Oxford University Press, 1981), xviii–xix, xxix).

116. Consider T. S. Eliot's reflections on canonicity in 'Tradition and the Individual Talent', which describes the canon as not fixed but changing with each new addition, so that 'the past [is] altered by the present as much as the present is directed by the past', *The Sacred Wood: Essays on Poetry and Criticism* (London: Methuen, 1920), 42–53 (44–5).

117. Edward Thompson argued that lyric is the most appropriate genre for devotional expression as 'Religion rises in solitude, when the soul is face to face with God'. Thompson, ed., *O World Invisible: An Anthology of Religious Poetry* (London: Ernest Benn, 1931), v. For a

The roots of the English lyric

Each of the theo-lyric reflections of the main chapters emerges out of a discussion of a significant period in the history of the English lyric, which is focussed on one of the four key characteristics of the lyric poem and interpreted through the insights of contemporary lyric theory. As an illustration of this approach, and a gesture towards some of the major themes explored below, this Introduction concludes with a brief reflection on the Anglo-Saxon roots of English lyric tradition. Through four possible origin-stories for the English spiritual lyric, it offers an alternative starting point for reflection to the Romantic model of affective-expressivism, sketching an outline of a lyric tradition located in public worship and rooted in community, a musical discourse that sits on the threshold of orality and literacy, the secular and the sacred.[118]

Most of the surviving Old English poetry is transcribed in four tenth-century manuscripts, which record poems that circulated orally for generations. The vagaries of chance through which these texts were preserved impart a sense of fragility, mystery and even miracle to the gift of what remains of the poetic heritage of Old English. Situated between the Latin of the monasteries and the Germanic influences of Saxon poetry, this was a poetry shaped by the Christian scriptures, the conventions of classical verse and pagan mythology. Representing a transitional

---

similar attitude, see G. Lacey May, ed., *English Religious Verse* (London: J.M. Dent and Sons, 1937), vii. Levi believed that the height of Christian poetry is lyrical, 'individual and radically personal' (Levi, *Christian Verse*, 26), while Elizabeth Jennings praised religious lyrics as 'records of the spiritual experience of a poet', Elizabeth Jennings, ed., *The Batsford Book of Religious Verse* (London: B.T. Batsford Ltd., 1981), 9. R. S. Thomas follows a similar line by beginning his collection with poems that 'apostrophize God', addressing God through the individual lyric voice: Thomas, ed., *The Penguin Book of Religious Verse* (Harmondsworth: Penguin, 1963), 10. Hopler and Johnson also argue that the 'lyric I' is particularly suited to the expression of devotion and the relationship between the individual and God. Kimberley Johnson, '"A Heavenly Poesie": The Devotional Lyric', in *Before the Door*, ed. Hopler and Johnson, xxv–xxx. S. T. Kimbrough might have privileged lyricality as musicality in his study of Wesley's hymns, but he stresses instead their lyrical affectivity and subjectivity: *The Lyrical Theology of Charles Wesley: A Reader* (Cambridge: Lutterworth, 2014), xii, 3.

118. There is a distinctive music to Old English verse but its four-beat rhythms, use of the cæsura, alliterative patterns, compound words and epithets are also seeded into the later history of English poetry. Consider, *e.g.*, the alliterative patterns to be found in medieval lyrics or the poetry of Gerard Manley Hopkins, or the influence of Old English verse on Ezra Pound, David Jones and W. H. Auden. See T. Cable, R. H. Osberg, G. T. Wright and R. McDonald, 'English Prosody', *PEPP*.

moment between orality and textuality, these texts retain many of the ritual features of a language adapted from liturgical performance.[119] It has echoes of performance, song, chant and music that draw the reader to listen beyond the text, leading them back into a mythical antiquity, on towards the ineffable or in towards the fireside of community, to hear its music and join in the song.

The quintessential origin-story for the English lyric is the legendary tale recounted in Bede's *Ecclesiastical History* about the oldest named poet of the English language. The miraculous story of Cædmon's reception of the gift of spiritual song has been recounted above, a story of lyric beauty received as a gift of divine grace and a work of human craft. Cædmon's only known poem is a hymn of creation recorded by Bede, not in English but in a Latin prose paraphrase.[120] The original poem is obscured, dislocated to the margins where the first Old English glosses of Bede's text reside.[121] Bruce O'Brien describes translation as a site of 'negotiation between cultures', and so this poem sits at the site of encounter between Latin and English, between 'high' culture and the vernacular, between textuality and orality.[122]

As the earliest dateable Christian English lyric, Cædmon's hymn inaugurates this genre with an epideictic poem, a poem of praise. This origin-poem is itself a tale of origins, a psalm in praise of the creator God as the great *scōp* or poet of the world. In Genesis 2.19, the gift of speech is revealed when Adam names the creatures. The poet turns this primitive gift back towards the giver through a series of epithets that both name and describe the God who is worthy of worship. God is praised as the 'hāleg Scepen' (holy Creator), the one who creates the earth for humanity, with the heavens their roof and the earth their fold. The alliterative music of the poem is heard in phrases such as 'Metudæs maecti' (the might of the creator God) or 'uerc Uuldurfadur' (the works of the father of glory). Forming one unit or half of a four-beat line divided by a cæsura, these pithy epithets craft a heartbeat rhythm that names and praises God with every beat.[123]

---

119. Heather Maring, *Signs That Sing: Hybrid Poetics in Old English Verse* (Gainesville: University Press of Florida, 2017), chaps 1 and 7.

120. Bede, *Historia Ecclesiastica* bk 4 chap. 24.

121. Ibid. Bede argues that a poetic translation would denigrate the beauty of the original poem, ironically obscuring the very vernacular that he means to celebrate. English translations appear *e.g.* in the *Moore Bede* (Cambridge University Library MS. Kk 5.16, fol. 128v); *Saint Petersburg Bede* (Saltykov-Schedrin Public Library MS. Q.v.I.18, fol. 107); *English Bede* (Bodleian Library, Tanner MS 10). It is debated whether these are faithful recordings of the original poem or retranslations from the Latin. For the former argument, see, *e.g.*, Paul Cavill, 'The Manuscripts of Cædmon's Hymn', *Anglia* 118 (2000): 499–530. For the latter, see, *e.g.*, Andy Orchard, 'Poetic Inspiration and Prosaic Translation: The Making of Cædmon's Hymn', in *'Doubt Wisely': Papers in Honour of E. G. Stanley*, ed. M. J. Toswell and E. M. Tyler (London: Routledge, 1996), 402–22.

122. Bruce R. O'Brien, *Reversing Babel: Translation among the English during an Age of Conquests, c. 800 to c. 1200* (Newark: University of Delaware Press, 2011), xii.

123. Old English taken from the *Moore Bede*, written in a Northumbrian dialect close to that of Cædmon. Translation my own.

According to Bede, while Cædmon's poems were composed in private, ruminated upon like a cow chewing its cud, they were commissioned by and produced for the edification of a community, who would recite poetry to the music of the harp passed round after a meal.[124] The opening phrase, 'Nū scylun hergan' (Now let us praise), is therefore more than a rhetorical flourish. It carries a tangible sense of exhortation, drawing the hearer to devotion as a member of a community of praise. It signals the poem as not only a description of God's mighty acts but an illocutionary act, a call to worship.

The mythology of songs shared around the mead-hall fire is equally vital to the second prototype for the English spiritual lyric, the affective-expressive mode of elegiac poems such as *The Seafarer* and *The Wanderer*. The former is the archetypal 'song of myself', the latter the soliloquy of a lonely traveller cast on the cold seas after losing their lord, kin and home.[125] These dramatic monologues might be read as lyrics of solitude and interiority, but such an interpretation would be anachronistic.[126] Their first-person voice is that of the lonely sufferer but also that of the *scop*, the bardic songster and word-crafter whose proper place was performing in front of the community. The Wanderer finds wisdom in solitude, but the wise exile yearns to return to the joy of community, although this home is ultimately found not on earth, where life is fleeting, but in the mercy of the Lord.[127]

The climax of *The Wanderer* is an expression of lament that centres on the Latin poetic commonplace *ubi sunt*. The conventional rhetorical questions 'Where has the horse gone? Where is the rider? Where is the giver of gifts?' are turned into straightforward lamentation through the cry *eala*, often translated 'oh' or 'alas': 'Gone is [Alas for] the bright cup. Gone is [Alas for] the mailed warrior. Gone is [Alas for] the glory of the prince.'[128] This word epitomizes the Old English elegiac tradition. *Eala* emits a sound that is close to a pure cry of pain, but its poetic use, particularly here through the intensificatory effect of repetition, highlights its phonaesthetic beauty. There is a curious sweetness to the term in this poetic context that captures a double sense of grief and longing. In the *Confessions*, Augustine condemned the enjoyment of vicarious grief through the arts, worried that it evoked a false compassion.[129] The Wanderer, though for different reasons,

---

124. Bede, *Historia Ecclesiastica* 4. 24. On the communal character of Cædmon's poetry, see Robert Stanton, *The Culture of Translation in Anglo-Saxon England* (Cambridge: D.S. Brewer, 2002), 117.

125. *The Wanderer* and *The Seafarer* are both found in the Exeter Book (Exeter Cathedral Library MS 3501). Note the allusion to *The Seafarer*, line 1, in the title of Walt Whitman's *Song of Myself* (1891–2).

126. See Craig Williamson's brief introductions to the poems of the Exeter Book in *The Complete Old English Poems* (Philadelphia, PA: University of Pennsylvania Press, 2017), Kindle.

127. *Cf.* similar themes in *Beowulf*, lines 35–47.

128. *The Wanderer*, lines 97–101, adapted from Williamson, *Old English Poems*.

129. Augustine, *Confessions* bk 3 paras 2–4.

similarly extols the wisdom of keeping one's counsel in grief, while at the same time sharing theirs with the audience. The danger of a grief shared with strangers, turned into a cathartic spectacle for others, is technically avoided, as the poem presents itself as an internal monologue reported by the poet and overheard by the audience. Through this poetic sleight of hand, the Wanderer uncovers the consolation to be found in the elegy that makes music out of grief, sweetness out of sorrow. Despite a broadly providentialist frame, this poem does not search for a justification of suffering but finds comfort in honouring the remembered good that forms a part of present sorrow, finding a language in which the pain of loss is bound up with gratitude for the memory of what is lost.

Another model for the English spiritual lyric is to be found in the 'paraliturgical' language of the Advent Lyrics.[130] This lyric sequence of twelve poems, once associated with the poet Cynewulf, is inspired by the Advent antiphons: 'O Sapientia', 'O Adonai' etc. Well established in liturgical use by the ninth and tenth centuries, the Advent antiphons may have been sung at vespers alongside the Magnificat. The Advent poems are not texts for liturgical use but poetic meditations on Christ and Mary inspired by the liturgy. These poems nevertheless retain many of the performative features of liturgical language, including the structure of the poems which follows that of the antiphons (an opening invocation followed by theological exposition and a final petition to Christ), and the cry 'O' (old English *eala*), that opens many of the poems.[131] Take, for example, the second of the Advent Lyrics, which elaborates upon the antiphon *O Clavis David*, extolling Christ as the one who unties the knot of life and opens the womb of Mary. The line 'Eal giofu gæstlic grundsceat geondspreot' ('all spiritual gifts – sprang up throughout the earth') recapitulates the opening 'O' (*eala*) of the poem, as it marvels at the overshadowing Spirit who brings to life the seeds of prophecy long hidden in the dark earth.[132] The word 'O' is triply significant for theo-lyric reflection. As described above, it comes as close as possible to the pure sound of the visceral cry. At the same time, it is a formalized feature of liturgical language and indicative of the vocative mode of address to God. As will be explored in Chapter 2, 'O' gets to the heart of lyric discourse by opening up the powerful dynamics of private words spoken in community. In this short word, the formal structures of ceremonial language and the sound of high emotion come together.

The final origin-story for the English spiritual lyric comes at the end of the Anglo-Saxon period. Reginald of Durham's twelfth-century account of the hermit Godric is the earliest manuscript containing English poems with their music. Reginald's story of Godric's poetic inspiration is comparable to Bede's history of Cædmon,

---

130. See Maring, *Signs That Sing*, 136–7; Lawrence Besserman, *Biblical Paradigms in Medieval English Literature: From Cædmon to Malary* (London: Routledge, 2012), 9. The poems are also known as 'Christ I' and are found in the Exeter Book.

131. See Jackson Justice Campbell, *The Advent Lyrics of the Exeter Book* (Princeton, NJ: Princeton University Press, 1959), 3, 11.

132. Campbell, *Advent Lyrics*, 47–8, line 25.

with a similar aim of celebrating the beauty of vernacular English.[133] In Reginald's story, it is not so much the words that are miraculous as the music, which comes first and to which the words are set. The repeated line 'Welcome, Simund' is basically a nonsense lyric; its main function is as a conduit for what Reginald describes as a sweet and intricate music, 'a voice of high jubilation'.[134] Unfortunately, this divine music did not survive. In the fragmented textual remains of the performed lyric, there is, as medieval literary critic Ardis Butterfield has argued, a sign of the depth and mystery of a form that still resonates with the 'silent and empty shape' of the song that has been lost.[135] The music that gives life to the poem may be silent but not absent, resonating through metre, rhythm and rhyme, through the sound of the words. The incompleteness of the poetic manuscript symbolizes the incompleteness of the textual lyric, which is not a deficiency so much as a sign of an unachieved plenitude. The written poem encapsulates the sense that what is core to lyric cannot necessarily be read directly off the page. The holes in the manuscript, its torn, burnt or disintegrated edges, draw the reader deeper into the poem in search for what is missing, the music that gives life to the text.

These four origin-stories for the English spiritual lyric correspond broadly to the four chapters below: lyric as a hymn of praise (Chapter 1), a prophetic cry from the heart (Chapter 3), a semi-liturgical form (Chapter 2) and a fragmented form (Chapter 4). They all share a trait of boundary-crossing between languages and genres, cultures and contexts, between immanence and transcendence. Regardless of their espoused theologies, the wisdom to which these poems call is not that of a spiritualized retreat from the world, but it is embedded in the human contexts of creative performance: of food, fire and song, of a community together in worship. If God is a poet and creation their song, then the Spirit who proceeds (is breathed out) from the Father must be heard not just in the breaths that intersperse the lines but in the musical vibration of air within the voice. Just as the hidden music of ancient poems resonates through their textual remains, so the Spirit's sound must reverberate in and through the corporeality of human creativity.

Chapter outline

Lyric does not lend itself to grand theoretical frameworks, so what follows is more along the lines of a lyric sequence, with interlocking motifs combining to build a kind of coherence, but with many thoughts left unfinished, threads left unpulled and avenues unfollowed. The four core chapters adopt a chronological structure, addressing key moments in the history of the English lyric in turn: the medieval

---

133. Reginald of Durham, *De Vita et Miraculis S, Godrici, Heremitæ de Finchale*, ed. J. Stevenson (London: Nichols, 1847), 306.

134. Ibid.; see also the translation in Ardis Butterfield, 'Why Medieval Lyric?', *ELH* 82, no. 2 (Summer 2015): 336–7.

135. Ibid.

lyric, early-modern metaphysical poetry, the Romantics and the modernist anti-lyric reaction. In each case, the history of the English lyric is reread in the light of contemporary lyric theory, and historical forms are brought into dialogue with contemporary British poetry as a way of expanding the canon. So, the multilingualism of the medieval macaronic lyric is brought into dialogue with code-switching Black British poetry, the liturgical character of lyric address in early-modern metaphysical poetry is explored in the light of the affectivity of modern charismatic worship, the prophetic subjectivity of the Romantic poets comes alongside the charisma of the spoken word artist, while the modern fragmentation of lyric is extended into the world of social media. The intention here is to open up alternative perspectives on the canon and to invite a reconsideration of the implications of historic lyric forms for modern theological reflection and practice.

The four core chapters also contemplate in turn one of the four main features of lyric outlined above: musicality, affective expression, the lyric 'I' and shortness. These standard features are inflected throughout by an interpretation of lyric as public, epideictic, rhetorical, performative discourse, informed by Culler and contemporary lyric theory. Hence, musicality is explored in relation to sweetness but also rhetorical persuasion, the discussion of affective expression focusses on the 'triangulated' nature of lyric address, the lyric 'I' is examined as socially oriented through the prophetic voice of testimony, while the disintegration of the lyric voice in modern poetry is explored through its epideictic role.

Throughout the chapters there is a listening for the voice of the Spirit who is heard in the creative performance of human speech, a sensing after the sweetness that is both integral to and transcendent of language, a receptiveness to the *charismata* conveyed through the gift of communication. Behind much of this lies a scriptural poetic of the Spirit as wind and breath, informed by Romans 8 as interpreted by contemporary feminist and systematic theology, alongside Genesis 1.2, Acts 2.1-8, Joel 2.28-9, Ezekiel 37.1-14, John 3.1-8 and John 20.22. Discernment of the Spirit as mixed up in the structures of human language, art and culture, will encounter much that is not holy, not life-giving. There is throughout the book an acknowledgement of the dangers of language and the risks associated with its misuse: whether that be the deceptive persuasiveness of music in spite of sense, the passionate affectivity that slides into emotional abuse, the irrepressible egotism of the 'I' or a chastening of language that results in the collapse of all sense and meaning. Through attentiveness to contexts where the gift of speech is most susceptible to misuse, a conviction emerges that it is important even, perhaps especially, here, to listen for the sound of the Spirit.

Chapter 1

MELOS OR BABBLE – LYRIC BEAUTY AND THE SPIRIT OF PENTECOST

Introduction

This chapter explores lyric beauty as *melos*, or the music of words, which is heard most clearly in poetry with a strong rhyme and rhythm. Orpheus, the classical patron of music and poetry, combines Apollonian attributes of beauty and harmony with Dionysian characteristics of passion and disorder. This chapter explores these two faces of lyric beauty through an examination of *melos* alongside its equivalent term 'babble', as a sweet sound combined of euphony and cacophony, a mixture of heavenly and earthly music. It reflects on the materiality of *melos* alongside its gestures towards transcendence through a discussion of poetry that foregrounds the relationship between sound and sense, specifically nonsense, macaronic (multilingual) and code-switching medieval lyrics and modern Black British poetry. Interweaving this argument is the sound of the Spirit as described in Acts 2.2: sometimes heard as a roar, sometimes a sweet song that inspires the apostles with eloquence. Through this discussion, a model of lyric beauty emerges that is characterized by the glorious disorder of the Pentecost story. These reflections on lyric sound are further developed by bringing the Pentecost miracle into conjunction with the babble of Babel in Genesis 11.1-9. Listening for the voice of the Spirit in the harmonious order of the song of heaven and the rough rhythms of sensuality, embracing the power and danger of lyric beauty, this chapter concludes by addressing the political and ethical implications of the music of language in theological discourse.

Melos: *Sweetness and power*

Melos comes from the Greek term for 'limb', providing both a corporeal metaphor for the sounds that are the substance of words and a sense of these sounds as part of a greater whole, the building blocks of language. The sound of words is formed through the body, a preverbal or primitive element of language that is rooted in the body and connected with language's capacity to rouse the passions and move the affections. *Melos* carries connotations of the inarticulate, but also of the inarticulable, in language. A constantly repeated word will lose its sense, becoming a sound alone, while a repeated sentence might be heard not as words but as melody. Jean-Luc Marion concludes from this that the enjoyment of verbal sound for its own sake, and not as a sign of semantic sense alone, reveals the 'excess' or transcendence of language.[1] *Melos* combines immanence and transcendence, pointing within and beyond itself to the joy of sound as the primal vocation of speech.

The pleasure afforded by *melos* is rightly described in terms of beauty. The phonaesthetic beauty of lyric sound has often been portrayed by the synaesthetic metaphor of sweetness, a term that evokes an intense enjoyment not unlike that of sexual delight. Pure and unmixed, sweetness can be an uncomplicated feeling, perhaps at risk of the saccharine. In combination with sorrow, as in lament, it can express more complex emotions such as nostalgia or regret. In combination with desire, as in the love song, it can evoke the sweet pain of yearning. Lyric sweetness is, according to Scottish poet Don Paterson, made up of a similarly complex balance of similarity and difference, repetition and variation.[2] What Paterson calls the 'lyric weave' arises out of the harmonious warp and weft of consonantal repetition and vowel variation.[3] This creates a balance not only of sounds but of fixity and fluidity, meaning and mystery, where the consonant represents the definitive knowledge of denotative sense and the vowel the expressive cry.[4] Paterson has explained how the clear articulation of the vowel-sound in poetry minimizes the *schwa* of the indefinable vowel, encouraging enjoyment in the sound of words and foregrounding variation in a way that invests the repetition of sound with particular significance. This is beauty not just as entertainment but as a carrier of meaning, part of, in Paterson's terms, 'a lyric process through which we work out what we think'.[5]

The cogency of *melos* lies in its persuasiveness: what Jonathan Culler has called 'charm' (an attractiveness combining beauty and influence), M. K. Blasing has called 'lyric power' and Roman Jakobson has called 'the spell of speech sounds'.[6] *Melos* takes language beyond description or denotation towards a ritual or even magical performativity, capable of shaping thought and provoking action. Take, for example, political slogans such as 'yes we can' or 'make America great again', 'let's get Brexit done' or 'for the many, not the few'. Their rhetorical power lies not only or even primarily in the sentiments they express but the feelings conjured

---

1. Jean-Luc Marion, *The Visible and the Revealed*, trans. Christina Gschwandtner (New York: Fordham University Press, 2008), 128–9.
2. Don Paterson, *The Poem: Lyric, Sign, Metre* (London: Faber, 2018), 92.
3. Ibid., 88.
4. Ibid., 92–3.
5. Ibid., 99.
6. Culler, *Lyric*, 258; Blasing, *Lyric Poetry*, 3; Roman Jakobson, *The Sound Shape of Language* (Bloomington, IN: Indiana University Press, 1979), 181.

by the music of the words. The musicality of a phrase may invest an idea with authority, a policy with legitimacy, a person with credibility, based not on rational argument but a pleasing sense of order or melody. For example, the UK government Covid-19 slogan, 'Hands. Face. Space' used single syllable words punctuated by a full stop to be clear and directive.[7] This firmness was rendered nonthreatening by the prominence of soft sibilants that intensify throughout the phrase, while the vowels open up from the short 'a' of hands to the long 'a' of 'space'. Operating at an often-subconscious level, the musical sense of a phrase can amount to little more than that it *feels right* but if, as George Steiner has suggested, 'form is content, content form', then such inarticulable feeling is integral to the meaning of a phrase.[8]

There is danger in melic power. As a component of lyric thinking, *melos* can support, complicate or even contradict the plain sense of a phrase, while the pre-eminence of sound over sense in nonsense or sound poetry can present a challenge to logical structures of discursive reasoning altogether. Julia Kristeva celebrated the subversive pleasure of *melos*, and its iconoclastic power to disrupt the making of sense, as the proper role of poetic language.[9] The power of music, in bypassing rational thought, is not to convince the hearer but rather, as if physically, to *move* them. What Friedrich Nietzsche called 'Dionyso-musical enchantment' can be compared to the song of the sirens or the music of the pied piper.[10] In the theological imagination, the connotations of error and deceit that these images associate with the rhetorical power of the music of language might be compounded by the spectre of heresy, a force that leads not on but astray.

Melos has been outlined here as a powerful combination of immanence and transcendence, corporeality and spirituality, an observation previously made from a sacramental perspective by Steiner and from an eschatological perspective by Jeremy Begbie. Steiner's sacramental approach defines music as the unparaphraseable and nonrational sense within all language, a mediation between body and air through the vibrations of throat and ear drum.[11] Begbie describes the interplay of tension and resolution in musical harmony as a gesture towards a final consummation, much as poetic rhyme schemes or the mid-line cæsura of the English lyric can construct a pattern of rising tension that constructs

---

7. Department of Health and Social Care, UK Government, 'New campaign to prevent spread of coronavirus indoors this winter' (9 September 2020), https://www.gov.uk/government/news/new-campaign-to-prevent-spread-of-coronavirus-indoors-this-winter.

8. George Steiner, *Real Presences: Is There Anything in What We Say?* (London: Faber & Faber, 2010), 250.

9. See Julia Kristeva, *Revolution in Poetic Language* (New York: Columbia University Press, 1984), 81; see also Friedrich Nietzsche's discussion of Schiller's poetic process as constructed out of a '*musical mood*', *The Birth of Tragedy* (New York: Dover Publications, 1995), 33.

10. Ibid., 34.

11. Steiner, *Real Presences*, 249–51.

a hopeful expectation of resolution.[12] This chapter adopts not a sacramental or an eschatological but a pneumatological perspective on melic immanence and transcendence, exploring the power of sound through the lens of Pentecost, and examining its implications for an understanding of divine beauty and power as embedded in history and culture.

Babble: Sound and sense

In *The Anatomy of Criticism*, Northrop Frye defines the musical and visual poles of lyric thought as 'babble and doodle'.[13] The primary meaning of babble is 'nonsense', a term that carries associations of both play and disorder. As a synonym for *melos*, it describes the mystifyingly anarchic process of drawing sense out of sound. Babble is onomatopoeic of an infant's early experiments with language and evocative of the experience of hearing unfamiliar or multiple overlaid speech patterns. It captures the joy of doodling with words, but arguably loses the connotations of music and therefore of beauty suggested by *melos*. According to Frye, poetry crafts a 'distinctively lyrical union of sound and sense' by drawing sense and form out of sonic resonances, through devices such as rhyme, alliteration, assonance and paronomasia (punning).[14] Nevertheless, the nonsensical features of babble remain a part of language, as in doggerel, where the rules of rhythm and rhyme may run roughshod over considerations of sense, value or refinement.[15]

Babble highlights the complexities and ambivalences of making linguistic sense out of sound. The connotative qualities of specific sounds are difficult to pin down, such that prosody is a notoriously difficult area of poetics.[16] The plosive 'b' of babble, for example, might communicate anything from excitement to anger to disgust to the sound of a brook. It is highly contested as to whether particular sounds contain any intrinsic meaning at all. Is the paradoxically apposite rhyming of 'womb' and 'tomb', for example, simply a happy accident or suggestive of a kind of linguistic doctrine of signatures, whereby sound and meaning are inextricably intertwined? The significance of the sound of language is also at the mercy of changing tastes and sensibilities. Frye alludes to this when discussing the poetic use of the pun, and its 'perilous balance … between verbal wit and hypnotic incantation'.[17] How is the full sense of a phrase to be discerned if it may be either

---

12. Jeremy Begbie, *Theology, Music and Time* (Cambridge: Cambridge University Press, 2000), 98–127.

13. Northrop Frye, *Anatomy of Criticism: Four Essays* (Princeton, NJ: Princeton University Press, 1957), 275.

14. Ibid., 272.

15. Ibid., 276–7. Consider, *e.g.*, the limerick where the meaning is often determined by the rhyme and rhythm.

16. See R. Winslow, 'Prosody', *PEPP*, 1117–20.

17. Frye, *Anatomy*, 276.

risible or charming, depending on whether it is received in a mode of detachment or commitment, scepticism or faith?[18]

Despite these difficulties, a cursory phenomenology of infant babble as a component of speech development reinforces the notion that poetic sound is more than mere noise. As Frye argues, babble is nothing like a '*cri de Coeur*'; it represents instead a progression from the instinctive self-expression of the cry towards the intentional crafting of communication.[19] It pushes the boundaries of speech, not, as metaphor does, beyond articulacy and towards transcendence, but beyond noise and towards the intelligibility of verbal articulation.[20] The joy of infant babble comes not just from the delight of making sound but also from the way these sounds point towards meaning, a promise fulfilled in the moment of epiphany when sense is both made and grasped.

It is here that a phenomenology of babble might connect with a theology of Pentecost, as brought into dialogue with Genesis 11.1-9. In the history of interpretation, the 'babble' (*balal* in Hebrew) into which humanity descends in Genesis 11.7 and 9 has often been described as a consequence of human pride, as the breakdown of communication and a sign of cultural separation. However, as biblical scholar Theodore Hiebert has argued, the 'babble' of this story is better understood less as a punishment than as accomplishing the divine plan for a 'polyglot world'.[21] The violence of enforced homogeneity and narrow self-preservation embodied in the aborted tower is overcome by the 'mixing' of languages. Babble is a blessing that realizes the promise and command of Genesis 1.28, for humanity to be fruitful, to multiply and fill the earth. In this interpretation, the xenoglossia of Pentecost is not the reversal of Babel but its fulfilment, a miracle of universal understanding but not of uniformity. The rest of the chapter explores how the song of the Spirit of Pentecost can be heard through the power of *melos* and the beauty of babble, through transcendent melodies that aspire towards a heavenly music and through demotic anthems that agitate for social transformation.

---

18. *NB* Helen Gardner defines religious poetry as characterized primarily by 'commitment', in *The Faber Book of Religious Verse*, ed. Gardner (London: Faber, 1971), 7. Religious language might be heard as risible to an ear that does not share that commitment.

19. Frye, *Anatomy*, 278. *Cf.* David F. Ford on the 'cry' of wisdom, see below, p. 48.

20. See, *e.g.*, the discussion of literal and metaphorical language in relation to descriptions of transcendence in Soskice, *Metaphor*, 117; *cf.* Rowan Williams, *The Edge of Words* (London: Bloomsbury, 2014), x, 146, 169, who describes metaphor but also rhyme and rhythm as poetic ways of probing the boundaries of language and making new meaning.

21. Theodore Hiebert, 'The Tower of Babel and the Origin of the World's Cultures', *Journal of Biblical Literature* 126 (2007): 47. For a similar interpretation of the text, see also Walter Brueggemann, *Genesis: Interpretation* (Atlanta: John Knox, 1982), 97–104.

The song of Heaven in the medieval lyric

Music as danger and divine beauty

Melos is nowhere more prominent than in the medieval religious lyric. Its carols, adaptations of European *canzone* and vernacular translations of Latin hymns were primarily oral, performative and musical forms of poetry.[22] The lost music of these lyrics can still be heard in the conventional formalism of their acoustic world, marked by devices such as a four-stress rhythm inherited from Old English poetry, quantitative metre and end-rhyme schemes often attributed to troubadour ballads, and alliterative patterns more often associated with Anglo-Saxon poetry.[23] This poetry played an integral role in devotional culture. In what has been termed a lyric preaching style, Franciscan preachers drew on contemporary poems, not just as a mnemonic or structural device, but because of the power of poetry to move a congregation.[24]

Although music was deeply integrated into devotional culture, the spiritual literature of the period displayed a conflicted attitude towards it, seeing music as both an echo of the song of heaven and a dangerously sensual medium. This reflected in part a dualistic perspective on the relationship between the carnal world of the body and the intellectual world of the spirit. In his treatise 'Of the Song of Angels', Walter Hilton contrasted the harmony of heaven which is 'above all … imagination and reason' with the sensory experience of song, concluding that any claim to have actually *heard* the song of angels must be delusory, however ingenuously rooted in a desire to hear the voice of God.[25] For Hilton, the sensual

---

22. Butterfield discusses the distinctive musicality of the medieval lyric as part of a discussion of the importance of music to lyric more generally in 'Why Medieval Lyric?': 324, 327; on the musicality of the medieval lyric, see also David Fuller, 'Lyrics, Sacred and Secular', in *A Companion to Medieval Poetry*, ed. Corinne Saunders (London: Wiley-Blackwell, 2010), 263–5; *cf.* Christina Whitehead, 'Middle English Religious Lyrics', in *A Companion to the Middle English Lyric*, ed. Thomas Gibson Duncan (Cambridge: D.S. Brewer, 2005), 96, for a view of the Harley lyrics as expressivist or 'personal' lyrics.

23. For a summary of the development of middle English verse forms, see K. Davis *et al.*, 'England, Poetry Of', *PEPP*. For an earlier perspective on the conventional formalism of English lyric musicality, see Rosemary Woolf, *The English Religious Lyric in the Middle Ages* (Oxford: Clarendon, 1968), 3. See also Andrew Albin's discussion of the scholarly debates surrounding alliterative verse in *Richard Rolle's Melody of Love*, trans. Andrew Albin (Toronto: Pontifical Institute of Mediaeval Studies, 2018), 34.

24. On the connection between the medieval lyric and Franciscan spirituality, see David Lyle Jeffrey, *The Early English Lyric and Franciscan Spirituality* (Lincoln, NE: University of Nebraska Press, 1975), 2. Friar John of Grimestone included translations of Latin poems in his preaching handbook, while the sermons of the Northern Homily Cycle were written in verse, see Siegfried Wenzel, *Preachers, Poets, and the Early English Lyric* (Princeton, NJ: Princeton University Press, 1986), 102–18.

25. Walter Hilton, 'Of the Song of Angels', in *The Cell of Self-Knowledge: Seven Early English Mystical Treatises*, ed. Edmund G. Gardner (New York: Cooper Square Publishers, 1966), 66.

dangers of earthly music were so serious as to require an utter divestment of the theoretical perfection of the unheard music of heaven from any hint of verbal materiality.[26] On the other hand, music played an important role in mystical texts of the time. Margery Kempe wrote of the mystical audition that led her to renounce the marriage bed in favour of the contemplative life, as 'a sownd of melodye so swet and delectable, hir thowt, as sche had ben in paradyse' (a sound of melody so sweet and delectable, she thought she had been in paradise), while Julian of Norwich recounted a vision of God on His throne, filled with the 'mervelous melody of endelesse love'.[27] These visions of heaven embraced the sensuality of sound, depicting the beauty and power of the Spirit as a sweet melody.

The peril and power of music came together in Richard Rolle's theology of song or *canor*, which described the transforming power of the Spirit as a sweet melody capable of turning grief into joy, prose into praise, 'thought … into song; and the mind … into full sweet sound'.[28] Rolle's position on music was, on the surface, somewhat inconsistent. Reflecting the anxieties of the time, he claimed to eschew all earthly forms of music (even the liturgical singing of psalms), but expressed these sentiments in an intensely alliterative, melodious Latin prose.[29] The sometimes

---

26. A musicology stretching back through Boethius and Augustine to Pythagoras viewed the mathematical harmony of the heavenly spheres as a purely spiritual or intellectual, and therefore non-auditory, beauty. See, *e.g.*, Augustine, *De Musica* 6.1.1–6.2.2, 6.17.58; Boethius, *De Institutione Musica*. However, recent studies of Augustine and Boethius argue that these works resist a simple dualism between spirit and body and actually embrace the sensory experience of music. See Carol Harrison, *On Music, Sense, Affect and Voice* (London: Bloomsbury, 2019), 8–10; Stephen Blackwood, *The Consolation of Boethius as Poetic Liturgy* (Oxford: Oxford University Press, 2015), 1, 11–12.

27. Margery Kempe, *The Book of Margery Kempe*, ed. Lynn Staley (Kalamazoo, MI: Medieval Institute Publications, 1996), bk 1 part 1 chap. 3; Julian of Norwich, 'the sixth revelation', *Revelations of Divine Love* (long text), chap. 14, in *The Writings of Julian of Norwich*, ed. Nicholas Watson and Jacqueline Jenkins (University Park, PA: Pennsylvania State University Press, 2006), 173. *NB* given this chapter's focus on sound, medieval quotations retain the original spelling, but clarificatory notes are provided where they might aid comprehension. Clarificatory notes for the Duncan extracts are from Duncan; the rest are mine.

28. Richard Rolle, *The Fire of Love or Melody of Love and The Mending of Life or The Rule of Living*, trans. Richard Misyn, ed. Frances Comper, 2nd edn (London: Methuen, 1920), bk 1, chaps 14–15.

29. The most convincing assessments of Rolle's attitude to music include Katherine Zieman's notion of textual sacralization or the ritual construction of the affections through music, and Andrew Albin's notion of Rolle's 'canoric aesthetics'. Both argue that Rolle was not seeking to imitate the song of heaven but rather, through analogy with it, to incite in the reader a desire for God. Katherine Zieman, 'The Perils of Canor: Mystical Authority, Alliteration, and Extragrammatical Meaning in Rolle, the Cloud-Author, and Hilton', *The Yearbook of Langland Studies* 22 (2008): 145; Andrew Albin, 'Listening for Canor in Richard Rolle's Melos Amoris', in *Voice and Voicelessness in Medieval Europe: The New Middle Ages*, ed. I. R. Kleiman (New York: Palgrave Macmillan, 2015), 179.

overwhelming impact of this melic device is revealed in Andrew Albin's stylistically faithful translation of Rolle's *Melos Amoris* (*Melody of Love*), in which he describes the heavenly music of the Spirit as a converting power, as follows:

> Let material magnificence diminish in their minds; let the Muse enamor modern men with music so their mourning over misfortune transmutes into melody ...[30]

The dense consonance of sound in passages such as this crafts a kind of monodic euphony that is reminiscent of plainchant, a sacralized sound evocative of the music of heaven. Much as Rolle used the melody of language to convey the beauty and transfiguring power of the Spirit, the following section explores how the devotional lyric wove the materiality of sound into a vision of the kingdom of heaven, lending substance to the echo of heavenly song through nonsense-lyrics and macaronic poetry.

The joy of sound as an act of praise

The sound of joy in the medieval lyric conveys the joy of sound as an act of praise. In medieval liturgy, the most joyful noise was heard in the *jubilus* or melisma, a variegated melody sung on the final syllable of the alleluia in the high mass. The term *jubilus* is rooted in Augustine's notion of *jubilatio* or the Spirit-filled song of praise. This sound plays on the borders between inarticulacy and transcendence, described in his exposition of Psalm 33.3 as 'a sound signifying that the heart laboureth with that which it cannot utter'.[31] While the medieval *jubilus* was sung on a single-syllable note, Augustine took as his model for *jubilatio* the joy of the harvest song. Work songs such as these are not typically made up of a single sound but a babble of nonsense syllables or performative phrases like the 'way hey' of the sea shanty (potentially referring to weighing anchor) or the 'lullay' of the nurse or caregiver.[32] There is form and structure to nonsense-lyrics such as these that transcends the pure expressivity of the single-syllable cry, and in the context of worship, crafts out of word-like sounds an offering of praise to God.

Even so in medieval poetry, it is not only alleluias but nonsense-lyrics also carry the illocutionary force of praise. Consider, for example, the nonsense-refrains (known as 'burdens') of the carol.[33] The word 'nowell' (a common burden

---

30. Rolle, *Melody of Love*, chap. 16.

31. Augustine, *Expositions on the Book of Psalms*, trans. J. H. Parker, vol. 1 (Oxford: F. and J. Rivington, 1847), Psalm 33, second exposition, para. 8, verse 3.

32. Consider, *e.g.*, the lyric 'way hey' in 'Blow the Man Down' or the refrain to 'John Kanaka'. The latter is a macaronic poem whose refrain was derived from Hawaiian or Polynesian languages. See Stan Hugill, *Shanties from the Seven Seas* (London: Routledge and Kegan Paul, 1961), 203–4, 288.

33. The difference between a refrain and a burden is that a burden is independent of the stanza, usually appearing at the head of the lyric.

drawn from the French word for Christmas) was a generic sound of praise in the English carol, appearing also in carols on other subjects.[34] Its bell-like sonority is almost onomatopoeic of joy, particularly in repetition, where all sense is lost in its ringing chime. The sixfold repetition of 'nowell' in the lyric 'Owt of your slepe aryse and wake' is a particularly striking example.[35] Performative of a peal of bells, this burden awakes a sleeping audience to announce a new dawn of gladness.[36] The nonsense-burden that opens the Christmas carol 'Abowt the fyld thei pyped full right' imitates the sound of shepherds' pipes. This cry, '*Tyrlé, tyrlo*', is described in the lyric itself as a 'merry' noise, delighting the ear through its combination of consonantal repetition and vowel variation. It is a representation of shepherds' music, but as the carol progresses it becomes clear that this noise is also an echo of heavenly song. Each stanza is punctuated by this melodic burden, as the subject moves from the shepherds of the nativity story to the angels' song, to the song of heaven, concluding with the exhortation 'to syng and mak good chere' here and now. This charming phrase goes beyond earthly delight, as the carol brings the singer to the realization that the cheerful song they sing is in fact a participation in the song of heaven: 'Than may we syng in paradice,/ "Tyrlé tyrlo."'[37]

Carols were not exclusively Christmas songs; they are more accurately understood as songs that originate in the form of a circle dance, bound up with the sensuality of bodily movement.[38] If there is peril in the melic power of this form, it is not that of sensuality but rather of rendering deep truths ridiculous. In his seminal study of the medieval carol, Richard Leighton Greene notes that what he calls 'charm' modern ears might hear as silly. Nonsense, light-hearted noise and onomatopoeia, all sit on the edge of risibility for the modern reader. For Greene, this reflects a change in sensibility from a period 'when one could be pious and merry at the same time' to one where the two are divided.[39] Treading the thin line between the sweet and the grating, the beautiful and the risible, carols such as 'Abowt the fyld' reveal not just changing cultural mores but also something of the nature of melic power. *Melos* may conceal wisdom in plain sight, embedded in the humility and humour of babble. Its danger is that of courting scorn, the peril that the hearer may miss the sweetness of heavenly song and hear only noise.

---

34. See Richard Leighton Greene, *Early English Carols*, 2nd edn (Oxford: Oxford University Press, 1977), xxvii–xxviii.

35. A more well-known example is of course 'The First Nowell'.

36. MS. Oxford, Bodl. Arch. Selden B.26 in Thomas G. Duncan, ed., *Medieval English Lyrics and Carols* (Cambridge: D.S. Brewer, 2013), 226.

37. Bodl. MS. Eng. Poet. E. I, f. 60^r in Duncan, *Medieval English Lyrics*, 230–1.

38. Greene, *English Carols*, xi.

39. Ibid., xii.

Lyric eloquence as a gift of the Spirit

This chapter develops its pneumatological account of melic beauty and power in dialogue with the story of Pentecost, where the apostles are inspired by the sound of the wind and a vision of tongues of fire to preach the gospel in all the languages of the empire. Early and middle English interpretations of this passage often connected the coming of the Spirit with the gift of eloquence, identifying the Spirit of Pentecost with the charm of sweet words, the power of wit and wisdom and the promise of peace and unity. These three lyric qualities of the Spirit shape the reflections of the following three sections.

The sweetness of the Spirit in the lullaby carol The sound of the Spirit in Acts 2.2 is usually translated as the rushing or roaring of the wind, but it has also been interpreted as a song or in Bede's terms a *sono suavissima*: the 'sweetest sound'.[40] Sweetness is a common theme in medieval accounts of the Spirit at work. Bernard of Clairvaux described the Spirit's presence as a sweet kiss, while the N-Town Pentecost Play described the apostles as 'enbawmyd' (embalmed) with sweetness by the Spirit.[41] Rolle's mystical journey towards knowledge of God was marked by the trilogy of *fervor*, *dulcor* and *canor*, the experiences of heat, sweetness and melody. These have been likened to the medieval banquet hall with its fire, food and song, a foretaste of the heavenly kingdom, but might equally be read as signs of the Spirit from Acts 2: the flames that alight on the disciples, the sweet taste suggested by the tongues of fire and the music of the Spirit's sound.[42] These descriptions of the gift of the Spirit evoke the most powerful forms of sensory delight, as melody in the ear, warmth in the heart and sweetness on the tongue.

The sweetest of the medieval spiritual poems are the lullaby carols, through their combination of lyric beauty and intense emotion. Consider, for example, the spiralling repetition of sense and sound in the burden to 'I saw a fair maiden':

Lullay, myn lyking,	my beloved
my dere sone, myn sweting,	sweet one
Lullay, my dere herte,	dear heart
Myn own dere derling.[43]	darling

---

40. In this hymn for Pentecost, the Spirit who is heard as a melody inspires a song of praise in return. Bede, Hymn 7, *Venerabilis Opera; pars 4, opera rhythmica*, ed. J. Fraipont, CCSL 122 (Turnhout: Brepols, 1955), 424–5.

41. Bernard of Clairvaux, Sermon 89 ('Concerning the Holy Spirit's Kiss'); Douglas Sugano, ed., 'Play 40, Pentecost', in *The N-Town Plays* (Kalamazoo, MI: Medieval Institute Publications, 2007), online, https://d.lib.rochester.edu/teams/text/sugano-n-town-plays-play-40-pentecost, line 7.

42. See Rosamund S. Allen, *Richard Rolle: The English Writings* (New York: Paulist Press, 1988), 26.

43. MS: London, BL Sloane 2593, in Duncan, *Medieval English Lyrics*, 134.

These repeated variations on the theme of 'lullay, my dear one' intensify the song's potent combination of joy, desire and grief, evoking emotions associated with caring for a young child. The 'ing' rhymes mark the end-line pauses with a sound like a catch in the throat, while the extension of '*sone*' to '*sweting*' in line two (with its combination of the consonants *s – n*) and of '*dere*' to '*derling*' in line four evokes the expansiveness of love. This intensity of feeling is softened by the pleasing combination of sonic consonance and variation crafted by the alliterative patterns that structure the text.

The charm of a lullaby is intrinsic to its performative function, to lull a child to sleep. Lullaby carols foster a sense of added pathos by juxtaposing this sweet sound with a contemplation of Christ's death. 'As I lay upon a night' is another poem in which the love-longing of the songster is intensified through repetition:

Lullay, lullay, lay lay, lullay:
Mi derë moder, sing lullay,   *my dear mother*[44]

The irony of this carol is that it is not the mother but the Christ child that sings the lullaby. The child is attempting to draw the mother into song, a call that commands a response through its claims to parental love and obligation:

'sing now, moder,' seide that child,
'What me shal befalle
Here after whan I come to ild,   *when I grow up*
So don modrës alle.   *so do all mothers*

The Christ child in this carol, unlike some others, is not blessed with foreknowledge of his end.[45] He yearns to be comforted with sweet words, while the hearer understands that there can be little comfort for the child destined for the cross. At the same time, by reciting the soothing sounds of the lullaby the infant Christ brings comfort to the poem's speaker and its audience.

In this carol the world is turned upside down, the roles of mother and child are reversed, the relationship between babble and speech, sound and sense is inverted. The stanzas in which the child speaks to the mother are rendered in grammatical English, turning the sound of infant babble into a semantic form. The burden, on the other hand, which puts words into the mouth of the mother, is made up of nonsense words. In the mouth of Christ, babble becomes song, gesturing forward to the redemptive turning of all sound into sense, noise into sweet music. Mary is called to babble back a lullaby that is heard as nonsense but in its melic sweetness expresses a power and wisdom that transcends intelligibility. This babbling

---

44. MS: Edinburgh, NLS Advocates 18.7.21, in Duncan, *Medieval English Lyrics*, 135–7.

45. See, *e.g.*, 'Lullay, lullay, litel child, child rèstë thee a throwe', in Duncan, *Medieval English Lyrics*, 137–8.

dialogue expresses the mystery of a God who is encountered not just as Father but as Son, the Word heard not in the voice from heaven but in the babbling infant.

Wit and wisdom in the macaronic lyric The multilingual or macaronic lyric opens up the second feature of the coming of the Spirit that is manifest in the gift of lyric eloquence: the twofold gift of wit and wisdom. Xenoglossia was often described in terms of wit, a miraculous knowledge obtained without learning, such as in the story of Kempe's German confessor, who was able to understand her confession in English after thirteen days of prayer.[46] John Mirk's festival sermon on the day of Pentecost described the apostles' miraculous knowledge of other languages as making them like 'þe best clerkes yn all þe world'.[47] However, the gift of the Spirit was more than knowledge alone. John Skelton's early sixteenth-century poem *Speke, Parrot* confronted the limitations of a wit that lacks the heavenly wisdom of virtue, ridiculing the fashion for knowing multiple languages as like the indiscriminate parroting of a bird.[48] According to the Northern Homily Cycle, the Spirit's gift to the apostles was 'witte and wisdome' combined, a theme developed through a pun on the term 'Whitsun'. This was in fact a sevenfold gift, inspired by Isaiah 11.2: the gift of wisdom, understanding, counsel, strength, 'conandschipe' (keeping from bad company), 'reuthe of hert' (compassion/remorse), 'Goddes doute' (fear of the Lord) and contemplation of Christ's passion.[49]

Multilingualism has been of particular interest to critics of medieval literature. It grants insights into a society that was not only impacted by Latinate influences on the English church but was an evolving culture marked at the beginning by the imposition of Anglo Norman on Anglo-Saxon English and at the end by the polyglossic humanism modelled in Skelton's *Speke, Parrot*.[50] Macaronic texts reveal the vibrant multiplicity of English culture in this period, as well as its fault lines of class, nationality and religious status.[51] Critics have noted how medieval Christian

---

46. Kempe, *Booke*, 1.1.30.

47. John Mirk, Sermon 39, *Mirk's Festial: A Collection of Homilies*, ed. Theodor Erbe (London: Kegan Paul, 1905), f. 93a, p. 160. See also ibid., Sermon 38 'De Vigilia Pentecost Sermo', f. 91a, p. 156.

48. John Skelton, *Speke, Parrot*, stanzas 7–8, lines 46–56.

49. 'Homily 33, Pentecost', in *The Northern Homily Cycle*, ed. Anne B. Thompson (Kalamazoo, MI: Medieval Institute Publications, 2008), https://d.lib.rochester.edu/teams/text/thompson-northern-homily-cycle-homily-33-pentecost, lines 1–3, 24–46; see also Mirk, Sermon 38, 'De Vigilia Pentecostes', f. 91a-91b, pp. 156–7, which lists a similar sevenfold gift of knowledge, understanding, virtue and devotion.

50. See, *e.g.*, Judith Jefferson and Ad Putter, eds, *Multilingualism in Medieval Britain (c. 1066–1520): Sources and Analysis* (Turnout: Brepols, 2012), xvii, xxii, which applies modern theories of code switching to medieval culture, noting that 'the ability to move between languages opened up a wealth of possibilities: possibilities for subtle changes of register, for counterpoint, for linguistic playfulness'.

51. See ibid., xi–xxiv.

culture connected the multilingualism of the time with the stories of Babel and Pentecost, but the distinctive contribution of lyric poetry to this discourse has been underacknowledged.[52]

The macaronic lyric not only mimics the multilingualism of the period, it also gestures towards the miraculous babble of Pentecost. On the surface it is a form dominated by wit, but in devotional application it also seeks to convey something of the wisdom of the Spirit. The fifteenth-century Italianate term 'macaronic' comes from *macaroni* and carries the sense of a mixture of languages, just as the dish contains a mixture of ingredients. In its strict definition, macaronic poetry is a witty form that combines different languages to delight an audience. Most commonly a humorous form of verse, in the medieval period macaronic devices were also a feature of devotional poetry and preaching.[53] Wit remains a strong element of the devotional macaronic lyric, but at its best this form uses melic devices to draw together the distinct linguistic worlds of secular and sacred life, to inspire the hearer with knowledge of God and lead them into praise.

The most common combination of languages in medieval macaronic poetry is English and Latin. Latin was the language of scripture, liturgy, scholarship and the law, so Latin tags were used to imbue a poem with spiritual authority.[54] The didactic lyric 'Tutivillus', for example, admonishes the vice of chattering in church ('*Ad missam garulantes*') using the same language that would have been heard on a Sunday morning, with each tercet concluding with a line in Latin.[55] Latin could be the voice of authority; it could also elevate a poem towards spiritual song. The Latin burden of 'When Cryst was born of Mary fre' turns a nativity narrative into an act of devotion through its call to worship: '*Christo paremus cantica:/ "In excelsis gloria."*'[56] This spiritual capital could be exploited or degraded; the lyric 'Omnes gentes plaudite' is one example, as essentially a drinking song that incorporates a psalmic exclamation into its burden.[57] Such corruptions were only effective because of the status of the Latin language. 'In noontide of a somers

---

52. For reflections on multilingualism in Old and Middle English literature that address connections with Genesis 11 and Acts 2, see, *e.g.*, Dekker, 'Pentecost and Linguistic Self-Consciousness'; Stanton, *Culture of Translation*, 64–70; Major, *Undoing Babel*, 6; Albrecht Classen, ed., *Multilingualism in the Middle Ages and Early Modern Age: Communication and Miscommunication in the Premodern World* (Berlin: De Gruyter, 2016), 5–6; O'Brien, *Reversing Babel*, 23–5.

53. For definitions of macaronic poetry, see Siegfried Wenzel, *Macaronic Sermons: Bilingualism and Preaching in Late-Medieval England* (Ann Arbor, MI: University of Michigan Press, 1994), 2–4; Elizabeth Archibald, 'Macaronic Poetry', in *A Companion to Medieval Poetry*, ed. Corinne Saunders (Hoboken, NJ: Wiley-Blackwell, 2010), 285.

54. See Carol J. Harvey, 'Macaronic Techniques in Anglo-Norman Verse', *L'Esprit Createur* 18, no. 1 (Spring 1978): 70.

55. Bodl. MS. Douce 104, f. 112ᵛ, in Duncan, *Medieval English Lyrics*, 300–1.

56. MS: London, BL Harley 5396, in ibid., 228.

57. MS: London, BL Sloane 2593, in ibid., 178.

day' requires only one repeated word, '*revertere*' (return), for the whole poem to reverberate with the weight of this call to repentance.[58] It remains uncertain how much of these Latin phrases the audience would have comprehended; they may have been commonly understood or heard by uneducated people as pious nonsense, gesturing towards the ineffable.[59] Regardless of its intelligibility, Latin was not merely religious or scholarly linguistic seasoning but integral to English devotion. In 'Jesu, for thi precious blood', the English conjunction 'and' in the Latin refrain 'Pater noster and Ave' is indicative of how deeply Latin was integrated into vernacular devotional culture.[60]

In the macaronic lyric, the use of Latin went far beyond the exploitation of its spiritual capital. It involved an interlingual interplay that was not purely ornamental but deeply theological, crafting through the intermingling of English and Latin a picture of human wit with heavenly wisdom combined. This is particularly evident in lyrics concerning Mary, whose role as intermediary between earth and heaven, body and spirit resonates with a macaronic poetic. In 'Of on that is so fayr and bright', an English rhyme scheme of aabbc is interspersed with Latin couplets dominated by the titles and attributes of Mary. The Latin lines could be heard as an echo of heavenly song, sounding behind the vernacular, but they also comment or expand upon the English. The English is denotatively self-sufficient but its meaning is amplified by the Latin additions, and would be diminished by their absence. This is seen particularly in the final three stanzas, as in the following description of the birth of Christ:

Thuster night, and com the day	*dark night; came*
Salutis;	*of salvation*
The wellë spingëth out of thee	*well*
Virtutis.	*of virtue*[61]

Similarly, a cursory reading of '*Ecce, ancilla Domini!*' (behold, the handmaid of the Lord) might assume that its Latin burden's only function is to cast a sacralizing sheen upon an English religious lyric.[62] The repetition of the line creates an identical rhyme that chimes across the poem, making the demotic Anglo-Saxon tones resonate with the song of heaven. However, the rhyme scheme also draws

---

58. Balliol College, Oxford, MS. 354, f. 155v, in Douglas Gray, ed., *English Medieval Religious Lyrics*, 2nd edn (Liverpool: Liverpool University Press, 1992), 82–3.

59. According to Christina Whitehead, Latin tags created a 'sense of mystifying incomprehension' as part of an overinflated aureate style, but vernacular facility with Latin may have invested such passages with a greater meaning and significance, Whitehead, 'Middle English Religious Lyrics', 117–18.

60. Bodl. MS Bodley 789, f. 148ʳ, in Gray, *Medieval Religious Lyrics*, 55–7.

61. MS: London, BL Egerton 613, in Duncan, *Medieval English Lyrics*, 128–9.

62. C.U.L., MS. Add. 5943, f. 182v, in Gray, *Medieval Religious Lyrics*, 3–4.

the Latin and the vernacular together. In the first stanza, the Latin refrain occurs on both first and last lines, so that in this stanza the ballade rhyme scheme of ababbcbc takes the symmetrical form of ababbaba. The Latin '*Ancilla domini*' in lines 1 and 8 rhymes with the English words 'gracyously' and 'myldely' in lines 3 and 6. There is a resonance in both sound and sense between these lines as they draw together a hymn to Mary as the handmaid of the Lord with two of her attributes: graciousness and mildness. In the following stanzas, the refrain is formed from the antepenultimate English and the final Latin line: 'Then sayde the virgine so myldely .... *Ecce, ancilla Domini*'. The rhyming of English and Latin in these Marian lyrics evokes the drawing together of the voice of praise with the song of the Spirit, suggestive of the coming of the Spirit upon Mary in the incarnation as like the creative intermingling of sonic worlds.[63]

There remains a perilous ambivalence in the wit of the macaronic lyric. The babble of the lullaby carols is illustrative of a gospel norm: that divine wisdom is to be found amid the apparent folly of humility and simplicity.[64] The notion that the wisdom of the Spirit might be found under the guise of human wit is somewhat different. Many of the onlookers of the miracle of Acts 2 saw only the marvel of unlettered Galileans speaking all the languages of the empire. The remarkable wit displayed blinded them to the true miracle of the message they proclaimed concerning 'God's deeds of power' (Acts 2.11). In the devotional lyric, the delight and wonder elicited by the linguistic dexterity of drawing sweet music out of diverse languages might similarly risk obscuring the wisdom to which it points. The power of the poem may rest precisely in that danger, where it employs *melos* not to persuade but to render truth beautiful, to enable the discovery of wisdom through delight.

Multilingualism and the Spirit of peace and unity The final feature of the gift of the Spirit relevant to a reflection on lyric eloquence is found in the idea of the Spirit of Pentecost as a Spirit of peace and unity who inaugurates the global church. Although, as discussed above, the song of the Spirit was often interpreted as a purely spiritual sound, the babble of Pentecost was commonly read not as the outpouring of a heavenly language but as a multilingual miracle.[65] The sociocultural implications of this interpretation were not lost on the medieval mind. The Northern homily on Pentecost applied the miracle to the contemporary

---

63. In a similar way, the birth of the church at Pentecost might also be heard as a harmony composed of the sound of the Spirit and the babble of human voices.

64. For sources of Christian reflection on wisdom hidden in apparent folly, consider *e.g.* Matthew 11.25; 1 Corinthians 1.18.

65. For Old English precedents for this interpretation, see Gregory the Great, Homily 30, *Homiliae in Evangelia*, ed. Raymond Étaix, CCSL 141 (Turnhout: Brepols, 1999), 259-60; Bede, *In Genesim*, ed. Charles W. Jones, CCSL 118a (Turnhout, 1967), 11.8-9b, both cited in Dekker, 'Pentecost and Linguistic Self-Consciousness', 349, 352.

context by replacing the languages mentioned in Acts 2 with languages known to the audience:

Thai spak Latin, Franche, and Grewe,	Greek;
Sarzenay, Danhsse, and Ebrewe,	Saracen; Danish; Hebrew;
Inflihsse, Walhsse, and Pikarde,	[English;] Welsh; Picard;
Gascoyne, Toskayne, and Lombardie.	Gascon; Roman; Lombard;[66]

Mirk's festival sermon on Pentecost emphasized the gift of the Spirit in Pentecost as a gift of peace and unity, through the purging flame of the tongues of fire that would 'so anonynt hom [the apostles] wyth þe swetnes of his grace, þat þey schuld … leue words of envy and debate, and speke of rest and pes'.[67]

Christine Cooper Rompato has discussed how medieval sermons on Pentecost utilized multilingualism to 'enact the experience of Pentecost' by drawing their hearers into an imagined global fellowship.[68] If this was true of sermons, it was even more so of macaronic verse, where poetic sweetness emulated the sacred eloquence of the Spirit. Much has been made of the fact that the sense of a phrase in the macaronic lyric often carries through with correct grammaticality from one language to another.[69] This knitting together of Latin and English is most comprehensive in later medieval poems such as *Veni Coronaberis* (Come, you shall be Crowned), a love song from Christ to Mary at the Assumption.[70] The Latin in this poem is not confined to separate lines but is intertwined with the English. The refrain is in Latin, but each stanza also incorporates a Latin title for Mary, mostly taken from the Song of Songs Chapter 4 as used in the antiphon for vespers on the feast of the Assumption.[71]

In this poem, the crossing of linguistic boundaries occurs not just through the denotative sense of the words but also through musical resonances of rhythm,

---

66. 'Homily 33, Pentecost', *Northern Homily Cycle*, ed. Thompson, lines 7–10 (notes apart from those in square brackets in Thompson's edition).

67. 'so anoint them [the apostles] with the sweetness of his grace, that they should … leave words of envy and debate, and speak of rest and peace', Mirk, Sermon 39, 'De Dominica Pentecostes', f. 94b, p. 162.

68. Christine Cooper Rompato, 'Xenoglossia and Multilingualism in Middle English Sermons on Pentecost', in *Multilingualism in the Middle Ages and the Early Modern Age: Communication and Miscommunication in the Premodern World*, ed. Albrecht Classen (Berlin: De Gruyter, 2016), 235.

69. See Archibald, 'Macaronic Poetry', 279–81; Chrisopher Lecluyse, 'Sacred Bilingualism: Code Switching in Medieval English Verse' (PhD, University of Texas, Austin, 2002), iv.

70. B.M., MS. Cotton Caligula A. II, f. 107vb-108ra, in Gray, *Medieval Religious Lyrics*, 63–5.

71. Carleton Brown notes this in his edition of the poem, drawn from the Harley MSS. 2251, f. 18^{r-v}, *Religious Lyrics of the XVth Century* (Oxford: Clarendon, 1939), 65–7.

rhyme, assonance and alliteration. Within each line, the two languages are closely interconnected through internal alliteration. Consider the following lines from the first two stanzas:

Surge mea sponsa, so swete in syghte …	*arise my bride, so sweet in sight*
Cum, clene crystal, to my cage,	
Columba mea, I the calle!	*my dove*

The sense flows between Latin and English, crossing linguistic boundaries as if they are not there and creating a multilingual music through alliterative patterns on 's' and 'c'. There is a sense of ease in these transitions that hints at a fulfilment of the Pentecost promise, constructing a global community through a macaronic poetics.[72]

Douglas Gray has criticized this poem as 'marred by flat lines and heavy diction' symptomatic of the fifteenth-century aureate style.[73] A closer consideration reveals a sweet melody hidden in plain sight and a complex negotiation between sound and sense that exploits the coming together of distinct linguistic worlds. There is a songlike sweetness to the rhyme scheme that exploits both the sonic and semantic affinities between rhyming words, such as the connectivity between 'syghte' and 'bryghte', 'shene' (beautiful or glorious), 'qwene' and 'clene' in the first stanza, or 'mayden mylde' and 'nevur defylde' in the fifth, or the chiastic structure of 'flower', 'towre', 'honowre' and 'bowre' in the third. The English end-rhymes within each stanza are dominated by long vowels and voiced lateral, nasal and sybillant closing consonants that express the love-longing of the bridegroom and linger in the sweetness of His song. The Latin refrain concludes with the short closed vowel ending of the phrase '*Veni coronaberis*', which gives a sense of accomplishment to the end of each stanza. These lines stand apart sonically from the rest. Their distinctive sound presents not a counterpoint to the English lines but rather their heavenly desire drawing to its conclusion. The ballade rhyme scheme gives weight to this final line but also connects it back to the English antepenultimate line. '*Coronaberis*' is rhymed with 'blysse' in four out of nine stanzas. Variations on this pattern in the other stanzas add a sense of surprise and delight to the fulfilment of expectation in the repeated refrain.

In the final four stanzas, a greater frequency of Latin phrases creates a sense of elevation, rising from two per stanza to three in the final stanza and culminating in a reference to Mary as '*Regina celi*'. As the verses draw Mary up into her rightful place as queen of heaven so the intensification of macaronic lyricism moves the hearer further into heavenly sweetness. In the final stanza, the English and Latin come together in a harmonious unity that echoes the song of heaven, through lines

---

72. On the promise of universal community, see, *e.g.*, Isaiah 45.23, Romans 14.11 and Philippians 2.11.

73. Douglas Gray, *Themes and Images in the Medieval English Religious Lyric* (London: Routledge, 1972), 149.

that uniformly end with a sibilant, and with rhyming pairs so close in sound they could almost be considered as mono-rhymes.

> *Que est ista* so vertuus,
> The is celestyall for her mekenesse?
> *Aurora consurgens* gracyous,
> So benygne a lady of fyne bryghtnesse,   *benign*
> That ys the colour of kynde clennesse,
> *Regina celi*, that nevur shall mysse.
> Thus endeth thys songe of gret swettenesse,   *great sweetness*
> *Veni coronaberis.*

Mary, who was described in the second stanza as singing the infant Christ to sleep with a lullaby, has progressed from dear mother to the queen of heaven through the sweet song of the Son.

Lyrics such as this give a sense of what Robert W. Barret Jr has called 'a multilingual redemption' in medieval macaronic literature.[74] The nature of this redemption is not, as J. Scappettone has styled xenoglossia, about the 'eras[ure of] cultural difference' but the gift of understanding across difference through the knitting together of linguistic worlds.[75] The performance of heavenly harmony in the medieval macaronic lyric occurs not through escape from body and culture but by delighting in the materiality of speech and tuning into the sonic resonances of the world. David F. Ford has described the song of heaven in the book of Revelation as a wordless melody, a purely expressive 'crescendo of cries'.[76] It might equally be imagined as a creative babble of joyful sound, a celebration of distinct linguistic cultures brought into harmony through mutual understanding, and of the craft through which sound is transformed into sense, babble into sweet music.

Conclusion

The babble of lyric music arises out of an instinctive joy in the physicality of sound, but goes beyond the cry towards a crafted vocalization, a poetic act of praise. This understanding of babble is suggestive of a vision of human creatureliness in which the purity of self-expression is accompanied by an instinct towards creativity. Poetry exploits and enhances the joy of sound through devices of rhyme and rhythm, through the delight of repeated resonance and the beauty of variety. This lyric sweetness can be distorted or disregarded, experienced not as delightful but as risible or nonsensical, a vulnerability of language that reveals the

---

74. Robert W. Barrett Jr., 'Languages Low and High: Translation and the Creation of Community in the Chester Pentecost Play', in *Translating the Middle Ages*, ed. Karen L. Fresco and Charles D. Wright (London: Routledge, 2012), 67.

75. J. Scappettone, 'Xenoglossia', *PEPP*, 1543–4.

76. David F. Ford, *Christian Wisdom: Desiring Freedom and Learning in Love* (Cambridge: Cambridge University Press, 2007), 264.

extent to which the sonic world of speech is embedded within social structures of communication.[77] The linguistic barriers to understanding across difference go well beyond grammar and syntax to include cultural associations, sonic stereotypes and the power relations that lie behind them. At the same time, *melos* has the capacity to confound and transcend these expectations, stretching the boundaries of communicability.

This section has reflected on the power and beauty of *melos* as a gift of the Spirit through medieval readings of the Pentecost story. The vision of *melos* that has emerged is not a pale shade of the eternal song of heaven but a performative discourse that turns thought into praise, not through an escape from the body but by delighting in the materiality of speech and tuning into the sonic resonances of the world. This interpretation of lyric eloquence has implications for theological discourse, which might consider the virtue of sweet words, the wisdom of wit and the power of language to make for peace and unity.

Heteroglossia and hybridity: Melos *in code-switching Black British poetry*

This section continues the discussion of *melos* in the multilingual lyric through a reflection on code-switching in modern Black British poetry. Code-switching, or flipping between language forms, is a common feature of speech for multilingual people. For members of immigrant populations, this might include switching between the languages of the 'host' and 'home' cultures, both of which may be felt as integral to the individual's cultural identity. Code-switching is also a linguistic-cultural process by which the idioms of one culture may be transplanted into or adopted by another.[78] The term 'code-switching', unlike the intermingling implied by the term 'macaronic', evokes a relationship between languages marked by their differences. Code-switching poetry can work creatively with these differences, exhibiting the wit and wisdom of a multilingual poetic through devices of contrast, counterpoint, harmony and fusion.

In postcolonial poetry, code-switching can be a means of addressing the legacy of empire by highlighting, exploiting, subverting and transforming the

---

77. Infant babble may bear universal features but is also already culturally encoded with the phonemes of the mother tongue. See, *e.g.*, Andrew M. Colman, 'Babbling', in *A Dictionary of Psychology*, 4th edn (Oxford: Oxford University Press, 2015), https://www.oxfordreference.com/view/10.1093/acref/9780199657681.001.0001/acref-9780199657681-e-855?rskey=AeWbKO&result=3; Janet F. Werker and Richard Tees, 'Influences on Infant Speech Processing: Toward a New Synthesis', *Annual Review of Psychology* 50 (1999): 509–35.

78. Tom McArthur, Jacqueline Lam-McArthur and Lise Fontaine, eds, 'Code-Mixing and Code-Switching', in *The Oxford Companion to the English Language*, 2nd edn (Oxford: Oxford University Press, 2018), online, https://www.oxfordreference.com/view/10.1093/acref/9780199661282.001.0001/acref-9780199661282.

sociopolitical features of the music of language. Code-switching poetry involves not just swapping vocabularies but the meeting of cultural imaginations. This poetic encounter might involve the celebration of undervalued vernaculars, critiquing the ideology behind a dominant language, providing a conduit for social resistance or crafting an emblem of trans-local identity. The progressive dimensions of these poetic processes are located within a context of ongoing tension, struggle and power-imbalance between language worlds. The code-switching poetry of the Caribbean diaspora, which is the focus of this section, illustrates such a complex coming together of cultures in the often dialogical, sometimes conflictual relationship between vernaculars and Standard English (hereafter SE).

This section explores the power of the Spirit at work in the subversive music of code-switching lyrics and the beauty of the Spirit manifest in the so-called vulgar features of oral discourse, before reflecting on the hope of Pentecost as a rebuilding of Babel through lyric babble. The story of Pentecost narrates the birth of a global church that crosses linguistic boundaries. As discussed above, interpretations of this passage have long regarded multilingualism as a mark of cross-cultural unity. In Acts 2, the sound of the presence of the Spirit is heard first as a roar like a hurricane (2.2), and next in a babble of multilingual praise and proclamation. This is a sound that makes sense not through the clarity of the lone voice, or the homogony of voices in unison, but through the intelligent interplay of different sonic worlds. Its beauty might be imagined as a lyric sweetness that does not just place difference in balance and proportion, like the lyric weave described above, but is a transformative aesthetic that hears babble as song.[79] For all its utopian connotations, the miracle of xenoglossia occurs within human history and culture, using language systems that are bound up with power, ideology and oppression. Hybrid poetic forms knit together different acoustic worlds in a manner that could be read as a proleptic sign of the intercultural unity to which Pentecost points but, as discussed below, none of these processes escape the politics of language. Melic power emerges through a creative interplay of cultural worlds that is marked by the ongoing reclamation, renegotiation, sharing and giving up of the power of words.

Chanting down Babylon: Melic power and cultural transformation

Melic power has been described above as magic or charm, a mysterious and persuasive force. Postcolonial code-switching poetics refashions *melos* as a political power that is embedded in body, culture, history and place, a power that can be exploited, resisted, subverted and transformed by the poet. *Melos* has long been a tool of intercultural encounter between nation languages and SE, as illustrated by the work of the Caribbean Artists Movement (1966–72), which was founded in London to celebrate and promote Caribbean art among poets and artists resident in the UK.

---

79. *NB* Daljit Nagra subverts the derogatory term 'babble' in 'Look We Have Coming to Dover', in which a newcomer to England refers to their own language as 'babbling', *Look We Have Coming to Dover* (London: Faber & Faber, 2010).

James Berry's Caribbean poetics brought 'the vibrancy, wisdom and pleasure of our culture sounds into the mainstream', while founding member Edward Kamau Brathwaite influentially defended the 'riddims' (a term that encompasses a poem's sound as well as its rhythm) of nation language poetry.[80] Brathwaite memorably described the difference between SE and Caribbean poetry through a reference to the weather, arguing that, like the sound of the hurricane native to the Caribbean islands and unlike the iambic pentameter of Palgrave's *Golden Treasury* that was taught in Caribbean schools, nation language poetry 'does not roar in pentameters'.[81]

The force of this argument is felt in the Jamaican poetry of Louise Bennett, which provides a good example of the power of *melos* in postcolonial poetics. Bennett raised the status of Caribbean vernaculars on a local and global stage, defending them against the pejorative stereotyping of 'creoles' as inferior forms of language. The subversion of iambic pentameter was an important element of this mission. The poem 'Colonization in Reverse' celebrates the overturning of cultural convention in more ways than one. The second stanza honours the Windrush generation who travelled to England 'By de hundred, by de tousan'. This line reverses the iambic rhythms of common metre that were set up in the first stanza, through the trochaic metre of Jamaican speech. On the page the line can be read two ways, but in performance the main stress is generally placed on the two 'by's' rather than on 'hun' and 'tou'. This rhythmic surprise can be amplified by the performer who savours the plosive sound of the 'b' and elongates the long vowel of 'By'. This overlaying of Jamaican speech patterns on an English poetic form creates a composite and conflicting rhythm that contributes to the mixture of delight and defiance communicated by the poem as a whole. The later line 'What an islan! What a people!' further celebrates the reverse colonization of SE by reinforcing and normalizing the trochaic rhythm, as in this line the emphasis can only be placed on the first and third syllable of each sentence, the exclamatory 'What' that expresses pride in the Jamaican people and their language.[82]

Jamaican poet Kei Miller exploits the same rhythmic contrast in his 2014 collection, *The Cartographer Tries to Map a Way to Zion*, which is an extended debate between an Iyaric-speaking 'rastaman' and SE-speaking 'cartographer', concerning the values that guide the 'mapping' of places, people and their histories. Following Brathwaite, poem 'xvii' draws attention to the difference between the two heartbeat rhythms of nyabinghi beat and iambic pentameter. Miller styles the Rastafarian beat 'the riddim of cutlass and cane ... the terrible metre of hurricanes', a noise that combines the violent history of work on the plantations with the

---

80. James Berry, cited in Sarah Lawson Welsh, 'Vernacular Voices: Black British Poetry', in *The Cambridge History of Black and British Asian Writing*, ed. Susheila Nasta and Mark Stein (Cambridge: Cambridge University Press, 2020), 329.

81. Edward Kamau Brathwaite, *History of the Voice: The Development of Nation Language in Anglophone Caribbean Poetry* (London: New Beacon Books, 1984), 10.

82. Louise Bennett, 'Colonization in Reverse', in *Jamaica Labrish* (Jamaica: Sangsters, 1966), 179, lines 5, 13.

elemental destructiveness of island weather.[83] This poem serves as a warning against the imposition of one culture's music on another. The cartographer of the poem is attracted, if not converted, by the nyabinghi rhythm, drawn into a richer relationship with both body and place through a very different cultural expression of the universal human experience of the heartbeat.

Linton Kwesi Johnson's politico-musical aesthetics draws on melic power for the task of cultural transformation, through poetry that is saturated in the riddims of dub and reggae. Johnson's famous essay 'Jamaican Rebel Music' developed a bass poetics that was descriptive of his own poetry, which is a powerful combination of lament and apocalypse, 'oscillating' like a bass line 'between the psychic states of despair and rebellion' and drawing on the tension between different linguistic codes just as the bass melody in reggae provides a deep counterpoint to the chanting line.[84] Johnson's assertion that 'the revolution is usually felt first as a perceptible change in the bass' is brought to life in the poem 'Bass Culture'.[85] The line 'di bubble an di bounce' of the 'bubblin bass' is almost onomatopoeic of the bass, exploiting the plosive sound of the letter 'b', while the following line imitates the rhythm of 'di leap an di weight-drop'.[86] This underground, subversive music is babble turned against Babylon, *melos* turned against the walls of exclusion and oppression, where rooms vibrating to the noise of sound systems become as trumpets against the walls of Jericho.

Infused by a Dionysian spirit of rage and jubilation, Johnson uses interlingual wordplay as fuel for the revolutionary tasks of deconstruction and re-creation. 'Bass Culture' is not a noticeably code-switching poem, but it does combine features of Jamaican, London Jamaican and SE.[87] The poem is dominated by the metaphor

---

83. Kei Miller, 'xvii', from *The Cartographer Tries to Map a Way to Zion* (London: Carcanet, 2014), 40, © Kei Miller, reproduced by kind permission of David Higham Associates.

84. See Linton Kwesi Johnson, 'Jamaican Rebel Music', *Race & Class* 17, no. 4 (1976): 397–8, 405, 407; ibid., 'Reading Bass Culture: Linton Kwesi Johnson in Conversation with Paul Gilroy', interview by Louisa Layne, Postcolonial Writing and Theory Seminar, Great Writers Inspire at Home Series (The Oxford Research Centre in the Humanities, 26 April 2018), audio, https://www.torch.ox.ac.uk/reading-bass-culture-linton-kwesi-johnson-in-conversation-with-paul-gilroy-1., 1:01:00-1:02:43; on Johnson's poetic exploitation of the tension between languages, see Andrew Salkey's Introduction to ibid., *Dread Beat and Blood*, introduction by Andrew Salkey (London: Bogle-L'Ouverture Publications, 1975), 7–9.

85. See Johnson, 'Rebel Music', 401.

86. Linton Kwesi Johnson, 'Bass Culture', in *Selected Poems* (London: Penguin, 2006), Kindle, loc. 251–76.

87. NB while the term 'Jamaican Creole' is still in common usage, it has been accused of reinforcing derogatory perceptions of the language, so this book uses the term 'Jamaican' in recognition of its distinct linguistic status. See McArthur, Lam-McArthur and Fontaine, eds, 'Jamaican Patois, (Jamaican English Creole, Jamaican Creole English, Jamaican, Patwa, Nation Language)', in *Companion to the English Language*, https://www.oxfordreference.com/view/10.1093/acref/9780199661282.001.0001/acref-9780199661282-e-644?rskey=jWLrST&result=5.

of reggae as a 'muzik of blood', expressing the passion and anger of the 'rebel generation' of Black youth. This conceit is developed through the intriguing phrase 'blood klaat pressure'. In colloquial Jamaican, 'blood klaat' is used performatively as a curse. Although literally translated 'blood cloth' in SE, its use in this poem seems to suggest the aural SE resonances of a 'blood clot' behind which pressure is building, threatening to burst. Miller exploits the multilingual resonances of the same phrase in his poem 'The Blood Cloths'. Translated literally into SE, the phrase becomes a perhaps uncomfortably literal but relatively straightforward term for a menstrual pad. The performative power of the curse word is nevertheless retained and even amplified in translation, becoming a symbol of female resistance and power as the poem narrates how the cloths are used to ward off the threat of would-be attackers in the cane fields.[88] In both of these examples, interlingual punning illustrates the kind of cultural transformation to which Johnson's poem 'Bass Culture' points, by bringing languages together in a new, surprising and creative unity through a play on the sound of words.

Punning is such a powerful poetic device because it brings the hearer to the point of new understanding by exploiting the sound of words. Puns uncover the unreliability of verbal reasoning, exposing how words are constructed out of phonemes with several semantic possibilities. They produce a situation where there are two possible interpretations of a phrase, thereby bringing the hearer to a moment of confusion and ignorance. The moment the audience gets the joke, there is the delight of comprehension and the expansion of understanding as these multiple meanings are embraced simultaneously, with each sense changed by the other.

Interlingual punning goes one step further in creating new understanding across difference, by bringing cultural worlds together. Take, for example, Caribbean theologian Michael Jagessar's manifesto for intercultural theology as '*Dis*-Place Theologizing'. This phrase puns across the negative connotations of the SE term 'displacement' and the contrasting deictic sense of 'this place' to describe a theology where one feels simultaneously dislocated and at home. Jagessar's neologism complicates simplistic definitions of identity and reorients standard divisions between 'centre' and 'margins'.[89] It is suggestive of the power of interlingual wordplay to generate what Homi Bhabhi calls a hybrid 'Third Space' between cultures, a space of connection, contradiction, multiplicity and 'ambivalence', where experience is rendered complex, cultural symbols translatable and identity multiple.[90]

As a resource for intercultural theology, interlingual punning is suggestive of the benefits of attentiveness to the cultural particularity of the sound of language, as a music of blood rooted not only in universal bodily rhythms but also in the

---

88. Miller, 'The Blood Cloths', *Cartographer*, 59.

89. Michael N. Jagessar, '*Dis*-Place Theologizing: Fragments of Intercultural Adventurous God-Talk', *Black Theology* 13, no. 3 (2015): 259.

90. Homi Bhabha, *The Location of Culture*, 2nd edn (London: Routledge, 2004), 53–6.

particularity of place and history. The poetic bringing-together of sonic worlds, not antagonistically nor in a homogenizing unity but in a dance of competing and complementary riddims, crafts a space of movement and meaning, a coherence capable of constant reshaping, a playful transmutation of power into beauty.

Orality, vulgarity and the sweetness of the Spirit

The relationship between Caribbean and SE poetry can be understood as a dialogue not only between different languages but between the supposed vulgarity of sound foregrounded by oral literature, and supposedly civilized textuality.[91] In making this argument, postcolonial feminist critic Carolyn Cooper retrieves the Latin sense of vulgarity as common or popular (rather than uncouth). Her 'politics of noise' uncovers the power of orality as capable of 'challeng[ing] the smug equivalence of class/language/intelligence' through a witty and subversive poetry.[92] These dynamics are evident in Michael (Mikey) Smith's poem 'Mi Cyaan Believe It', which is a celebration of culture through sound. The title is also the refrain, an expression of frustrated incredulity that intersperses the narrative of a life that lists an increasingly shocking litany of injustice and oppression. In performance, the word 'cyaan' is savoured, its long vowel becoming ever more pronounced as the poem progresses, a gradual turning of word into sound that simultaneously intensifies the emotion and revels in the sound of the word. This performative device does not diminish the word's sense but foregrounds its melic power, so that the word 'cyaan' becomes an act of resistance, conveying joy and empowerment in the midst of a story of injustice.[93]

What Brathwaite and Cooper term 'noise' is *melos*, the power and beauty of the sound of words. While Black poetry may have been often associated with oral literature, it is important to note that it has frequently crossed and re-crossed the boundaries of orality and literacy, in a manner that Cooper has termed '*oraliterature*'.[94] Kwame Dawes influentially resisted the ghettoizing of Black voices under the sometimes-dismissive label of 'performance poetry', Johnson became the first Black poet to be included in the Penguin classics series, while Jean 'Binta' Breeze and Roger Robinson have similarly reached wide audiences through publication alongside spoken performance.[95] Taking into account the intersections of orality and literacy, the use of code-switching in Black British poetry might be imagined more like dancing across a linguistic spectrum than a binary dialectic

---

91. Carolyn Cooper, *Noises in the Blood: Orality, Genre and the 'Vulgar' Body of Jamaican Popular Culture* (London: Macmillan, 1993), 4–5, 8–9.

92. Ibid., 9; see also Brathwaite, *Voice*, 17, 46n59.

93. Michael Smith, 'Mi Cyaan Believe It', '*Mi C-YaaN beLiēVe iT*' (Island LP #ILPS 9717, 1982), audio.

94. Cooper, *Noises*, 4–5, 8–9.

95. Kwame Dawes, 'Black British Poetry, Some Considerations', *Wasafiri* 18, no. 38 (2003): 44–5.

between languages. Nevertheless, the representation of vernacular voices in code-switching poetry has often exploited the conceit of a binary relationship between orality and literacy in order to defend the lyric beauty of languages that have been heard as 'vulgar'.

Consider, for example, two poems by Breeze and Robinson, both narrated in SE with Jamaican appearing as represented speech. 'Simple Tings' is a reflection on what Breeze has termed the multiple personalities of translocal identity.[96] The poem begins with the refrain: a grandmother's assonantal Jamaican maxim regarding 'Simple Tings', which chimes like a tinkling bell across the poem, representing the voice of wisdom. The transition to SE in the next verse is gentle but marked, evoking a distance between languages and cultures that is emphasized by the description of the grandmother yearning for home, 'miles of travel in her stare'.[97] Robinson begins his poem 'Grace' in SE. Grace is the name of the Jamaican nurse who cared for his preterm baby son in hospital. Her voice frequently interrupts the narrative, a voice of authority that embodies the warmth of human compassion on a cold and sterile neonatal ward, through phrases such as '"No baby must dead/ wid a hungry belly."'[98] The affectionate and respectful representation of Jamaican in these poems is akin to that described by Carol Tomlin as common to second-generation reception of the language of their parents, uniting a respect for voice and culture with veneration for one's elders.[99] The lyric beauty of the voices represented poetically here also stands as an act of resistance to their historically dismissive reception, both in British culture and within Caribbean communities where SE was preferred to Jamaican as the language of social advancement.[100]

The complex politico-aesthetic landscape of code-switching poetry illustrates the power and vulnerability embedded in the sound of words. Whether audibly or silently, a lyric poem must be voiced for the music of the words to be appreciated. Cooper has noted how the phonetic transcription of oral languages in poetry can upturn the conventional power-relations of language, undoing the literacy of the reader who is only familiar with SE who must work out the words by sounding them out.[101] At the same time, the code-switching poem takes a risk, expertly managed by poets such as Breeze and Robinson but present, nonetheless, that within a context historically dismissive of vernacular voices, the important distinction between mimicry and mockery might be missed. Translated onto

---

96. Jenny Sharpe, 'Dub and Difference: A Conversation with Jean "Binta" Breeze', *Callaloo* 26, no. 3 (Summer 2003): 610.

97. Jean "Binta" Breeze, 'Simple Tings', in *Third World Girl* (London: Bloodaxe, 2011), 25.

98. Roger Robinson, 'Grace', in *A Portable Paradise* (Leeds: Peepal Tree Press, 2019), Kindle loc. 777.

99. Carol Tomlin, 'Speaking Jamaican, British Black Talk and Code-switching in Preaching', in *Preach It! Understanding African-Caribbean Preaching* (London: SCM, 2019), chap. 3.

100. Ibid.

101. Cooper, *Noises*, 13.

the page, the spoken word is divorced from the performer's own voice and their creative choices, exposed to the reader's interpretation of tone, rhythm, pace and dialect.[102] The sound of a poem can therefore have an effect that goes beyond the intentions or hopes of the poet, perhaps susceptible to misinterpretation but also displaying the inherent dignity of the sound of words.

Grime and the performance of heteroglossic identity Another example of the power of *melos* in code-switching poetry is found in Grime, a musical British art form largely in Multicultural London English (MLE), which celebrates the influence of Black British poetry and its Caribbean and African roots.[103] Debris Stevenson's *Poet in Da Corner* (2018) uses Grime to develop a heteroglossic aesthetic that explores the multifaceted nature of identity within a multicultural community. This work, which was first a stage production, followed by a book and album, tells the story of Stevenson's coming of age in London. Stevenson is White, and so the work addresses the contentious issue of cultural appropriation. The narrator's voice is peppered with Black British Talk (BBT) (the opening track 'Sitting Here – Blud Line', for example, uses words such as 'skank', 'mandem', 'blood' and 'dere' instead of 'there') but it is not the vocabulary of BBT so much as the artistic borrowings that are examined in the work.[104] Stevenson uses rhythms, tones and lines drawn from Dizzee Rascal's seminal album *Boy in da Corner* (2003), in a manner common to Grime. In 'The Clash', SS Vyper, played by Grime MC Jammz, challenges Stevenson's right to do this and the authenticity of her voice, accusing her of 'Cultural theft-sans-force.'[105] 'Respect my Struggle' is another Grime clash that debates the issue further. Using the title line in both attack and defence, Grime's syncopated rhythms and jumping tones allow Stevenson to place extra emphasis on the middle word 'my' in her response to Vyper, as she claims that regardless of the cultural appropriateness of her profiting from Grime, it 'saved' her from an oppressive Mormon upbringing.[106]

The beauty of a heteroglossic aesthetic is found not in the euphony of a fusion of languages or the harmony of polyglossia but in the creative clash of words. As appropriated from Mikhail Bakhtin by womanist literary criticism, heteroglossia (as opposed to polyglossia) signifies not just linguistic multiplicity

---

102. On the various voices that make up a poem, including the oral traditions behind a text, the poem in performance and the poem on the page, the reader's internal voicing of the poem and the reception of vernacular voices in society, see Rachel Gilmour, 'Doing Voices: Reading Language as Craft in Black British Poetry', *The Journal of Commonwealth Literature* 49, no. 3 (2014): 355–6.

103. See Dan Hancox, *Inner City Pressure: The Story of Grime* (London: HarperCollins, 2018), 36–8, 43–4.

104. © Debris Stevenson, feat. Jammz, *Poet in da Corner* (London: Oberon, an imprint of Bloomsbury Publishing Plc, 2018), 3–5.

105. Ibid., 51.

106. Ibid., 26–7.

but an internal embracing of otherness and marginality, an incorporation of brokenness and ambivalence.[107] In Virginia Burrus' terms, heteroglossia is language 'split or doubled by the awareness of other "tongues", spaces and temporalities'.[108] Stevenson's track 'I Luv U – God Luvs U' is performative of heteroglossic identity by juxtaposing the sexualized lyrics of Dizzee Rascal with the religious language of the poet's home, an incongruity highlighted by the colloquial spelling of the title. This track further illustrates the features of a heteroglossic identity by mimicking an argument between daughter and mother, code-switching between the narrator's MLE and the overpronounced SE of the mother's imitated voice.[109]

'I Luv U – God Luvs U' evokes an internal conflict using the Grime conventions of clashing or 'murking', a battle of words in which two poets compete against each other. The explicit and sometimes violent lyrics often used in these poetic scuffles have at times contributed to the criminalization of its practitioners.[110] At the same time, Grime's appeal owes much to the energy of this verbal combat; Dan Hancox calls it 'Punch and Judy' and Richard Bramwell an aesthetics of the 'grotesque', while Grime poet D. S. Marriott has described it as a violence that is 'no more or less than beauty'.[111] The danger of violent words cannot be glossed over. Nevertheless, the self-perception of many Grime artists is that this poetic is not malicious but playful, finding a subversive delight in turning harsh realities into a creative medium.[112] If there is redemptive potential here, it might be found in Grime's confrontation with poverty and violence, apathy and rage. Its raw but faithful account of urban life arguably provides a foundation for the hopeful projects of cultural empowerment heard in Stormzy's more transcendent lyrics or in the work of such as George the Poet.[113]

---

107. See, *e.g.*, Mae Gwendolyn Henderson, 'Speaking in Tongues: Dialogics, Dialectics and the Black Woman Writer's Literary Tradition', in *Colonial Discourse and Post Colonial Theory: A Reader*, ed. P. Williamson and L. Crisman (New York: Columbia University Press, 1994), 258–9.

108. Virginia Burrus, 'The Gospel of Luke and The Acts of the Apostles', *A Postcolonial Commentary on the New Testament Writings*, ed. Fernando Segova and R. S. Sugirtharajah (London: T&T Clark, 2009), 147–8.

109. Stevenson, *Poet in Da Corner*, 41–2; ibid., 'I Luv U – God Luvs U', in *Poet in da Corner*, Debris Stevenson feat. Jammz (London: Accidental Records, 2020), audio, track 13.

110. See Lambros Fatsis, 'Policing the Beats: The Criminalisation of UK Drill and Grime Music by the London Metropolitan Police', *The Sociological Review* 67, no. 6 (2019): 1300–16.

111. Hancox, *Story of Grime*, 134; Bramwell, *UK Hip-Hop, Grime and the City* (London: Routledge, 2014), cited in Hancox, *Story of Grime*, 133; D. S. Marriott, 'Murking (after Stormzy)', in *Duppies* (Oakland, CA: Commune Editions, 2019), 17.

112. Consider, *e.g.*, the laughter and joking at the end of Stormzy's track 'Wiley Flow', www.youtube.com/watch?v=ItNm4MdykBE (accessed 31 January 2023).

113. Consider, *e.g.*, Stormzy, 'First Things First' and 'Blinded by Your Grace, Pt. 2', *Gang Signs & Prayer* (#Merky; Warner; ADA, 2017), audio, tracks 1, 10; ibid., 'Superheroes', *Heavy Is the Head* (#Merky; Atlantic, 2019), audio, track 14; George the Poet, 'Have You Heard George's Podcast?' (BBC, 2019), audio.

Grime is characterized by an emotional intensity that is carried in the pace, rhythm and tone of the lyrics, embracing what Cooper has characterized as the vulgarity of sound.[114] This aspect of Grime is encapsulated in Stevenson's description of a rave in 'Temple', which combines sensuality with the uncouth: 'Vibrations our Holy Spirit,/ Spitting in tongues with every lyric.'[115] 'Spitting' is a common verb for Grime lyricizing, onomatopoeic of its speed and staccato rhythms and suggestive of crudeness and anti-sociality. To SE-speakers unused to Grime's vocabulary and velocity, it might sound like a cacophony. As described here, it is Spirit-inspired speech. Given its often crude subject matter, to imagine Grime lyricizing as apostolic speech may feel an overreach bordering on the sacrilegious. To listen for the sound of the Spirit in and through obscene and violent words presents ethical difficulties to say the least, to say nothing of Stevenson's sexualized language of encounter with the Spirit, an issue addressed further in the next chapter. Nevertheless, is such perturbation after all so very far from the medieval apprehensions about poetry discussed above? If the infusion of the Spirit in human voices is to be taken seriously as, in Sonderegger's terms, 'ingredient down into the very sighs of our ignorance and our faith', then it may prove not only possible but imperative to listen for the sweet sound of the Spirit through the vulgarity of forms such as Grime.[116]

The celebration of noise in code-switching poetry, whether it be that of misprized vernaculars, oral discourse or the aesthetics of the uncouth, is a reminder of the rootedness of sense in sound, sound in the body, and the body in place and history. In playing with what Cooper calls 'the politics of noise', code-switching poetry embraces the subversive potential of melic power. This so-called vulgar noise does not drown out the song of heaven, but rather invites a rehearing of babble as the sweetness of lyric song. Infused by the Spirit of Pentecost, who is both transcendent as the wind and 'ingredient' in the sounds that make up words, this babble of speech may also be heard as the sound of the hurricane: embedded in culture and community, time and place, but also part of the sonic circumambience that embraces all of human experience.

Building Babel anew: Pentecost as a macaronic miracle

Several of the themes discussed above in relation to *melos* – the forming of sense out of nonsense, the vulgarity of sound, the excess or transcendence of speech, the power and danger of words – are encapsulated in poetic interpretations of glossolalia. As a linguistic phenomenon, glossolalia has long been of poetic as well as theological and philosophical interest.[117] Speaking in tongues has been variously interpreted as a spiritual or utopian form of language, a regression to infant babble or primitive speech, or as xenoglossia (sometimes known as missionary

---

114. Cooper, *Noises*, 9.
115. Stevenson, *Poet in Da Corner*, 38.
116. Sonderegger, *Trinity*, 463.
117. See H. Feinsod, 'Glossolalia', *PEPP*, 573–4.

tongues). Taking account of the corporeality of words and the 'politics of noise', the Pentecost towards which the code-switching poem points might be imagined not as a purely spiritual or transcendent language but as a heteroglossic, hybrid or mixed conversation that breeds justice as well as peace.

Miller's poetic reflection on 'Speaking in tongues', from his earlier collection *There Is an Anger that Moves*, recounts a childhood memory of seeing his grandmother speaking in tongues in a revivalist meeting in Jamaica.[118] The poem both evokes and rebuts a secularist discomfort with the practice, through a description that is reminiscent of W. E. du Bois' account of revivalist 'frenzy' at the turn of the twentieth century: 'scenes [that] appear grotesque and funny, but as seen they are awful.'[119] Like the poem itself, which 'is waiting on its own Day of Pentecost', the speaker remains on the edge of the experience, half-envious, half-desiring of those able to cross the threshold into transcendence. The difference between the ridiculous and the awful lies, in this poem, in the way that sounds can seek after meaning and hope for grace. The speaker describes his grandmother going through a process of 'unbecoming', signifying not only a loss of decorum but a metamorphosis into the 'grunt and rumble' of the earthquake, a sound connected with the power and elemental reality of the earth. This later becomes an agricultural metaphor, in which tongues are described as not 'pulling words out of dust' but 'pulling up fresh words to offer as doves to Jehovah'. As the poem argues, 'what is language but a sound we christen?' Rather than trying to harvest crops out of dry earth or, to draw an analogy with Genesis 11, trying to make bricks without water, the poem's sonic landscape is watered with tears and harvested in a sacrifice of praise. In Miller's poem, glossolalia connects the transcendent with the primitive or elemental, describing the excess of language as rooted in body and in ground, in the sound of words.

Miller's poem depicts glossolalia as heteroglossia, the disruptive force of female revivalist spirituality that undermines the authority of the masculine secular world of the speaker. This heteroglossic interpretation of tongues is rooted in the work of Black feminist literary critic Mae Gwendolyn Henderson, who, inspired by revivalist Christianity and the work of Black women writers, has described true glossolalia as a heteroglossic, apostolic discourse.[120] The subversive political power of the ecstasy of sound has long been part of Pentecostal tradition, which has read the gift of tongues as a sign of revolution and renewal; what Robert Beckford following Mike Dyson has called 'a radical language of equality', or James K. A. Smith has called 'a discourse of resistance'.[121] Understood as heteroglossic

---

118. Kei Miller, 'Speaking in tongues', in *There Is an Anger That Moves* (London: Carcanet, 2012), 33.

119. W. E. B. Du Bois, 'Of the Faith of the Fathers', in *The Souls of Black Folk*, ed. Brent Hayes Edwards (Oxford: Oxford University Press, 2007), 129.

120. Henderson, 'Speaking in Tongues', 262.

121. Robert Beckford, *Jesus Dub: Theology, Music and Social Change* (London: Routledge, 2006), 125; James K. A. Smith, *Thinking in Tongues: Pentecostal Contributions to Christian Philosophy* (Grand Rapids, MI: Eerdmans, 2010), 147. Beckford has also drawn on Henderson's work in his 'dub' hermeneutics to describe how the Spirit is at work in society, *Jesus Dub*, 128.

speech, this disruptive force does not only descend from above but includes an internal undermining of the authority of the dominant discourse from within speech itself. Michel de Certeau describes this as the *'noises of otherness'*, the vocal sounds that interrupt or 'dub' speech (such as 'um' and 'er'), through which 'the major voice … appears caught up in a doubling that compromises it'.[122] This heteroglossic nature of even ordinary speech is suggestive of the transformative potential held within the sound of words.[123] In this way, the postcolonial concept of heteroglossia provides a significant resource for an interpretation of the babble of Pentecost.

Hybridity is another useful concept, which is evoked by literary critic Jahan Ramazani's account of postcolonial code-switching poetry as a 'code-stitching' fusion of languages (in contrast with the binary relationality of code-switching), situating it within the broader canon of macaronic poetics.[124] As posited above, and as suggested in Miller's poem, the transcendence of babble is not that of words moving apophatically beyond sense into silence. Instead, like infants learning to speak, babble moves beyond sound towards sense, beyond incomprehension towards intelligibility. Jay Bernard's poem 'Patois' describes the development of the hybrid language of MLE in these terms, as a progression from a subvocal understanding of language that is felt in the body, towards a language that is shared, if not fully understood. Bernard is a London-born poet with a Jamaican heritage, and in this poem the speaker remembers in their youth their mother cursing white people in Jamaican, reasoning in justification that they did not understand her: 'Which is why she said it, knowing they felt every word.' There is power in the sound of words, a universal resonance in the emotion of speech, but it is used in this passage to emphasize the alienation between languages and cultures. Now, as the speaker notes, there are Asian youths in south London using the same Jamaican curses. The hybridization of language has transformed the speaker and these characters, in a slant-rhyming phrase that expresses the surprise of kinship, into 'sudden cousins', a kind of macaronic miracle.[125]

Bernard describes the incorporation of Jamaican into MLE as a 'dubbing' of English by England's immigrant populations. The British now speak in multiple voices, and the poem mimics this hybrid language, written in SE and scattered with Jamaican expressions. It is left unclear whether the youths of the poem understand the words they speak or appreciate the cultures and histories behind them. Their understanding may remain at the subvocal level of performative meaning.

---

122. Michel De Certeau, 'Vocal Utopias: Glossolalias', *Representations* 56 (Autumn 1996): 30.

123. It also raises questions about lyric subjectivity that will be explored more fully in a later chapter. As literary critic Jahan Ramazani suggests, such doublings of language challenge the notion of a singular lyric 'I' by highlighting the 'always-already dialogic nature' of human identity. Jahan Ramazani, 'Code-Switching, Code-Stitching: A Macaronic Poetics?', *Dibur Literary Journal* 1 (Autumn 2015): 40.

124. Ibid.

125. Jay Bernard, 'Patois', in *Surge* (London: Penguin, 2019), Kindle.

They nevertheless represent what Sarah Lawson Welsh has described as a poetic revolution that challenges 'monologic notions of Englishness', demonstrating how linguistic hybridity, previously identified with the translocal or transcultural, has entered into the heart of British culture.[126]

Alongside heteroglossia and hybridity, mixture also proves a suggestive term for a pneumatological account of *melos* informed by postcolonial poetry. Macaronic poetry signifies a mixing of languages reminiscent of the story of Genesis 11. Looking beyond this passage, *balal* (babble) is most commonly used in the Hebrew Bible with reference to the mixing of flour or grain with oil to make cakes as a gift offering to God.[127] The 'mixing' of languages in Genesis 11.7 and 9 has sonic resonances not only with 'Babel' and babble but also with the mixing of ingredients to make bricks (which are also baked) in verse 3.[128] God's mixing of languages, like the ingredients in a cake, might be read as an alternative to the baking of bricks for the tower, a divinely offered sacrifice of praise that replaces the failed monument to human supremacy. Babel is fulfilled in the multilingual miracle of Pentecost, which might be similarly sensed as the sweet savour of bread, received as a gift and offered back to God.

This is a subversively beautiful image of the eloquence of intercultural encounter, but the entwinement of the metaphor of mixing elsewhere in the Bible and in the history of interpretation with the politics of exclusion must also be acknowledged. Hosea 7.8, for example, condemns the 'mixing' of Israel with other peoples through intermarriage as 'a cake not turned', burnt on one side and raw on the other. This passage turns the sweet taste of multilingualism into the bitter charcoal of division, serving as a reminder of the negative interpretations of the mixing of languages often applied to Genesis 11. Texts influenced by the Vulgate, such as the King James Bible, translate Genesis 11.7 and 9 as the 'confounding' (*confundamus*) or 'confusion' (*confusum*) of languages, turning mixture into a paradoxical sign of cultural separation. These translations are influenced by the LXX version of Genesis 11.7, where συγχέωμεν (pouring together) carries the sense of being 'stirred up', suggestive of unrest and violence.[129] The fact that the same term, συνεχύθη, is used to describe the crowd who are united in their confusion in Acts 2.6 opens up the possibility that these same hearts and minds may be stirred up to love and action by the sound of the Spirit. Negative representations of multilingual mixing have nevertheless also contributed to interpretations of the Pentecost miracle that have reinforced cultural divisions. One example is the justification of apartheid by the South African Dutch Reformed Church, whose 1975 report, *Human Relations and the*

---

126. Lawson Welsh, 'Vernacular Voices', 347.

127. See, *e.g.*, Exodus 29.2, Leviticus 2.4, Numbers 6.15.

128. On the wordplay in Genesis 11.3 and 7 between 'Come, let us make bricks' (*nilbĕnāh*) and 'Come, let us mix/confuse' (*nābĕlāh*), see Andrew E. Steinman, *Genesis: An Introduction and Commentary* (Downers Grove, IL: InterVarsity Press, 2019), 77.

129. See James Strong, *The Exhaustive Concordance of the Bible* (New York: Abingdon-Cokesbury Press, 1947), G4797.

South African Scene in Light of Scripture, argued that Acts 2 presents not the coming together of cultures but rather the declaration of the gospel in distinct, and therefore separate, languages.[130]

Commonly celebrated as a sign of the cultural diversity of the global church, interpretations of Pentecost have the capacity to affirm the collective work of human creativity. Jamaican-born Joel Edwards, the first Black person to head the UK Evangelical Alliance, referred to Pentecost as 'the sanctification of difference ... God's way of saying, "I talk your language"', but also a phenomenon in which 'human cultural agency has a critical role to play'.[131] American Black theologian Willie James Jennings also affirms this sense of agency, the human aspiration for construction, while critiquing the building-up of the self-sufficient individual in Western culture. Jennings calls instead for a 'New Babel', a building 'with noise/ A cacophony of voices' sounding in praise of the God through whom we understand one other.[132] Through a postcolonial perspective on babble, the hope of Pentecost might be imagined as building the kingdom of heaven with bricks of sound, inspired by the hurricane roar and the sweet song of the Spirit, while acknowledging a mixing of culture, politics and power in the language of praise. This macaronic miracle is not only a celebration of difference but also a subversion of the forces that invest difference with inequality and an invitation to cultural transformation. Interpreted through a lyric poetics of babble, incorporating concepts of hybridity, heteroglossia, mixture and the creative agency of 'wit', the Pentecost miracle becomes a public and performative language embedded in body, place and history and marked by the politics of sound, manifesting mutual understanding as both the fulfilment of the abortive Babel project and proleptic of human community in the kingdom of heaven.

Conclusion

It has long been debated whether Pentecost is a miracle of speech or hearing. Do the apostles speak in other languages, or is the miracle that whatever language they are speaking, they are understood? Imagined through a macaronic poetics of the Spirit, Pentecost might be understood as both a miracle of speech, crafting new meaning through the fusion of languages, and a miracle of hearing by which the babble of uncomprehended language is heard as song. The lyric beauty of the

---

130. Nederduitse Gereformeerde Kerk, and Algemene Sinode, *Human Relations and the South African Scene in the Light of Scripture* (Cape Town: National Book Printers, 1976), 87.

131. Joel Edwards, 'Foreword', in *Intercultural Preaching*, Congregational Resources vol. 1, ed. Anthony Reddie, Pamela Searle and Seidel Boanerges (Regent's Park College Oxford: Centre for Baptist Studies in Oxford, 2021), 11.

132. Willie James Jennings, *After Whiteness (Theological Education between the Times)* (Grand Rapids, MI: Eerdmans, 2020), chap. 3, loc. 1536–47.

Spirit is found here not in the fixity of balance and proportion but in the ongoing creative evolution of culture, moving from incomprehension towards the wisdom of mutual understanding through the wit of interlingual wordplay.

The model of human community embodied in the macaronic lyric opens up ways in which theological discourses might take better account of their responsibilities towards global contexts, through attentiveness to the sound of words and everything that implies. The awkward term 'babble' invites theologies to confront their blindness to the heavenly song manifest in forms of speech otherwise heard as 'nonsense'. A macaronic poetics of the Spirit might contribute to the work of restoration and reconciliation by bringing together the sonic building blocks of language and culture in a way that demonstrates their interconnectedness without damaging their integrity. This is a demanding process, one that requires a continuing openness to emendation (the making of amends), attentiveness to the minutiae of language, courage to rest in disjuncture or disconnection, and acceptance of the ambivalence of multiplicity. It is a historical process and so remains incomplete, committed to the ongoing task of the recognition, reclamation and redistribution of power.

The reflections on *melos* in this chapter have taken on a particular inflection through the discussion of the multilingual lyric, but they also have more general implications for a consideration of the tone of a lyric theology. *Melos* has been discussed as the sound of joy and the joy of sound, an act of praise. Interpreted as what de Certeau has called '*originary joy*', an unrestricted plenitude of meaning similar to Augustine's *jubilatio*, *melos* might be seen as the building blocks of a temple of praise.[133] The beauty and power that it embodies is accompanied by a peril, historically addressed through discussions of the dangers of sensuality. To confront the commingling of body and spirit, earth and heaven, wit and wisdom, inarticulacy and transcendence in *melos* might entail an embracing of corporeality and historicity, ambivalence and ambiguity in theological discourse. It might also mean exploring the unavoidable capacity of words to move the hearer, with implications for theological reflection on the power, perils and virtues of rhetoric, a theme that will be further addressed in subsequent chapters.

---

133. De Certeau, 'Vocal Utopias', 41.

Chapter 2

'O!' LYRIC ADDRESS AND PRAYER IN THE SPIRIT

Introduction

This chapter examines lyric as the genre of prayer. Through an account of the 'O' of lyric address to God, it reinforces the notion of lyric discourse not as a monological soliloquy but as a fundamentally relational, dialogical and communal form. It argues that, as a model of prayer, lyric address goes well beyond the straightforward appeal of 'I' to 'Thou'. John Stuart Mill famously defined the lyric voice as '*over*heard', but this chapter draws on theories of lyric address to describe lyric as an utterance that is heard, overheard and participated in.[1] It delves into the mysterious interrelationships of God, pray-er, church and world through a Trinitarian reading of the Spirit of Romans 8 as the One who hears, overhears and joins in with the cries of the children of God.

This chapter foregrounds the corporeality and affectivity of lyric sound through a focus on the vocative 'O'.[2] The letter 'O' is a visual representation of its sound, imitating the shape of the lips when they speak the word. This form echoes the meaning-making connectivity between the body and the air that moves through it in speech, a consonance that evokes the way the Spirit moves through the believer in prayer. 'O' is a term capable of a multiplicity of meanings; its circular shape can signify fullness or emptiness, enclosure or expansion, the border of the circle or the space that fills it.[3] This ambivalence extends into its use in prayer, where the 'O' of the versicle 'O Lord open thou our lips' might be heard as an affective-expressive cry, an exhortation to God or the congregation, or a formal liturgical invocation.[4]

These three possible readings provide the framework for an account of the multiplicity of lyric address in this chapter. Lyric has been often read as an

---

1. Mill, 'Thoughts on Poetry', 95 (original italics).
2. See above, pp. 28, 38, on *eala* and *jubilatio*.
3. See 'o, adv.', *OED*, https://www.oed.com/view/Entry/129449?rskey=f94Rp0&result=7&isAdvanced=false#eid.
4. Opening Sentence for Morning and Evening Prayer, *BCP* (Psalm 51.15). *NB* there is an argument for distinguishing the liturgical/scriptural 'O' from the expressive 'Oh', but it is difficult to detect a consistent distinction between these two in the poems discussed in this chapter.

expressive language of sincerity, interiority and affectivity, suited to conveying the intimate colloquy between the believer and God.[5] At the same time, lyric has ritual roots that connect it firmly with the poetics of public prayer, from the Hindu Vedas to the Psalms. This chapter focusses on early-modern prayer-poems, whose indebtedness to the rhetoric of Petrarchan love poetry also raises difficult questions about the dynamics of love and power in prayer. The complex relationality of prayer is drawn out in this chapter through an assessment of the vocative 'O' as not a purely affective cry but a combination of the sincerity of expressivity, the persuasiveness of rhetoric and the authority of community and tradition embodied in its ritual or liturgical aspects.

Many critics and theologians have stressed the differences between the fictional discourse of poetry and the sincerity of true prayer, but this chapter argues that it is precisely the poetic characteristics of fictionality, ambiguity and multiplicity that illuminate the complex entanglements of address to God in and through the Spirit.[6] It draws out the historical connection between love poetry and the devotional lyric through a focus on the sonnet, which situates lyric address within the context of a loving relationship.[7] From the Italian *sonetto* or 'little sound', a sonnet is a fourteen-line poem derived from medieval Petrarchan poetry that embodies what Stephen Regan identifies as the classic lyric attributes of 'brevity, musicality, and intimacy'.[8] Regan has discussed the sonnet's 'discursive' structure, noting how the *volta* or turn between octave and sestet sets up a dialogical framework suited to representing the evolution of a thought or the struggle between competing thoughts and feelings.[9] This dialogical structure to an internal soliloquy suggests a mind properly seen as in relationship: to itself, to the world or to another, whether human or divine. The devotional sonnets discussed in this chapter describe the relationship between the believer and their God as characterized by a freedom and audacity made possible by the presumption of love as the basis of address to another.[10]

5. See, *e.g.*, K. J. E Graham, 'Devotional Poetry', *PEPP*; Hopler and Johnson, *Before the Door*, xxi–xxii.

6. On the similarities and differences between poetry and prayer, see, *e.g.*, Jahan Ramazani, *Poetry and Its Others: News, Prayer, Song, and the Dialogue of Genres* (Chicago, IL: Chicago University Press, 2013), 126–8. For a fuller discussion of the relationship between poetry and prayer, with some preliminary reflections on lyric address, see Elizabeth S. Dodd, 'Silence, Breath, Body, Cry: Poetry and Prayer', in *T&T Clark Handbook of Christian Prayer*, ed. Ashley Cocksworth and John C. McDowell (London: T&T Clark, 2021), 583–600.

7. The sonnet derived a predilection for the theme of love from Petrarch and Dante.

8. Stephen Regan, *The Sonnet* (Oxford: Oxford University Press, 2019), 14.

9. Ibid. The English sonnet adapted the Italian Petrarchan form (abbaabba cdecde or cdcdcd) to a language with fewer rhymes. It is generally classified as Spenserian (abab bcbc cdcd ee) or Shakespearean (abab cdcd efef gg). Both forms include three quatrains and a concluding couplet whose final *volta* may surprise, subvert or decisively conclude the poem.

10. For an introduction to the devotional lyric as a 'vehicle of spiritual discourse', which emphasizes its roots in love poetry, see Louis William Countryman, *The Poetic Imagination: An Anglican Tradition* (Maryknoll, NY: Orbis Books, 1999), 25, 28. Countryman sees the 'overheard' character of the lyric voice as a device for avoiding a didactic tone in devotional poetry.

Lyric address

Culler's seminal work in lyric theory famously centres on the device of apostrophic address, the 'O' by which the poet appears to address an absent, silent or inanimate other. Through apostrophe, poets have addressed everything from lovers to flowers to dead friends and death itself. According to Culler, apostrophe is not merely a formal poetic convention but a sign of the ritual or religious core of lyric discourse.[11] From Percy Bysshe Shelley's 'O wild west wind' to John Keats' 'O solitude!', its 'hyperbolic' overtones have an almost spiritual capacity to 'animat[e] the world, investing mundane objects or occurrences with meaning'.[12] When applied to poetic address to God, this 'conjuring' into being of the silent object of address by the poetic act raises fundamental theological questions.[13] For Philippe Lacoue-Labarthe, the God-like figure of the imagined other is a 'no one whom it is (still) possible to address'.[14] For the devotional poets of this chapter, God is the One who has always addressed humanity first, who may be felt to be silent but is never truly absent. The poetic of apostrophic address nevertheless confronts the reader with the possibility of the absence of the silent God, of the invisible addressee constructed by the act of poetic address.[15]

The implicit dialogism of the vocative of lyric address has important implications for reflections on the language of prayer. Even as an instinctive cry of woundedness or joy, 'O' intimates relationality, acknowledging the impact of the other upon the speaker and reaching out to them through speech.[16] This dialogism is vital to lyric discourse. Von Balthasar's dramatic model of prayer as a dialogue between 'I' and 'Thou' neglects the observation that while in a drama both sides of the conversation are heard, in the public language of prayer the 'Thou' remains ostensibly silent.[17] God speaks but often indirectly, through the foregoing words of scripture and liturgy, through the motions of the believer's heart or through the transformational coming together of the community of faith. As seen below, the

---

11. Culler, *Lyric*, 186–8.

12. Percy Bysshe Shelley, 'Ode to the West Wind' (1820), line 1; John Keats, Sonnet VII (1816), line 1; Culler, *Lyric*, 34–8.

13. Ibid., 219.

14. Ibid.; Philippe Lacoue-Labarthe, *Poetry as Experience*, trans. Andrea Tarnowski (Stanford, CA: Stanford University Press, 1999), 80.

15. NB Paul Alpers has questioned the applicability of Culler's theory to the devotional Renaissance lyric, where apostrophe is addressed to God not as a fiction but as something real, 'Apostrophe and the Rhetoric of Renaissance Lyric', *Representations* 122, no. 1 (Spring 2013): 1–22.

16. On lyric address not as an appeal to an 'unhearing' audience but as a communicative act that makes a connection with the reader, see William Waters, *Poetry's Touch: On Lyric Address* (Ithaca: Cornell University Press, 2003), 1–4.

17. See Von Balthasar, *Theo-Drama* II, 56.

structures of lyric address open up this experience of the indirect revelation of God through prayer.[18]

Lyric address also raises the issue of sincerity. Culler calls apostrophe 'indirect address', emphasizing that it is not, in fact, the addressee but the eavesdropping audience who is the secretly intended hearer whose hidden presence looms over the page, their shadow cast across it.[19] The reader who 'overhears' the apparently private meditation of lyric address is reassured that what they hear is sincere, precisely because it is not directed at them. This is, of course, an illusion, since the poet (even in poems not intended for publication) always writes for an audience. Culler describes the pretence of indirect address as an artistic sleight of hand that 'winks' at the reader, who is thereby implicated in its fictionality.[20] In contrast, Frye describes indirect address as a performance whereby the poet 'turns his back on his listeners' like a priest celebrating mass facing the high altar. Frye notes that the reader, like the congregation in public prayer, takes on the poet's words for themselves by sounding them out.[21] Drawing on Frye as well as Culler, this chapter confronts the relationship between fictionality and sincerity in lyric address through the priestly role of the poet. It examines the curious ventriloquism of the lyric voice, as taken into the mouth of the reader, to address the didactic purposes of prayer-poems and the horizontal as well as vertical relations that they delineate. Taking on Culler's notion of 'triangulated address', the argument culminates in a discussion of the Trinitarian structures of prayer, through which humanity is drawn into the conversation of Father, Son and Spirit.[22]

A silent God? Apostrophe beyond expressivity

When directed to the poet themselves or an absent lover, lyric address may be heard as eavesdropping on an inner monologue, directed to rocks or trees, it may be heard as artistic affectation. When directed to God, lyric address evokes the 'I-Thou' posture of private prayer. This apparently monological poetic discourse raises fundamental theological questions about the nature and existence of God. When God remains silent in the poem, it raises the spectre of prayer as pure introspection and of God as a psychological projection. In poems where God's voice is represented, such as Herbert's (1593–1633) 'A True Hymne' or 'The Collar', God becomes an overtly fictional character, a construct of the poet. Early-modern devotional poets were intimately aware of the issues with poetic address to God. Beyond the potential idolatries of representation, questions of how to address a holy, good and loving God were also tied up with theological and pastoral

---

18. Frye draws out the devotional connotations of lyric address, defining it as 'what in religion is called the "I-Thou" relationship'. Frye, *Anatomy*, 249–50.
19. Culler, *Lyric*, 34, 211–43.
20. Ibid., 206.
21. See Frye, *Anatomy*, 249–50.
22. Culler, *Lyric*, 8.

anxieties over assurance and providence.[23] This section explores the paradoxical presence of the God who is silently heard in and through the expressive cry of the soul in turmoil, through the sonnets of Ann Lok and the elegies of Mary Carey. It also provides a wider perspective on these questions by highlighting the ritual and fictional features of otherwise highly affective-expressive lyrics.

Hearing the mercy of God in Ann Lok's sonnets on Psalm 51

Ann Lok's (c. 1533–90) *A Meditation of a Penitent Sinner* (1560) is an extended reflection on Psalm 51 and the first sonnet sequence written in English. Lok was a devout Protestant who migrated to Geneva at the behest of John Knox during the reign of Mary I, taking her two children with her (one of whom died on arrival) and leaving her husband behind. Lok's *Meditation* was published after her return to England in 1559, to accompany her translation of Calvin's sermons on Isaiah 38.[24] There was a long heritage to poetic translation of the Psalms, which were considered an acceptable aid to devotion even when vernacular translations of the scriptures were banned, while congregational singing of the metrical Psalms was a central feature of sixteenth-century Protestant worship.[25] The Psalms were considered both a pattern for common worship and a map of the heart: what Calvin called '"An Anatomy of all the Parts of the Soul"'.[26] The penitential Psalms held a crucial role in early-modern Protestant devotion as an expression of the need for grace and an appeal to the God of mercy.

Lok's decision to translate a psalm designed for public worship into a sonnet form commonly associated with the amorous adventures of courtly life might seem surprising, but the sixteenth-century sonnet was frequently turned to religious subjects.[27] Regan has noted how its intricate rhyme schemes provide a

---

23. For a discussion of Herbert's *Temple* in relation to a theology of assurance, discussing how God responds either explicitly or implicitly to the poet's cry, see Rowan Williams, 'Inside Herbert's *Afflictions*', in *Anglican Identities* (Lanham, MD: Cowley Publications, 2003), 57–72.

24. Ann Lok, *A Meditation of a Penitent Sinner*, appended to *Sermons of John Calvin, upon the songe that Ezechias made after he had been sicke* (London: John Day, 1560).

25. Exemplified in England by Thomas Sternhold and John Hopkins' vastly popular if pedestrian translation, *The Whole Book of Psalms Collected into English Metre* (London: John Day, 1562), which was used well into the eighteenth century. On the uses of the Psalms in this period, see Hannibal Hamlin, *Psalm Culture and Early Modern English Literature* (Cambridge: Cambridge University Press, 2004).

26. John Calvin, *Commentary on the Book of Psalms*, trans. James Anderson, vol. 1 (Edinburgh: Calvin Translation Society, 1845), preface, p. xxxvii.

27. Consider, *e.g.*, the spiritual sonnets of Henry Lok (Ann's son) and Barnabe Barnes. The classic collection of erotic sonnets was Tottel's *Miscellany* or *Songes and Sonettes* (1557). On the Psalms in the early-modern religious lyric, see Elizabeth Clarke and Simon Jackson, 'Lyric Poetry', in *The Oxford Handbook of Early Modern English Literature and Religion*, ed. Andrew Hiscox and Helen Wilcox (Oxford: Oxford University Press, 2017), 151–65; Deirdre Serjeantson, 'The Book of Psalms and the Early Modern Sonnet', *Renaissance Studies* 29, no. 4 (September 2015): 632–49.

structure for the performance of complex thoughts and feelings, while Malcolm Guite, a modern practitioner of the devotional sonnet, similarly describes it as a 'form whose discipline, brevity and concentrated "muscle"' is appropriate for metaphysical reflection'.[28] As a model of lyric reasoning, the sonnet form could ably follow the shifting sands of the psalmist's soul, following them from praise to despair, from frustration to hope and back to praise.

Lok's poetic translation of Psalm 51 illustrates a Calvinist perspective on the difficulties of address to God, through the words of an anxious yet repentant sinner. The preface summarizes the conflicted character of prayerful address as it appears throughout the poem:

> From troubled sprite I send confused crye,
> To crave the crummes of all sufficing grace.[29]

The sonnet for Psalm 51.1 provides an example of this 'confused crye'. It contains a marginal transcription of Psalm 51.1, which brackets out the key vocative phrase: '*Have mercie upon me (o God) after thy great merci*'. This striking editorial insertion into the scriptural text problematizes address to God, demonstrating the equivocation of the penitent soul caught in tension between the desire to cry for mercy and the 'dred' of addressing God with sinful lips. The line 'O God: my God, unto my shame I say' reveals a speaker turned back upon themselves into introspection, ruminating on their own sin.[30] While repeatedly crying to God for mercy, the sonnet also describes the difficulty the soul finds in addressing God. It asks in the first place not just for mercy, but for the ability to cry for it.

This opening stands in sharp contrast to Thomas Wyatt's earlier paraphrase of Psalm 51 and to Mary Sidney's later translation, neither of which vacillates over the propriety of crying to God. Adopting the traditional Latin title 'Miserere mei, Domine', Wyatt's poem presents the natural and dutiful supplication of subject to king, in confidence of being heard.[31] Sidney's rhyme royal draws on a similar Protestant tradition to Lok, influenced by the Geneva Bible and the Psalm translations of Theodore of Beza and Clément Marot. Unlike Lok, it shows no discomfiture in opening the poem with the apostrophe, 'O Lord, whose grace no limits comprehend'. In Sidney's translation, the impassioned plea of the vocative 'O' reaches almost the tone of command. The strength of the cries, 'O, cleanse, o, wash', rests in an utter confidence in God's unchanging grace.[32]

---

28. Malcolm Guite, *After Prayer: New Sonnets and Other Poems* (Norwich: Canterbury Press, 2019), i.

29. Anne Locke, 'A Meditation', in *The Collected Works of Anne Vaughan Locke*, ed. Susan M. Felch (Tempe, AZ: Arizona Center for Medieval and Renaissance Studies and Renaissance English Text Society, 1999), 62–71, lines 72–3.

30. Ibid., line 88.

31. Thomas Wyatt, 'Miserere mei, Deus', *Paraphrase of the Penitential Psalms* (1536/1541).

32. Mary Sidney, 'Psalm 51', in *The Sidney Psalter: The Psalms of Sir Philip and Mary Sidney*, ed. Hannibal Hamlin *et al.* (Oxford: Oxford University Press, 2009), 97, lines 1, 5.

Lok's Sonnet 1, by contrast, proceeds in a manner of conflicted reticence, continuing to address God while seeming to decline to do so. The penitent sinner's cry is one word: 'mercy'. The hesitance expressed in line 9 ('That scare I dare thy mercy sound againe') is consistently overruled, as each line in the final sestet contains this term.[33] This apparently irresistible desire to cry for mercy continues throughout the sequence, which repeatedly, seemingly directly and increasingly unashamedly, addresses God in ever more strident cries, with the word 'mercy' repeated sixty-eight times in all.

This repetitive cry for mercy can become oppressive, its circularity imitative of a mind in turmoil. As the sequence progresses, the addresses grow in hope and confidence, but not without the occasional relapse into despair. For example, Sonnet 17 on Psalm 51.15 ('Lord, open thou my lippes, and my mouth shal shewe thy praise') begins somewhat surprisingly in despair. It leaves praise to the final couplet, which looks forward to a future when finally:

> … findyng grace with open mouth I may
> Thy mercies praise, and holy name display.[34]

The final sonnet concludes its octave with a hymn of praise from God's people that extends into line nine:

> We praise thee, God our God: thou onely art
> The God of might, of mercie, and of grace.

Crossing the Shakespearean rhyme scheme, this device moves the volta to line ten. This line ('That I then, Lorde, may also honor thee') pointedly distinguishes the collective praises of the church from the individual speaker's present inability to praise. The final quatrain turns back from a vision of heavenly praise to the call for mercy that has dominated the sequence, circling back to leave the reader where they started, but perhaps with greater hope than when they began:

> Releve my sorow, and my sinnes deface:
> Be, Lord of mercie, mercifull to me:
> Restore my feling of thy grace againe:
> Assure my soule, I crave it not in vaine.[35]

The final line ends with a hope of assurance, and of the fulfilment of the desire for grace, although the final word 'vaine' echoes in the mind with an ongoing sense of unease.

---

33. Locke, 'Meditation', line 95.
34. Ibid., lines 323–4.
35. Ibid., lines 374–80.

Psalm 51 was commonly read as David's song of repentance after being reproved by the prophet Nathan for the sins of adultery and murder in 2 Samuel 12. Lok's sequence is a kind of expansion of an expansion. 2 Samuel 12.13 records only a brief declaration of penitence: 'I have sinned against the Lord'. Psalm 51 is made up of nineteen verses, which Lok stretches out over twenty-one sonnets. The cumulative effect of this long sequence is to leave the reader gasping for a mercy that, despite the more positive tone of the final couplet, remains undeclared. In the Hebrew narrative, mercy arrives swiftly in the prophet Nathan's declaration of absolution. The silence of the Lord in the context of this lyric monologue leaves a mind that, in the words of Sonnet 10 (on Psalm 51.8), hears instead the 'thonders of the law', the echoes of their guilt that drown out the sweet song of mercy.[36]

Although highly pensive, the voice of this poem is not purely introspective. There are three key ways in which, by going beyond expressivity, the poem whispers God's grace and conveys a sense of assurance, if indirectly, to the reader. The first is its narrative hinterland. The story of David, as just outlined, is one in which an appeal for mercy receives a response of grace. This poem was appended to a translation of Calvin's sermon on Hezekiah, another story where a sinner is confronted with a prophecy of doom but after repentance, God relents. This wider narrative context presents the character of God as one of mercy and faithfulness, attributes that may be relied upon by the repentant sinner, even in the midst of their anguish.

The second way in which this poem conveys the grace of God is through the ritual features of the text.[37] In early-modern Protestant devotion, assurance of salvation was often sought through a sense of peace and trust in God's favour, but assurance could also be conveyed through the performance of penitent anguish.[38] Calvin's commentary on Psalm 51.3 stresses that true repentance requires a 'deep inward feeling' of one's sins, without which the sinner's cry for mercy is mere hypocrisy.[39] Following Calvin's advice, the mental turmoil communicated through Lok's *Meditation* can serve as evidence of a sincerity that, in itself, gives hope of redemption. In the liturgical reperformance of a Psalm, the voice of the reader merges with that of the speaker. Lok's poem is entitled *A Meditation of a Penitent Sinner*, a nonspecific voice who is explicitly identified neither with David, Hezekiah nor the poet. This enables the reader to take on the poem's address to God as their own, and so to share in both the agony of guilt and the hope of redemption.

In the *Institutes*, Calvin associates assurance with the 'testimony of the Spirit' in Romans 8.15. Through the Spirit the believer is given the words with which to cry

---

36. Ibid., line 214.

37. Roland Greene has discussed sixteenth-century psalters as lyric sequences that sit on the ritual end of the ritual and fictional poles of the lyric genre. Roland Greene, *Post-Petrarchism: Origins and Innovations of the Western Lyric Sequence* (Princeton, CA: Princeton University Press, 1991), 3–21 (16).

38. See Calvin, *Institutes* 3.2.7.

39. Ibid., *Psalms*, Psalm 51.3-4.

to God, 'Abba, Father!'[40] The very act of address to God is evidence of the presence of the Spirit, who prays with and through the pray-er. Seen in this light, Lok's opening sonnet can be seen not as an example of anxious spiritual introspection but a charting of the soul's transition from a state of damnation to a state of grace, through the process of coming to the point of being able to cry for mercy. To hear the cry for mercy as the 'testimony of the Spirit' is to see the silent Other of the lyric prayer-poem as not silent at all but to hear the voice of God in every word of the penitent sinner.

Intimacy and ambivalence in Mary Carey's elegies

Of her seven children, Mary Carey (*c.* 1609–80) lost five as infants and the other two in early adulthood, as well as having at least one miscarriage.[41] Her poems on these subjects were not printed but neither were they a private affair. They began as a mother's legacy (a testimonial in case of death in childbirth) addressed to her second husband, and were later transcribed in a presentation copy intended for circulation.[42] The intensely intimate tone of address to God in this poem is all the more striking given the suggestion of a wider audience, which raises questions about the public role of apparently private prayer.

Carey's manuscript is a mixture of poems, including elegies for her children, and prose meditations, both of which combine a depth of emotion with an assertion of absolute submission to God's providence. After the death of her first three children, Carey wrote a 'Dialogue betwixt the Soul, and the Body', in which the body complains of its sorrows and the soul responds with a sense of lasting peace, while God is presented as a loving father who acts in wisdom and faithfulness.[43] After the loss of all of her first five children, Carey declared herself to be 'in greatest Sorrows, content, & happy'.[44] This dominant theme of peace and acceptance is accompanied by an ongoing sense of agitation and anguish. In the 'Dialogue', for example, the voice of Satan seeks 'to tempt me, terrify, upbraid, & challenge me for his own', unsettling Carey's trust in God's providence by speaking in whispers that are suggestive of concealment and deceit, but also of the heart's internal monologue.[45]

---

40. Ibid., *Institutes* 3.1.1, 3.1.3.

41. See '*Upon the Sight of My Abortive Birth the 31th of December 1657*', in *Lady Carey's Meditations, & Poetry* (Bodl. Oxf., MS Rawl. D. 1308), fols 215–22.

42. Sara H. Mendelson, 'Carey [née Jackson], Mary, Lady Carey', in *Oxford Dictionary of National Biography* (Oxford: Oxford University Press, 2004), online, https://doi.org/10.1093/ref:odnb/45811.

43. Mary Carey, 'February, 11th 1649. A Dialogue betwixt the Soul, and the Body', in *Flesh and Spirit: An Anthology of Seventeenth-Century Women's Writing*, ed. Rachel Adcock, Sara Read and Anna Ziomek (Manchester: Manchester University Press, 2014), 45–51.

44. Ibid., 'May, 14th 1652', in ibid., 51.

45. See Ibid., 'A Dialogue' and 'A Meditation, or Commemoration of the Love of God the Father, Son, & Holy Ghost', in ibid., 48–50, 53.

In the poems, the device of lyric address adds a sense of pathos, ambivalence and even a hint of reproach to this combination of sorrow and contentment. In the elegy 'on the Death of my 4th, & only Child, Robert Payler', Carey surrenders her dead son to God, but asks for God's Son Jesus Christ in return. This oblation and petition for a gift that has already been given is a model of right devotion that goes well beyond a shallow providentialism. The poem is framed by the opening and closing couplets as a one-sided dialogue with God:

1. My Lord hath callèd for my Son, My heart breathes forth, thy Will be done …
6. Give him to me; & I'll reply Enough my Lord; now let me die.[46]

The voice of the Lord is never represented within the poem, but God has already spoken through it. First God 'calls' her son to heaven, then appears to speak through the gift of His Son, an act to which the poet 'replies'. There is an intimate and instinctive character to the poet's response, which Carey terms the heart's 'breathing forth', but the words of this spiration are thoroughly conventional: the liturgical phrase from the Lord's prayer, 'thy will be done'. This is the prayer that Jesus taught, both a rote prayer and the cry of God to God. With reference to this allusion Helen Wilcox describes the lines 'as though the Lord is praying beside her'.[47] The apostrophized Lord is far from a silent Other. He is, on the contrary, deeply present to the poem.

It is perhaps the posture of faithful and loving address that gives the poet strength to challenge God. The address to God as 'my Lord' and not 'O Lord' in the first and last lines connotes not only filial duty and submission but also the expectation of love and favour. After the first quatrain, in which the speaker surrenders their son to God, the poem turns from submission to request: your child for mine. The following couplet marks this *volta* and the beginning of the second half of the poem:

4. Change with me; do, as I have done, Give me thy All, even thy dear Son:

The centrality of this line to the poem is marked by the inverted repetition of the rhyme-words from the first couplet, 'Son' and 'done'. The speaker asks for no miracle or material recompense but only what God has already given in sending Jesus Christ. At the same time, the tone is blunt and directive, expressed through monosyllables, the plosives of 'do' and 'done' and the stark duality of exchange which is reinforced by the devices of the rhyming couplet and cæsuras. In this bald demand there is the honesty of a straight speech that is only possible within a context of intimate relationship.

46. Ibid., 'Written by me at the same time on the Death of my 4th, & only Child, Robert Payler', in ibid., 52.
47. Helen Wilcox, '"Your Suit Is Granted": Performing Prayer in Early Modern English Poetry', in *Prayer and Performance in Early Modern English Literature: Gesture, Word and Devotion*, ed. Joseph Sterrett (Cambridge: Cambridge University Press, 2018), 164.

This poem is more than a straightforward act of prayerful address to God. Narrative elements at the beginning and end enclose the lyric monologue in a dramatic frame, so that the words appear not as direct but as represented speech. The opening past-tense phrase ('My lord hath called for my sonne') locates the poem within a narrative context, before proceeding to a present-tense description of the action ('My heart breathes') and thence to the prayer. This device has a distancing effect that contextualizes and somewhat contains the strength of emotion conveyed in the central passages. More importantly, this device highlights the multiplicity of prayerful-poetic address. The prayer may be addressed to God, but the poem is addressed to a human reader, an anonymous audience who is, it seems, invited to judge, approve or imitate the speaker's response to God's providence. This poem is not, as it appears, an intimate colloquy with God, a private expression of grief and devotion, but a public display of piety and a lesson in prayer. It serves as a reminder that the evident intimacy of direct address in the cry, 'Abba', in the Lord's Prayer in Matthew 6.9-13 or the Spirit's prayer in Romans 8.15 is also a representation of and a pattern for prayer. The transparency of poetic representation in this poem does not distinguish it from an act of prayer. Rather, it reflects the multiple levels on which prayerful address to God might be heard: as a personal cry, an exhortation to others, a joining with the prayers of the saints and an address of God to God.

The repetition of the dramatic device at the end of the poem places a particular emphasis on the final line: 'Enough my Lord; now let me die.' This allusion to Luke 2.29, a New Testament poem used in the liturgical context of common prayer, turns the settled contentment of 'Lord, now lettest thou servant depart in peace' into a stark 'Enough' that communicates nothing of the peace that the poet elsewhere claims to enjoy. Carey's 'let' conveys an emphatic longing for relief from pain that is not usually read into the Song of Simeon. The counterpoint between these two voices highlights the contrast between the aged man joyfully accepting death after the fulfilment of his desires and the fatigued desolation of the bereaved mother who has had her hope and future taken away. Resting upon the authority of the scriptures and encompassed by the prayers of the church, which provide both bassline and counterpoint to the poem's melodic line, the speaker finds freedom to suggest a sense of hurt, anger and betrayal to God, within a broader context of trust and submission to God's providence.

In the poems of Lok and Carey, the personal expressivity of lyric address is situated within a ritual and fictional framework that extends its voice beyond the individual speaker to embrace a community of prayer. The sincerity of this lyric voice is not located in the apparent directness of address of 'I' to 'Thou' but rather in the multiplicity of apostrophic address, an ambivalent space where the self in its relation to the other may be broken open, interrogated and offered up precisely in its brokenness and suffering. To read the figure of God as silent or even absent in devotional lyrics such as these is to misunderstand not only the poetic and devotional traditions on which they draw but also their theological underpinnings. The implicit dialogism of these poems is, most importantly, a dialogue with a beloved other. The Spirit who is, as Augustine describes them, the bond of love both within the Trinity and between God and the world, dwells within these poems as the declaration of love that precedes every act of prayer.[48]

Persuading God? The rhetoric of lyric address in Donne's devotional poetry

The power of the vocative 'O'

Culler has described the vocative lyric 'O' as not a pure expression of emotion but a fundamentally rhetorical as well as ritual poetic device.[49] In Cicero's classic definition, rhetoric had three purposes: to teach, delight and move, of which the latter was the most essential.[50] In the context of lyric address, this persuasive power has been described as a form of 'coercion', closer to the forcefulness of magical invocation than the submissiveness of prayerful intercession.[51] This section explores lyric address's potential for rhetorical violence through the devotional poetry of John Donne (1572–1631). By asking who it is that the voice of indirect address is seeking to persuade, it explores the messy entanglement of human and divine relations in prayer, listening for the sighs and groans of the Spirit in humanity's distorted cries to God.

Although Phillip Sidney wrote only of teaching and delight in his famous definition of poetry, the power to move was by no means alien to early-modern understandings of the poetic vocation.[52] John Milton, for example, described lyric poetry as possessing a 'power beside the office of a pulpit to inbreed and cherish in a great people the seeds of virtue and public civility ... and set the affections in right tune'.[53] Milton's likening of the poem to the sermon was not incidental. What Eliot termed the 'oratorical' features of Donne and Herbert's poetry arose out of their academic training in rhetoric and intersected with their priestly vocation of preaching.[54] The exhortatory quality of their lyric 'O' is intimately bound up with the liturgical contexts behind its utterance, which include the pulpit.[55]

48. Augustine, *De Trinitate* 6.1.5.
49. Culler, *Lyric*, 213, 215–16.
50. Cicero, *De Optimo Genere Oratorum* 1.3.
51. Thomas M. Greene, 'Poetry as Invocation', *New Literary History* 24, no. 3 (Summer 1993): 499.
52. Phillip Sidney, *The Defence of Poesie* (London: William Ponsonby, 1595), f. 14. On the importance of rhetoric in early-modern poetry, particularly its power to move the audience, see Brian Vickers, 'Rhetoric', in *The Cambridge Companion to English Poetry, Donne to Marvell*, ed. Thomas N. Corns (Cambridge: Cambridge University Press, 1993), 101–20.
53. John Milton, *The Reason of Church-Government* (London: John Rothwell, 1641), 39.
54. T. S. Eliot, *George Herbert* (Tavistock: Liverpool University Press, 2018), 24. NB Herbert was praelector in rhetoric and University Orator at Cambridge before he was priested.
55. According to Joseph Sterrett, Donne considered the sermon 'an important collective performance of prayer', central to the liturgy, 'Introduction', in *Prayer and Performance*, 7.

The often-acknowledged rhetorical power of Donne's *Holy Sonnets* is evident in its varied uses of the lyric 'O', which convey the strong emotions of an anxious soul.[56] The metaphysical poets and their readers would have been familiar with what Henry Peachum's rhetorical primer, *The Garden of Eloquence*, called *exclamatio*, the incitement of heightened emotion through 'figures of exclamation'.[57] Peachum warns the reader that such figures are only effective when uttered with sincerity, reflecting the true passions of the speaker. As one such figure, the apostrophic 'O' could convey, among other feelings, a passionate desire, a desperate appeal or a cry of grief or pain. For example, *Holy Sonnet* 3 ('O might those sighes and tears returne again') opens with a straightforwardly expressive cry of regret for tears sinfully 'spent', presumably in love-longing and not in repentance.[58] The opening 'O' of Sonnet 5 ('Oh my blacke Soule') signals an address to the self, but is also a passionate sigh that through the course of the poem is filled with the regret, reproach and self-love of the penitent sinner. In the final quatrain, the repeated 'O' of 'Oh make thy selfe with holy mourning blacke' recapitulates these feelings in an exhortation to the soul to turn from the darkness of sin, doubt and despair to the mourning colours of penitence.[59]

One of the most striking uses of 'O' in this sequence appears in Sonnet 9: 'If poysonous Minerals'. It marks the point where the poem turns from soliloquy to prayer; from a bitter complaint about the prospect of damnation to a petition to God to forget the speaker's sins:

> But who am I that dare dispute with thee
> O God? O of thyne only worthy blood
> And my teares make a heauenly Lethean flood[60]

Lines 9–11 mark a double turn: from protest to self-reflection and thence to a cry for mercy. This dramatic *metanoia* is performed through the jolting rhythm of the first half of line 10. The enjambment from line 9 brings the flow to a jarring halt at

---

56. Hugh Adlington describes Donne's poetic-theological style as a mixture of the rhetorical and the dialectical, reflecting Eliot's earlier assessment: Hugh Adlington, 'John Donne', in *The Oxford Handbook of Early Modern English Literature and Religion*, ed. Andrew Hiscock and Helen Wilcox (Oxford: Oxford University Press, 2017), www.oxfordhandbooks.com.

57. Henry Peachum, *The Garden of Eloquence Conteyning the Most Excellent Ornaments, Exornations, Lightes, Flowers, and Formes of Speech, Commonly Called the Figures of Rhetorike* (London: Richard Field for H. Jackson, 1593), 62–4.

58. John Donne, Sonnet 3, *Holy Sonnets*, lines 1–2. NB all citations from the *Holy Sonnets* are taken from the Westmoreland Sequence (*c.* 1620) as transcribed in *The Variorum Edition of the Poetry of John Donne*, ed. Gary A. Stringer and Paul A. Parrish et al., vol. 7, part 1 (Bloomington, IN: Indiana University Press, 2005), 11–20.

59. Ibid., Sonnet 5, lines 1, 11.

60. Ibid., Sonnet 9, lines 9–11.

the end of 'O God?' The reader must then stumble through the disruptive force of the two exclamations and the articulative hurdle of the repeated vowel sounds in 'O of', before the iambic rhythm resumes with the word 'only'. The point of conversion in this poem is marked by two lyric 'O's. These double 'O's in line 10 surround the name of God, encompassing it in a wordless cry that extends throughout the line through further assonance on the letter 'o'. In Romans 8.26, the Spirit is said to intercede for us in prayer, through sighs and groans 'too deep for words'. In Donne's poem it is as if, through the extended groan of line 10, the Spirit is heard to lift the speaker's prayer to the Father, transforming a selfish complaint into a cry for mercy.

In Sonnet 7, 'I ame a little World, made cunningly', 'O' laments first the unredeemed sinner's double death, of body and spirit, and then the purging fire that purifies the soul. In both cases ('and Oh both parts must dy', 'But Oh it must be burn'd') 'O' is an interjection or interruption but is also integral to the flow of the line, conforming perfectly to the poem's iambic meter. The final 'O' of this poem, 'And burne me O God with a fiery Zeale' works in a similar way, but sits less comfortably with the iambic rhythm, which if followed strictly would place the emphasis rather awkwardly on the 'O' of 'O God'. Inserted into a graphic petition for devotion to God, this conventional liturgical apostrophe combines formal address with rhetorical intsensity.[61] The quality of the exclamatory 'O' in this poem, as an interpolation that is integral to the poetic line, might provide a figure for the intervention of the Spirit in prayer, whose cry rises up from within, elevating and intensifying the prayer while making it whole.

Passion and persuasion in 'Batter my Heart'

The problematic intersection of passion and persuasion in rhetorical poetry, already raised in Chapter 1, takes on a particular complexion in relation to lyric address. American poet and critic Denise Levertov describes 'The poet's task' as follows:

> to hold in trust the knowledge that language … is not a set of counters to be manipulated, but a Power. And only in this knowledge does he arrive at … that quality of song within speech which is not the result of manipulations of euphonious parts but of an attention … to the latent harmony and counterpoint of language itself.[62]

Donne's *Holy Sonnets* are a masterclass in the art of lyric reasoning, exploiting every facet of the sonnet form to evoke a sinner's heart in anguished reflection on questions of life, death and salvation. However, it remains a vexed question to what extent his linguistic gymnastics sound the song of the Spirit, or to what extent he is ruthlessly manipulating the 'euphonous parts' of language, or simply enjoying the play of words.

61. Ibid., Sonnet 7, lines 4, 10, 13.
62. Denise Levertov, 'The Origins of a Poem', in *The Poet in the World* (New York: New Directions, 1973), 54.

Donne's *Holy Sonnets* appropriate poetic conventions from the love sonnet tradition in a manner that proved definitive for the metaphysical school of poetry, but has also been seen as theologically dubious. Donne had ample precedent for the spiritual employment of erotic motifs through literature inspired by the lyric world of the Song of Songs: from Origen to Bernard of Clairvaux to Teresa of Avila and John of the Cross. Nevertheless, as seen below, Donne's proficiency in the secular art of erotic poetry has long rendered theologically questionable his use of erotic spiritual motifs. From a modern perspective, the lover's rhetorical posture of persuasion may be problematic enough in Donne's secular lyrics. The translation of this device into the dynamics of prayerful address to God only adds an extra dimension to this difficulty.

A key poem in these debates is Sonnet 16, 'Batter my hart', which has been subject to extensive critiques for its spiritualization of the language of sexual violence. Many of the *Holy Sonnets* adopt the posture of private meditation, of the soul addressing itself. This is one of the few dominated by apparently direct address to God. The violence of this poem is bound up not only in its combination of martial and sexual imagery but in the forceful dynamics of its rhetorical address to God, with invocation at times straying into the imperative of command.[63] Following the conventions of mystical literature, this poem adopts the feminine voice of bride to bridegroom. This device reverses the lyric conventions of erotic persuasion, as the address not of lover to beloved but of beloved to lover. Stanley Fish has noted that despite its feminine voice, this poem embodies masculinist ideals of independence, power and control, while feminist theologians have used this poem about the 'three-person God' to exemplify patriarchal constructions of the Trinity that endorse oppressive power relations.[64] These moral and theological issues cannot be contextualized away. Neither historical context, poetic convention nor the scriptural hinterland can excuse its violent implications.[65] Nevertheless, from her own distinctive feminist

---

63. Brian Cummings makes this observation in his discussion of the poem, while also noting the irony that this forceful rhetoric comes from a position of impotence, as the speaker has no power over the God whom they invoke. Cummings describes this poem's theological grammar as 'noise' without a 'coherent "voyce"', in *The Literary Culture of the Reformation: Grammar and Grace* (Oxford: Oxford University Press, 2002), Kindle, chap. 9 section IV.

64. Donne, Sonnet 16, line 1; Stanley Fish, 'Masculine Persuasive Force: Donne and Verbal Power', in *Soliciting Interpretation: Literary Theory and Seventeenth-Century English Poetry*, ed. Elizabeth D. Harvey and Katharine Eisaman Maus (Chicago: University of Chicago Press, 1990), 228; see Mary Grey, 'The Core of Our Desire: Reimagining the Trinity', *Theology* 93 (1990): 362–72; Hannah Bacon, *What's Right with the Trinity? Conversations in Feminist Theology* (London: Routledge, 2016), 15.

65. It could be argued, for example, that the word 'batter' in line 1 refers only to the beating of a door, a reference to Revelation 3.20, but the final line's reference to 'ravishment' by God makes the connotations of sexual assault inescapable, nor does the conventionality of this imagery eliminate its problematic nature.

perspective Sarah Coakley has called for a more nuanced assessment of this poem. She acknowledges Donne's capacity to 'stare the entanglement of sexual desire and desire for God firmly in the face', even if only to emphasize the irretrievable 'disjunction' between human desire and the love of God.[66]

If there is more to be said about this poem in the context of a discussion of lyric theology, it might be to consider how the features of its lyric address illuminate the dynamics of prayer. In his sermons on the penitential Psalms, Donne described prayer, following Tertullian, as 'besieging God', or a kind of holy 'impudence', following Gregory of Nazianzus.[67] Herbert also picked up on the notion of prayer as a battle in poems such as 'Artillerie', which describes prayer as both seduction and 'combate', 'Prayer (I)', which depicts prayer as a military 'engine' or 'spear', and 'Prayer (II)', which speaks of 'invading' God's ears.[68] Deeply indebted to the Psalms, this imagery preserves a space for challenge and struggle in the life of prayer, and presents a picture of participation in God as akin to the sometimes stormy colloquy of lover and beloved. It also, as Michael Schoenfeldt has argued, opens up questions around the 'violence' and 'power structure' of prayer.[69] The strong rhetoric of Donne's Sonnet 14 – its extravagant metaphors (siege, betrothal, imprisonment), forceful plosives ('breake, blow, burne') or the witty paradoxes of the final couplet – may be read as a kind of prayerful impudence, more provocation than invocation.[70] The power dynamics in this prayer run beneath, even contradict, its forceful vocative. The God who is addressed *in* the poem is not necessarily the God *of* the poem. While the speaker may desire a forceful warrior, they encounter God in line 2 as the one who will 'but knock, breathe, shine, and seeke to mend' the door of the heart.[71] The God who, as Donne describes them in his sermons, is content to be besieged is not a weak God, nor necessarily one whose strength is revealed only in suffering, but one with power both to withstand (*i.e.* stand with) and to comprehend (*i.e.* understand/encompass) the force of human emotion.

The lyric address of this poem reveals much more of the speaker than the God to whom they pray. Many of Donne's *Holy Sonnets* portray a soul anxious for salvation and fearful of reprobation, aspiring to a 'holy discontent' while revealing the follies and corruptions of a sinner's desire for God.[72] Fish influentially labelled

---

66. Coakley, *GSS*, 296, 299.

67. John Donne, Sermon 50 'Preached upon the Penitential Psalms', in *The Works of John Donne*, ed. George R. Potter and Evelyn M. Simpson, vol. 2 (London: University of California Press, 1953–62).

68. Herbert, 'Artillerie', lines 19, 26; ibid., 'Prayer (I)', 5–6; ibid., 'Prayer (II)', 3. All citations from the poetry of George Herbert are taken from *The English Poems of George Herbert*, ed. Helen Wilcox (Cambridge: Cambridge University Press, 2007).

69. Michael Schoenfeldt, *Prayer and Power: George Herbert and Renaissance Courtship* (Chicago: University of Chicago Press, 1991), 92, cited in Wilcox, *English Poems*, 371.

70. Donne, Sonnet 14, line 4.

71. Ibid., line 2.

72. Ibid., Sonnet 3, line 3.

Donne a poet 'in bad faith', whose sacred poems lack sincerity, delighting in the power of words with little regard for their moral or theological implications.[73] Against the wider context of the sequence, Sonnet 14 might be read perhaps not as a poem in 'bad faith' but as the prayer of one who does not know how to pray, in thrall to sin, loving God but not knowing how. In Romans 8.26-27, the intercession of the Spirit is promised in support of those who 'do not know how to pray as they ought', a cry imagined in this chapter as heard through the wordless sighs and groans of the lyric 'O'. Sonnet 14's barrage of words leaves room for only one 'O', the *exclamatio* of 'but Oh to no end' in line 6.[74] This is a cry of frustrated desire, grief, despair and longing, one in which the 'O' of sexual desire and the 'O' of prayer become dangerously entangled. Its presence might be taken as a token of hope, of the presence of the Spirit even in the distorted words of a sinner's prayer.

There is a risk of violence in this poem that lies not in Donne's distinctive poetics but in more general features of lyric address. The reader of a first-person lyric becomes the 'I' of that poem, appropriating its words as their own. Renaissance critic Roland Greene has described this ventriloquism of the lyric voice as a form of 'violence', in which one subjectivity is 'superposed' upon another.[75] In the prayer-poem, the poet does not merely address the reader indirectly but co-opts them into sharing the poem's prayer. In prayer-poems such as Sonnet 14, which test the boundaries of prayer, the reader may be led despite themselves into an address to God that they find uncomfortable or even objectionable.[76] At the same time, the reader may impose their own subjectivity on the voice of the poem in ways never intended or imagined by the poet. These reciprocal impositions may lead both reader and poem down unexpected avenues, which may be discomfiting, even dangerous, but also potentially transformative.

Sonnet 14 can be read as a rhetorical lyric in which it is not God but the reader that the poet seeks to move. It could be read as an exhortation to the kind of passionate devotion modelled by its speaker, but it could also be interpreted as a poem that is conscious of its speaker's flaws. Read as such, this is a poem that gives the reader permission to examine the distortions of desire for God, and to explore the implications of a combative model of prayer inherited from the Psalms. C. S. Lewis described a sonnet sequence as 'much more like an erotic liturgy than a series of erotic confidences' and styled 'a good sonnet' as 'like a good public prayer: the test is whether the congregation can "join" and make it their own'.[77] A fruitful

---

73. Fish, 'Masculine Persuasive Force', 244–5.

74. Donne, Sonnet 14, line 6.

75. Greene, *Post-Petrarchism*, 5–6. This characteristic is one of the main sources of modernist critiques of lyric. See Helen Vendler, *The Given and the Made: Strategies of Poetic Redefinition* (Cambridge, MA: Harvard University Press, 1995), xi.

76. For other examples in this vein, one might consider, *e.g.*, satirical prayer-poems such as Thomas Hardy's 'The Bedridden Peasant: To an Unknowing God'.

77. C. S. Lewis, *English Literature in the Sixteenth Century, Excluding Drama* (London: Oxford University Press, 1954), 491.

'joining' of reader and poem may yet be possible with Sonnet 14, not through a blind parroting of its lyric voice but rather through a melding of the voices of the poem and its readers, by which words and thoughts might be purified and perfected through the more subtle shaping influence of a community of interpretation.

Feminist critic Barbara Johnson has described the lyric 'O' as a 'demand' for recognition akin to the cry 'Mama'.[78] The prayerful cry 'Abba' (Romans 8.16) may be similarly read as an implicit plea to be called a child of God, a claim to relationship and thereby to existence. This cry is not just a request to God to hear but also a demand for God to be: to be animate, personal and responsive, to be the creator who brings the creativity of the speaker into existence. The forceful rhetoric of the 'O' of lyric address finds a place in the life of prayer not as an assertion of dominance but as such a plea, whose very utterance is dependent upon the One who is addressed. Romans 8.15-16 speaks of the Spirit 'bearing witness' with this cry, upholding the plea of the one who does not know how to pray. Donne echoes this verse in 'A Litany', which invokes the Spirit to 'Heare Thyself now, for Thou in us dost pray'.[79] The challenging prospect that the Spirit might be heard through the distorted prayers of the sinner, even if only in counterpoint, rests in the hope that a sincere desire for God, however debased, cannot be devoid of God. Through the melding of the voices of pray-er, reader/congregation and Spirit, the excesses of Donne's poetic rhetoric may not be contained, sanitized or somehow baptized, but may be held within the infinite embrace of the Spirit as the one who takes broken words and raises them to God.

Liturgical apostrophe and triangulated address

The preceding discussions of the expressive and rhetorical features of lyric address to God both in different ways locate it within a ritual or liturgical framework. This final section turns more explicitly to an account of the lyric 'O' as akin to the liturgical 'O'. According to George Puttenham's *Arte of Poesie* (1589), 'Poets Were the First Priests, the First Prophets, the First Legislators and Politicians in the World'.[80] This section considers the priestly vocation of the poem, through Catherine Pickstock's liturgical theology and Heather Dubrow's notion of 'deflected' address, exploring how lyric address combines sincerity and performance and cuts across distinctions between private and public or expressive and formal prayer.[81] The chapter concludes with a discussion of the Trinitarian structures of triangulated

---

78. Barbara Johnson, 'Apostrophe, Animation, and Abortion', *Diacritics* 16, no. 1 (Spring 1986): 38.

79. Donne, 'A Litany', line 207.

80. George Puttenham, *The Arte of English Poesie* (London: Richard Field, 1589), chap. 3.

81. Heather Dubrow, *The Challenges of Orpheus: Lyric Poetry and Early Modern England* (Baltimore, MD: Johns Hopkins University Press, 2008), 59.

address, exploring lyric as a model of prayer drawn into the conversation of the Trinity, inspired by Levertov's account of poetry as a 'triple communion'.[82]

Poem as temple: The liturgical intersections of the lyric 'O'

The liturgical cry 'O Lord' is an invocatory term, imploring God to hear, be present and be at work. This 'O' might be heard as an expressive phrase – an emotional or emphatic cry, or as a conventional phrase – a purely formal invocation, but Catherine Pickstock's pioneering work in liturgical theology described 'O' as a 'gratuitous' phrase, a 'gift' or sacrifice of praise that transcends the structures of rational discourse.[83] The gratuitous grammar of 'O' might be read in terms of an unnecessary superfluity – as emotional hyperbole or empty formalism, but Pickstock read it as an abundance of passion that is central to the practice of prayer. Contrasting it with the 'empty' subjectivity constructed by a Cartesian dualism between 'I' and 'Thou', Pickstock described 'O' as constructing a space of encounter, in Shelley's words 'the "mutual confrontation of two realities"', through which the subject comes to know itself as created by the one who it addresses.[84] As a consequence, Pickstock argued, 'it is impossible to desire God emptily'; the liturgical 'O' is filled with the presence of the God who has made the prayer possible, 'such that to call upon God is always already to have entered into Him'.[85]

Pickstock drew subtle but important differences between poetic apostrophe and 'liturgical apostrophe', taking care to distinguish the latter as an address to that which is not absent but transcendent, and as not a monological but a '*communal* figure … both heard and overheard'.[86] Reading lyric through a ritual lens, it is the kinships rather than the differences between the lyric and the liturgical 'O' that stand out. The ritual readings of lyric provided by such as Culler, Greene and Dubrow describe the lyric 'O' as a paradigmatically religious discourse, as dialogical and communal, a public event in language designed for performance and reperformance.[87] The notion of the lyric 'O' as a liturgical space of encounter with the divine is opened up by Levertov's characterization of the poet as 'a priest' and 'the poem [as] a temple; epiphanies and communion take place within it'. The architectural conceit of the temple depicts the lyric voice not as a conversation addressed from 'I' to 'Thou' but as a place of meeting, what she calls a 'triple

---

82. Levertov, 'Origins of a Poem', 47.

83. Catherine Pickstock, 'The Apostrophic Voice', in *After Writing: On the Liturgical Consumption of Philosophy* (Oxford: Blackwell, 1998), 192-8 (193). *Cf.* Culler's critique of critical reception of lyric apostrophe either as hyperbolically expressive or as a merely formal poetic convention *Lyric*, 212-13.

84. Pickstock, *After Writing*, 194; *cf.* Culler's description of apostrophe as a 'gratuitous' or semantically 'empty "O"', *Lyric*, 217.

85. Pickstock, *After Writing*, 194, 196-7.

86. Interestingly, Pickstock associates apostrophe with dramatic rather than lyric poetic forms, ibid., 193-4.

87. See Culler, *Lyric*, 216-17, 219-20.

communion': 'between the maker and the needer within the poet; between the maker and the needers outside him – those who need but can't make their own poems … and between the human and the divine in both poet and reader'.[88] This triadic model of the lyric voice encompasses a relational multiplicity that incorporates internal relationships within the self, horizontal relationships between poet and community and the vertical relationship between humanity and God.

The exemplar of the poem as temple, and a likely inspiration for Levertov's account, is Herbert's famous lyric sequence, *The Temple: Sacred Poems and Private Ejaculations* (1633).[89] Encapsulated in the shape poem 'The Altar', Herbert presented this collection as a temple of prayer and praise, ultimately constructed not out of words but out of the sacrifice of the heart: 'A broken ALTAR … Made of a heart and cemented with tears'.[90] There is throughout Herbert's collection a wrestling with the tone of poetic and prayerful address to God, exploring the tension between the simplicity of sincere prayer and the craft and conventions of poetry. In 'Jordan (I)' the 'plainness' of the cry '*My God, My King*' surpasses all poetic invention, while 'A True Hymne' is to be found not in skilful rhyme but a sincere heart: 'As when the heart says, sighing to be approved,/ "O, could I love!" and stops, God writeth, "Loved"'.[91] The simplicity and sincerity of true prayer is encapsulated in the terse vocative of the apparently involuntary response to God that concludes 'The Collar': 'At every word,/ Methought I heard one calling, *Child!!*/ And I replied *My Lord.*'[92] While previous scholarship read such passages as embodying post-Reformation patterns of private devotion, the current critical consensus stresses the integration of private passion with liturgical performance in Herbert's poetry.[93] Similar to Lok's poetic allusions to the Lord's Prayer and Song of

---

88. Levertov, 'Origins of a Poem', 47. NB Levertov preserves the transcendence of the divine within this communion as 'something beyond both the making and the needing elements, vast, irreducible, a spirit summoned by the exercise of needing and making'.

89. On Herbert's status in anthologies of religious poetry, see Dodd, 'Why Lyric?'. On Herbert as both poet and priest, see, *e.g.*, Helen Wilcox, 'When Is a Poet Not a Priest?', in *George Herbert's Pastoral: New Essays on the Poet and Priest of Bemerton*, ed. Christopher Hodgkins (Newark: University of Delaware Press, 2010), 93–102.

90. Herbert, 'The Altar', lines 1–2.

91. Ibid., 'Jordan (I)', line 15; ibid., 'A True Hymne', lines 19–20.

92. Ibid., 'The Collar', line 36.

93. Ramie Targoff influentially argued that the 'first-person and subjective poetics' of the metaphysical poets 'emerged out of public devotional practice', targeting the earlier contributions of Louis Martz and Barbara Lewalski, who both, from Catholic and Protestant perspectives respectively, argued that the early-modern devotional lyric represented a post-Reformation renaissance of personal and private prayer, Ramie Targoff, *Common Prayer: The Language of Public Devotion in Early Modern England* (Chicago: University of Chicago Press, 2001), 102; ibid., 'The Poetics of Common Prayer: George Herbert and the Seventeenth-Century Devotional Lyric', *English Literary Renaissance* 29, no. 3 (1999): 469. On the early-modern devotional lyric as sitting 'on the cusp of the public and the private', see Clarke and Jackson, 'Lyric Poetry', 161.

Simeon, Herbert's apparently instinctive, involuntary cries of the heart also convey the language of common prayer.[94]

One way in which these poems draw together the worlds of lyric and liturgical discourse is through the sacred subversion of Petrarchan tradition. *The Temple* has been read as something akin to a sonnet sequence, which follows what Wilcox terms the 'ups and downs of a spiritual lover's joys and sorrows'.[95] These devotional poems draw on secular Petrarchan conventions but also critique Petrarchan tradition.[96] Herbert explores the rivalry between the lover's address and the passion that is properly directed to God in the two sonnets, 'Love I' and 'II', which lament the ease with which poets write to their lovers while neglecting to address the source of all life and love in God.

Immediately preceding these two poems is 'Antiphon (I)', which could be read as the culmination of a spiritualizing subversion of the sonnet tradition. This poem is not a sonnet; it is structured as a hymn (often sung to the tune 'Luckington') with a thrice repeated couplet chorus interspersed by quatrain verses in iambic trimeter, which cut across the standard sonnet structure of three quatrains and a closing couplet.[97] Nevertheless, this poem's fourteen lines seem more than incidental given its location in the collection. It might be read as a kind of perfected love sonnet, a response to the desire expressed in 'Love (II)' to 'in hymnes send back thy [God's] fire again', through unfeigned, unabashed and uncomplicated praise of the only true and lasting love.[98] Its vocative refrain 'Let all the world in ev'ry corner sing,/ *My God and King*' is not an expressive cry to God but a rhetorical exhortation to the world to praise, drawing the cry of the heart into a communal 'shout' of praise that encompasses all of creation.[99] Although located at a liturgical high point of the collection after 'The H. Communion', 'Antiphon (I)' is not Herbert's final word in praise, as the following sonnets on love illustrate the ongoing work of the heart in learning to direct its address to God.

Another example of the sonnet form perfected in a hymn of praise is Mary Sidney's translation of Psalm 150. The final poem and only sonnet in this sequence of poetic translations of the Psalms, it is divided into hymn-like quatrains but

---

94. On the 'liturgical' character of Herbert's poetry, see David Jasper, who highlights the connections and distinctions between the Petrarchan lyric tradition and the language of common prayer, defining Herbert's poetic as one that 'bleaches into prayer and worship', *The Language of Liturgy: A Ritual Poetics* (London: SCM, 2018), Kindle, chap. 3.

95. See Debra Rienstra, '"Let Wits Contest": George Herbert and the English Sonnet Sequence', *George Herbert Journal* 35, nos 1–2 (2011–12): 23–44; Helen Wilcox, 'George Herbert', in *Cambridge Companion to English Poetry, Donne to Marvell*, ed. Corns, 183–99 (184).

96. See, *e.g.*, Herbert, 'Dulnesse', 'Grief', 'Jordan (I)' and 'Jordan (II)'.

97. Wilcox lists fifteen sonnets in *The Temple*, of which 'Antiphon (I)' is not included, *English Poems*, xxiii.

98. Herbert 'Love II', line 8.

99. Ibid., 'Antiphon (I)', lines 1, 2, 8, 14.

preserves a Petrarchan-style rhyme-scheme (abba abba cdcd ee). Sidney turns a highly repetitive psalm that begins almost every line 'Praise Him', into a poem that never uses the same word twice in exhorting the hearer: 'Oh, laud the Lord, the God of hosts commend,/ Exalt his pow'r, advance his holiness …'[100] Read as a hymn, this 'O' might be a direct address from priest to congregation, in which they join to exhort each other to praise, but read as a lyric poem it is a form of indirect address whose eavesdropping audience is the God to whom praise ought to be directed and, as emerges in the final couplet, the global congregation of all creation ('all that air or life enfold').[101] The indirectness of address here is a gesture of expansion that draws the reader simultaneously into the presence of God and into the public performance of praise, as not only the work of the church but, in Herbert's terms, of 'all the world'. Herbert and Sidney's experiments in poetic form cross the boundaries between the cry of the heart and the craft of verse, between the sincerity of personal prayer and the performance of public worship, uniting the vocative 'O' of desire with the liturgical 'O' of invocation to craft a lyric address that is not a straightforward petition of 'I' to 'Thou' but a site of encounter with God, the world and the self.

Poet as priest: The priestly posture of deflected address

One of the priestly attributes of lyric address is its capacity to curate a space of encounter; another is its power to direct its hearer towards a transcendent other. Dubrow defines indirect address as 'deflected speech', likening apostrophe to the poetic 'turn' whereby each verse or strophe involves a dance-like 'turn' of voice, mood or sense.[102] This turning can be an expression of a soul in turmoil, turning and turning about, or of *metanoia*, a soul turned and tuned to the sound of heavenly harmony.[103] As a kind of stage direction for the reader, the art of deflected address might also be a means of turning the congregation to God.

This chapter has so far focussed on address in the devotional lyric as facing God while winking at the congregation, but the lyric voice in Herbert and Donne also at times turns *away* from God to address the self or the reader directly. This turn might be read as a kind of *contrapposto* dance-step, in which the dancer turns at once away from and towards their partner.[104] The pray-er who turns from God cannot do so absolutely, since to do so is to turn towards one of the many works that praise God's name, while even words of protest are filled with the God from

---

100. Mary Sidney, 'Psalm 150', *Sidney Psalter*, 286, lines 1–2.

101. Ibid., line 13.

102. Dubrow, *Orpheus*, 57.

103. On turning as tuning consider, e.g., John Drury's discussion of the musical influence on Herbert's poetics, in *Music at Midnight: The Life and Poetry of George Herbert* (London: Penguin, 2013), vi, cxxxi, cxlviii, clii.

104. This thought is inspired by comments of Ben Quash on the figure of Christ in Titian's *Noli me Tangere* (1514).

whom they turn. This dynamic can be seen, for example, in Herbert's 'Sighs and Grones', which begins and ends each stanza with an emphatic 'O do not', which is a desperate plea to God not to judge or punish, a kind of flinching address that turns towards God while looking away. The title's allusion to Romans 8.26 provides reassurance that its 'Sighs and Grones' may not be the speaker's alone, but are joined by the voice of the Spirit, through whose influence the final stanza finally turns from a fearful 'O do not' to the hopeful 'But O reprieve me!'[105] In the poem 'Dialogue', the pray-er constantly seeks to pull back from God and resign themselves to sin. In this dramatic dialogue, each verse involves a change of voice between the recalcitrant soul and the beckoning Christ. While the sinner has the final say, cutting off the voice of God in the final line, 'Ah! no more: thou break'st my heart', this last impassioned cry reveals them no longer broken by sin but by Christ's sacrifice of love.[106] Just as the previous declarations of despair are countered by God's hopeful promises of love, so this final line cannot be the last word. The Lord's unheard reply continues to echo in the reader's mind well after the poem is finished.

The irresistibility of prayer is also modelled in 'Deniall', which recounts the suffering of a soul that feels itself unheard by God. While seeking to cease to pray, the speaker can find no other recourse than increasingly desperate address to God, expressed through the apostrophic 'O' of incredulity ('O that thou shouldst give dust a tongue … And then not heare it crying!') and of petition ('O cheer and tune my heartlesse breast').[107] Similarly, the speaker who at the end of 'Affliction (I)' threatens to 'seek/ Some other master out' seems unable to follow through, falling immediately into the passionate address 'Ah my deare God!' The ambivalent final line 'Let me not love thee, if I love Thee not' indicates a heart, like any Petrarchan lover, suffering the torments of love but unable to break away.[108] These devotional lyrics may be read as an act of prayer even when they appear to pull away, the deflected voice turned back magnetically towards the ultimate Subject of address.

The art of deflection takes on particularly intriguing features in Donne's 'Good Friday, 1613, Riding Westward'. A forty-two-line poem in heroic couplets, this is a meditation on the impiety of riding west on business on Good Friday. Turned away from the east and from the figure of Christ crucified, the speaker initially appears to be addressing either themselves or the reader in a muttered monologue. The final octave turns suddenly to second-person address to Christ, heralded by the unexpected 'thou look'st towards me' and followed by the conventional apostrophic address 'O Saviour'.[109] While the speaker remains physically turned away from the cross, it transpires that in memory and in meditation Christ has been in full view all along. What appears to have been

---

105. Herbert, 'Sighs and Grones', lines 1, 25.
106. Ibid., 'Dialogue', line 32.
107. Ibid., 'Deniall', lines 16, 18, 26.
108. Ibid., 'Affliction (I)', lines 63–6.
109. John Donne, 'Good Friday, 1613, Riding Westward', lines 35–6.

an act of turning away has in fact been a face-to-face encounter. This double deflection illustrates the convolutions of the sinner's address to God. The conceit that the speaker's back is only turned to God to 'receive/Corrections' highlights the possible disjunction between appearance and reality when it comes to the posture of prayer. Those turned physically towards Christ may in their hearts be turned away, while those who appear to tread a winding path may in truth be directing their steps towards God.[110]

The poetic posture of prayerful address takes on particular significance in relation to Reformation debates over the direction in which the priest should face when leading worship.[111] The Tridentine mass preserved the medieval practice whereby the majority of the service was delivered facing the eastern altar (*ad orientem*), with occasional exhortations addressed directly to the congregation (*versus populum*) and much of the rest muttered or whispered privately to God, while Protestant churches across Europe removed their east-facing altars, and Martin Luther advocated that in 'the true mass' the priest 'face the people as Christ doutlessly did in the Last Supper'.[112] The situation in England was complex. The 1549 Book of Common Prayer retained the medieval pattern of facing the altar during communion, and many churches kept their eastward-facing altars, while the rubrics of the 1552 version, preserved in the 1662 Book of Common Prayer, dictated a communion table moved into the chancel with the priest presiding 'from the north side' surrounded by the congregation.[113] The poet-priest who is, metaphorically, deflected away from the east to address the people also stands with Christ, who is the mediator between God and humanity. This is an understanding of the priestly vocation expressed in Herbert's *Country Parson*, which defined priests as 'Deputies' of Christ whose 'Dignity' and 'Duty' is to imitate Him.[114] The poet-priest who addresses God, facing, as it were, towards the east, is deflected away from the people but also stands with them, interceding with the Spirit on their behalf and presenting them to God. Thus Herbert's priest again who, 'being truly touched and amazed with the Majesty of God, before whom he then presents himself [and] with himself the whole Congregation'.[115] An orientation 'from the north side' involves the capacity to address both east and west, God and people, through a mere turn of the head. Thus, Herbert's preacher, whose holiness is

---

110. Ibid., lines 37–8. Note Herbert's imagery at the end of 'The Church Militant', which argues that this church in its expansion into Europe did 'by going west / Still eastward go' in coming closer to Christ and the day of judgement, lines 275–6.

111. See Gilbert Cope, 'Posture', in *A New Dictionary of Liturgy and Worship*, ed. J. G. Davies (London: SCM, 1986), 437–8.

112. Eric Lund, *Documents from the History of Lutheranism, 1517–1750* (Minneapolis, MN: Fortress Press, 2002), 130.

113. 'The Order for the Administration of The Lord's Supper or Holy Communion', *BCP*.

114. George Herbert, *A Priest to the Temple, or, The Country Parson* (London: T. Maxey, 1652), chap. 1.

115. Ibid., chap. 6.

demonstrated 'by turning often, and making many Apostrophes to God, as, Oh Lord blesse my people, and teach them this point'.[116]

The liturgical significance of the direction of address has implications for interpretations of the lyric posture of prayer. Herbert's devotional lyric address might be read as speaking, as it were, from the north side, turning swiftly from self to God to congregation. 'Aaron', for example, appears to be a private meditation about the nature of priesthood, until the final line that turns to invite the congregation, 'Come people; Aaron's drest', while the sonnet 'The Holy Scriptures (I)' is mostly addressed to the Bible ('Oh Book!'), with a brief aside to the congregation in the middle, which exhorts them to join the poet in praise of the scriptures.[117] In 'Sin', God is addressed in the first line ('Lord, with what care hast thou begirt us round!'), only for the poem to descend into bitter introspection on the inescapability of sin, while 'Christmas' starts with a homiletic tale about the speaker stopping by an inn and finding Christ there, before turning to prayer addressed to Christ in the final sestet.[118] These swift turns, often abrupt and unannounced, enact a priestly turning-of-the-head, using deflection as an art not of turning away but of drawing together, the direction of address acting as a shifting line of sight that brings self and congregation into communion with God.

There is an element of performance in the figure of the priest who, in Herbert's words, 'composeth himself' to worship, 'lifting up his heart and hands, and eyes, and using all other gestures which may express a hearty, and unfeyned devotion'. Herbert mitigates the potential for hypocrisy, the irony of a performed sincerity, by stating that this performance must be 'hart-deep', 'that [the priest] being first affected himself … may affect also his people'.[119] This passage illustrates the capacity for public prayer to model the sincerity of the heart prized by Protestant reformers, but there was also a performed aspect to the discourse of private prayer in the devotional lyric, as illustrated by the semi-dramatic shifts and turns of deflected address.[120] Through lyric deflection the poem can voice at once the posture of the sinner who struggles to meet God face to face and that of the priest for whom the art of indirection is a way of drawing others to God. This might be seen not as a contradiction but as central to a life of faith lived as that of a redeemed sinner. Although in part an expression of the difficulties of prayer, deflected address is also a sign of its interweaving of the voices of the individual and the congregation, Christ and the Spirit in the apparently simple act of address to God.

116. Ibid., chap. 7.
117. Herbert, 'Aaron', line 25; ibid., 'The Holy Scriptures (I)', lines 8–10.
118. Ibid., 'Sin', line 1.
119. Ibid., *Country Parson*, chap. 6.
120. For a discussion of this issue, see Sterrett, *Prayer and Performance*, 1, 8.

A Trinitarian perspective on triangulated address

Apostrophe in Culler's lyric theory is also called 'triangulated' address.[121] This term replaces the connotations of deception or illusion in indirect address with those of understanding or illumination. In mathematics, triangulation is a method of finding the way to an intended goal through a diverted route, emphasizing both the connections between objects and the distance that separates them. Applied to devotional poetry, triangulation might be imagined as a way of charting the (infinite) distance between the human mind and the heart of God, of locating oneself in relation to God or of finding one's way to God, but it is treated here more in terms of the intimate interconnections it evokes. W. R. Johnson described lyric poetry as a 'lyrical triangle of speaker, discourse, and hearer', while this chapter considers the triad of lyric address: of speaking, hearing and overhearing.[122] Regardless of the taxonomy used, what is essential to these models is that, as Coakley has argued, 'threeness always challenges and "ambushes" the stuckness of established "twoness"'.[123] The triangulation of lyric address facilitates an opening up of the closed circle between speaker and addressee, not only towards an individual eavesdropper but towards a more global conversation. The triangulations of lyric address therefore have intriguing implications for a reflection on the Trinitarian dynamics of prayer in the Spirit. A Trinitarian perspective on triangulated address need not be concerned with identifying the three poles of 'I', 'Thou' and overhearer with the three persons of the Trinity.[124] Rather, it involves recognizing the lyric voice's multiplicity, lability and openness to the other as resonant of the relations within the Trinity and between the Trinity and the world.[125]

In two key poems about prayer, 'The Call' and 'Prayer (I)', Herbert evokes the intimacy and mystery of prayer not through the lover's whisper of 'I' to 'Thou' but through what William Waters describes as 'moments of wonder', where the structure of address breaks down and the multiplicity and lability of the lyric voice come to the fore.[126] 'The Call' is resonant of the threefold prayer to Christ in Revelation 22.17, with each of its three stanzas intoning a triple invocation: 'Come, my Way, my Truth, my Life'; 'Come, my Light, my Feast, my Strength'; 'Come, my Joy, my Love, my Heart'.[127] This poem evokes the Trinitarian dynamics of prayerful

---

121. Culler, *Lyric*, 186–7.

122. Johnson, *Idea of Lyric*, 34.

123. Coakley, *GSS*, 330. Coakley describes the prayer of Romans 8.26-28 as 'ineluctably, though obscurely, triadic', in *The New Asceticism: Sexuality, Gender and the Quest for God* (London: Bloomsbury, 2015), 86, 90.

124. On the development and critiques of the ontological Trinity, see Coakley, *GSS*, 106, 134.

125. On lyric address as 'multiple' and 'labile', see Dubrow, *Orpheus*, 57.

126. Waters, *Poetry's Touch*, 1–4.

127. Herbert, 'The Call', lines 1, 5, 9. For a Trinitarian reading of this poem see Helen Vendler, as cited in Wilcox, *English Poems*, 539.

address not just through these triadic structures but also through the apostrophic ambiguity of its unidentified voice. In this poem, Christ is addressed not as *'the'* way but through more personal, relational language as *'my'* way, truth and life. The 'I' of the poem is unidentified; they could be the individual soul, the church in prayer or the Spirit who breathes through both.[128] As Coakley describes it, Origen's Trinitarian model of prayer as addressed *to* the Father, *through* the Son and *in* the Spirit is a kind of *ménage à trois* in which the participants are drawn ever closer through the Spirit's bond of love.[129] Just as, in Revelation 22.17, the Spirit and the bride speak together to invoke the presence of Christ, so 'The Call' evokes the intimate interrelationship of voices merged in the act of prayer. Its labile voice echoes the mystery of God praying to God in God, the Spirit 'incorporating' the believer into God's Trinitarian life as God prays in the pray-er, hears their prayer and leads them into Christ.[130]

Herbert's famous sonnet, 'Prayer (I)', delves even deeper into the mystery of address to God in prayer by appearing to abandon address altogether. Surrounded in the sequence of *The Temple* by poems that address God clearly in the vocative mode, this omission is even more striking.[131] With no 'I' or 'Thou', what remains is a labile voice that could be read as a mere catalogue of prayer. Instead, the twists and turns of the sonnet form turn this poem from a description of prayer into a prayer itself that leads the reader toward its closing contemplation of 'something understood'.[132] It is notable that the first three lines attribute prayer first to the church, angels and God ('the Churches banquet, Angels age,/ Gods breath in man') before turning inward to the famous depiction of prayer as 'The soul in paraphrase'.[133] The idea of prayer as a heart in conversation with God is virtually absent. Without a clear voice or explicit apostrophe, the reader is invited to place themselves in the position of hearing, eavesdropping on and speaking the whispers of the Spirit, 'Gods breath in man' who is heard through the regular pauses that intersperse the lines.[134] The ambivalence embodied in this peculiar grammar is resonant of the 'middle voice' of Romans 8.16 ('that very Spirit bearing witness with our spirit'), the simultaneously active and passive verb that turns prayer into a kind of synergy with the Spirit.[135]

---

128. NB the personal 'my' in lines 1, 5 and 9 is balanced by the collective 'us' in line 2.

129. See Origen, *De Oratione* 33.1; Hebrews 13.15, Colossians 3.17, Ephesians 5.20, 1 Peter 4.11, Romans 7.25; Coakley, *GSS*, 113, 111.

130. Ibid.

131. The poem follows 'Repentance' and 'Faith', leading up to the climactic moment of 'The H. Communion'. *Cf.* also Herbert, 'Prayer (II)', which addresses a clearly dialogical and petitionary form of prayer.

132. Ibid., 'Prayer (I)', line 14.

133. Ibid., lines 1-3.

134. Ibid., line 2. For a more extended discussion of the use of breath pauses in 'Prayer (I)', see Dodd, 'Prayer', 593-4.

135. Sonderegger, *Doctrine of God*, 416-17, 463-4.

The lability and multiplicity of address in these two poems model a lyric grammar that conveys the intimacy and mutuality of prayer in the Spirit as described in Romans 8. In this passage, God is not only addressed directly by the pray-er (v. 15) but they also overhear the unspoken cries of the heart (v. 27) and give voice to those cries through the Spirit (vv. 15-16, 26). The prayer 'Abba!' is a claim to relationship, a request to be called a child of God. To imagine this cry as not only heard but *overheard* is a testament to the sincerity of this desire, as spoken from the heart. To hear the confirming cry of the Spirit joining in with this prayer is to understand the request as granted before it is asked. Romans 8 culminates in the promise that nothing 'will be able to separate us from the love of God in Christ Jesus our Lord' (vv. 38-39). The entanglements of loving address emerge through this passage as a mutual intertwining that cannot be unravelled, an ever-stronger reaffirmation of bonds that can never be broken. John of the Cross conveys this intimate inter-relationality of prayer in his description of the inspiration of the Spirit, by which the soul is incorporated into the Trinitarian life: 'This breathing of the Holy Spirit in the soul, whereby God transforms it in Himself, is to the soul a joy so deep, so exquisite, and so grand that no mortal tongue can describe it.'[136] The wonder of the prayer 'Abba!' is that it is never uttered alone: the Spirit 'bears witness' with the children of God (v. 15) and Christ 'intercedes' for them (v. 34), while all of creation also 'groans' in concert with them, both yearning for redemption (vv. 22-3). Through the expansive grammar of triangulated address, the ecstasy of prayer is seen to involve not only an intimate colloquy of the individual with the Trinity but also the communion of saints, the host of angels and the sounds of creation: in the words of Psalm 150.6, 'everything that breathes'.

Conclusion: A lyric theology of prayer in the Spirit

This chapter has argued that, far from distinguishing poetry from true prayer, the dynamics of lyric address provide a rich seam for reflection on the character of prayer in and through the Spirit. The very ambiguities, multiplicities, indeed fictionalities and hyperboles of lyric address illuminate the complex relationality of prayer as a communion with the self, the community of faith, creation and the Triune God. All of this is to suggest that, whether in personal prayer or public worship, there is a world contained within the apparently straightforward direct address: 'I love you.' The first-person voice of lyric address is deeply and intimately personal but is never uttered alone. Its passion is a passion shared with creation and the communion of saints who may hear, overhear or speak with the pray-er, as the Spirit also bears witness. The priest who addresses God in part to teach the congregation to pray, the preacher exhorting them through rhetorical exclamations, the liturgical prescription of emotion—all draw on the craft of lyric address to draw people into the presence of God. The sincerity of worship thus

---

136. John of the Cross, *Spiritual Canticle*, commentary on stanza 39.2.

performed may be found in its capacity to curate a sacrifice of praise that, with and through Christ, commends the offering of broken humanity to God.

These conclusions have contemporary constructive implications. Modern liturgical debates lie not far beneath the surface of much scholarship on early-modern metaphysical poetry.[137] Disputes between extemporary/expressive and formal/liturgical forms of prayer are as pressing for many today as they were for the likes of Donne and Milton.[138] The sometimes destructive duality of these disputes might be circumvented by an acknowledgement of the multiplicity of prayerful address.[139] In this light, for example, the intimate first-person address of modern worship songs might be read not as a myopic focus on subjective experience but as a communal 'I' capable of encompassing a community, helping to move debates away from anxieties about the dangers of modern individualism towards a consideration of how the unity of the body of Christ is expressed in public worship.[140] The rhetorical aspects of lyric address equally locate even private prayer in the context of participation in a community of faith, as an exhortation to self and others as well as an appeal to God. In this way, rhetoric provides a grammar for the sincerity of performed affection, even in the unheard words of private prayer.

From this perspective, the affectivity of lyric discourse may be viewed as much more than a tool for personal catharsis or a window into what L. William Countryman has called the 'hidden, interior realities of spirituality'.[141]

---

137. The modern relevance of historical criticism in this area stretches from Florence Higham's influential *Catholic and Reformed: A Study of the Anglican Church, 1559–1662* (London: SPCK, 1962) to Jasper's *Language of Liturgy* (2018). James Steven has discussed the similarities between modern charismatic worship and seventeenth-century dissenting traditions of free prayer in 'The Spirit in Contemporary Charismatic Worship' in Teresa Berger and Bryan D. Spinks, eds, *The Spirit in Worship – Worship in the Spirit* (Collegeville, MN: Liturgical Press, 2009), 245–59 (248–50).

138. For important voices in these debates, see, *e.g.*, Martin Percy, 'Sweet Rapture: Subliminal Eroticism in Contemporary Charismatic Worship', *Theology & Sexuality: The Journal of the Institute for the Study of Christianity and Sexuality* 6 (1997): 71–106; Bryan D. Spinks, *The Worship Mall: Contemporary Responses to Contemporary Culture* (London: SPCK, 2010); Graham Hunter, *Discipline and Desire: Embracing Charismatic Liturgical Worship* (Cambridge: Grove Books, 2017); Pete Ward, *Liquid Ecclesiology: The Gospel and the Church* (Leiden: Brill, 2017), 158–9.

139. For an attempt to overcome the stridency of liturgical differences through an ecumenical theological aesthetics, see Frank Burch Brown, *Good Taste, Bad Taste, and Christian Taste: Aesthetics in Religious Life* (Oxford: Oxford University Press, 2000).

140. What Pete Ward has styled the 'individual Romantic self' of modern charismatic worship has been tied to the problems of modern individualism. See Pete Ward, *Selling Worship: How What We Sing Has Changed the Church* (Bletchley: Paternoster Press, 2005), 151–62.

141. Countryman, *Poetic Imagination*, 28.

This chapter began by describing the affective cry of the lyric 'O' not in terms of emotional expressivity alone but as the enfleshment of air, the embarrassment of embodiment that is essential to the act of communication. The corporeality of affective discourse is central to the wisdom of worship, what James K.A. Smith has called 'erotic comprehension' or Origen called the experience of being 'mingled with the Spirit'.[142] In Herbert's terms, 'God's breath in man' is a breathing both in and out, a combination of incarnation and theosis, with carbon-dioxide exchanged for oxygen, with additional water vapour, saliva and the organisms that it carries.[143] This chapter has explored the melding of the call of God and the cry of the heart, alert not only to the human voice in prayer but also to its communal and cosmological connections. From this liturgical perspective, the 'O' of lyric address is a fundamentally embodied experience.

---

142. James K. A. Smith, *Imagining the Kingdom: How Worship Works* (Grand Rapids MI: Baker Academic, 2013), 31. Origen, *De Oratione* 10.2, cited in Coakley, *GSS*, 127. Eugene Rogers also highlights the eroticism of encounter with the Spirit as 'embodied' in bread and wine, oil and water, fire and flesh, or in von Balthasar's 'unspeakable "mouth-to-mouth" interchange between the Spirit of God and the human spirit, a kind of kiss', *Prayer*, 78–9, cited in Rogers, *After the Spirit*, 213.

143. Herbert, 'Prayer (I)', line 2.

Chapter 3

THE VOICE OF THE LORD – THE PROPHETIC SPIRIT IN THE LYRIC 'I'

Introduction

This chapter addresses the Romantic lyric 'I' and its implications for prophetic discourse. Continuing the discussion of lyric expressivity and affectivity, it turns to focus on the first person, reading the lyric 'I' of 'I love', 'I am' or 'I feel' as a prophetic declaration. The prophetic potential of the lyric 'I' is uncovered through a focus on the first person not as an isolated subject speaking to themselves but as a poetic voice, the voice of the bard, which is culturally constructed, socially located and speaks to a public audience. Read as such, the lyric 'I' not only surpasses the lonely solipsism of the modern subject but can be interpreted as a prophetic declaration of the voice of the Lord. This chapter focuses on Romantic poets for whom the prophetic spirit is affirmed as not only the preserve of a poetic elite but as that which can inspire all people.

Romantic poetry has been a major focus of lyric criticism to date, so much so that historicist studies of lyric in other contexts continue to refer to this still-dominant model.[1] A central feature of the Romantic lyric is the prominence of the first-person singular as the voice of the poetic subject, exemplified by Wordsworth's description of the poet's 'readiness and power in expressing what he thinks and feels'.[2] Hegel's *Aesthetics* contains a classic account of Romantic subjectivity, which describes lyric as the voicing of the inner world, so that the external object is perceived only through incorporation into the self and described only as it is 'felt' by the individual.[3] This lyric 'I' has been subject to a range of critiques in poststructuralist criticism and postmodern theology. These include critiques of the illusion of the supposedly rational, independent and stable Cartesian subjectivity

---

1. On the dominance of the Romantic lyric, see Abrams, 'Lyric as Poetic Norm'. For examples of the influence of post-Romantic criticism on the historical criticism of other eras see, *e.g.*, Butterfield, 'Why Medieval Lyric?', 324–5; Dubrow, *Orpheus*, 5.

2. William Wordsworth, Preface to the *Lyrical Ballads* (1802), para. 15.

3. See G. W. F. Hegel, *Hegel's Aesthetics: Lectures on Fine Art*, trans. T. M. Knox, vol. 2 (Oxford: Clarendon, 1975), 1116, 1118, 1123.

that is in fact socially constructed and contextually contingent, of the tyranny of the individual that subsumes otherness into itself, its false innocence and its pursuit of personal fulfilment through self-manifestation.

Developments in lyric criticism have complicated this picture by emphasizing the social location of the first-person voice.[4] Drawing on Adorno's Marxist theory, Culler highlights how the lyric subject subsists in relation to, dialogue with, conflict with or flight from the social.[5] The 'I' that is thereby constructed is capable of multiplicity, dialogism, self-interrogation and fragmentation. The seeds of these trends were already present in nineteenth-century Romanticism. Hegel's dialectic between epic (representing the social) and lyric (representing the individual), which culminates in the dramatic, communicates lyric's limitations as well as its indispensability to the progress of the soul. In his account of mystical poetry, Hegel presents a lyric self that is 'fragmented', 'disordered' and overwhelmed through its encounter with the divine other.[6] His discussion of odes, hymns and elegies locates the lyric poet in relation to society through the 'bardic' recitation of sublime thoughts before a public audience.[7] This chapter's focus on the social location of the performed lyric 'I' can therefore lay claim to consistency with an authentic albeit subsidiary legacy of Romanticism.

The lyric first person has been read as what Quash calls a 'poetic *perspective*', the inner mind's point-of-view expressed through the text, but in poetic criticism it is more often termed a poetic 'voice'.[8] 'Voice' is a conventional though contested term that gestures towards the oral roots of poetry and its attendant features of performance, presence and sound. Applied to a first-person prophetic poetic,

---

4. For a revisionist perspective on the Romantic lyric 'I', which sees women as the true visionary Romantic poets because they are more concerned with the eye than the I, see Stuart Curran, 'Romantic Poetry: The I Altered', in *Romantic Writings*, ed. Stephen Bygrave (Maidenhead, Berks: Open University, 1996), 279–93. Ian Balfour adopts the neologism 'subjecticity' to broaden the lyric 'I' into four types that avoid the egoistic and individualistic connotations of subjectivity: the autobiographical 'I', the epistemological 'I' of idealism, the divine 'I' and the aesthetic or poetic 'I', in 'Subjecticity (On Kant and the Texture of Romanticism)', in *Romanticism and the Insistence of the Aesthetic*, ed. Forest Pyle (College Park, Maryland: University of Maryland, 2005), online, https://romantic-circles.org/praxis/aesthetic/balfour/balfour.html. Andrea K. Henderson, *Romantic Identities: Varieties of Subjectivity, 1774–1830* (Cambridge: Cambridge University Press, 2008), expands and complicates definitions of the Romantic self that are focussed on interiority, through attentiveness to historical and social context. For an influential defence of the centrality of subjectivism to the Romantic lyric *cf.* Geoffrey Hartman, 'The Poetics of Prophecy' and 'Romanticism and Anti-Selfconsciousness', in *Beyond Formalism: Literary Essays 1958–1970* (New Haven, CT: Yale University Press, 1970), 160–8.

5. Culler, *Lyric*, 325, 330–1.

6. Hegel, *Aesthetics*, 1139–40.

7. Ibid., 1146.

8. Quash, *Drama*, 30; E. Richards, 'Voice', *PEPP*.

voice invites a consideration of how poetic or spiritual *in*spiration is accompanied by *ex*halation, the speaking out of poetic truth.⁹ As intimated in the conclusion to the previous chapter, attentiveness to the exhalation of the breath involves an acknowledgement of the partnership of body and spirit in the creative act. What Catherine Keller has termed a 'pneumatic oscillation' (the vibrating wings of the Spirit figuring the proximity of body and air as they hover over the waters of creation) is imagined here as a more intimate intermingling of air and body in the breath.¹⁰ This poetic of voicing involves a celebration of corporeality that in poetic and theological discourse has often been presented as superseding Romantic subjectivity.¹¹ It is not, however, necessarily incompatible with the voiced lyric 'I', which may be heard as rooted in society, in E. Richards' terms 'possessed by' the voices of tradition and, according to Blasing, articulating 'the communal personality of a people'.¹²

Also key to theories of poetic voicing is voice as a sign of presence and the idea that, just as a shout can sound out the hollow of a cave, voice is that by which interiors are revealed.¹³ Jacques Derrida's influential critique of the primacy of orality in interpretation argues that the appearance of the presence of the author in a poem is a purely textual construct and attacks the illusory sense that hearing a voice gives insight into the speaker's thoughts and intentions.¹⁴ Walter

---

9. On the exhalation of the Spirit as breathed out into the world through the church, consider John 20.22 and Acts 2.2-4. NB Kate Heffelfinger stresses voice and not subjectivity as a hallmark of lyric, highlighting the significance of the voice of the Lord as delivered in the first-person singular in the lyrical sections of Isaiah, *I Am Large, I Contain Multitudes*, 24-5, 33-5, 40.

10. Catherine Keller, *The Face of the Deep: A Theology of Becoming* (London: Routledge, 2003), 233-4.

11. Charles Olson's breath-based avant-garde poetics, for example, was concerned with 'getting rid of the lyrical interference of the individual as ego' through a poetic driven by sound and performance over thought and poetic intention, Charles Olson, 'Projective Verse' (1950), in *Collected Prose*, ed. Donald Allen and Benjamin Friedlander (Oakland, CA: University of California Press, 1971), 239-49; see also Rowan Williams, *Grace and Necessity: Reflections on Art and Love* (London: Continuum, 2005), 150-1: 'The "presence" in art is not some looming romantic/creative genius in the background, but a presence within what is made that generates difference, self-questioning, in the perceiving subject.' See also the supersession of the Cartesian subject through an appeal to poetry in Heather Walton, 'Re-visioning the Subject in Literature and Theology', in *Self/Same/Other: Re-visioning the Subject in Literature and Theology*, ed. Heather Walton and Andrew Hass (Sheffield: Sheffield Academic Press, 2000), 10-19; Nicola Slee, *Praying Like a Woman* (London: SPCK, 2004), 6.

12. Richards, 'Voice', *PEPP*; Blasing, *Lyric Poetry*, 12.

13. Walter Ong, *The Presence of the Word* (New Haven: Yale University Press, 1967), 125.

14. Jacques Derrida, *Of Grammatology: On Orality and Literacy*, trans. Gayatri Chakravorty Spivak (Baltimore: Johns Hopkins University Press, 1976), 259, 262.

Ong's *Presence of the Word*, which came out in the same year as Derrida's *Of Grammatology*, acknowledges the theological implications of this debate. Drawing on the connotations of *Logos* in the Hebrew Bible, Ong defines the Word as speech and speech as embodied, personal and living, an event in time and space. For Ong, to hear the voice of God is to experience God as personal presence.[15]

A connection between the voice of God and the presence of God is figured in the name, YHWH, which can be heard as a vocalized inhalation and exhalation, a breath that is a sign of life, presence and spirit. In English translations of Exodus 3.14, this word (*eh·yeh*) has commonly been rendered as the divine self-naming 'I AM'.[16] As both the sound of an exhalation and a statement of being, *eh·yeh* signifies not an elusive divinity, hidden behind the text, but a performance of presence manifest within the word.[17] God is encountered in this breath-like word not as the director behind events but as what Ong, Ford and David Kelsey, among others, have called the 'circumambient' presence around and among them.[18] If the name of God is the sound of a breath, then speech itself might be heard as a prophetic act, whispering the voice of the Lord.

This chapter focusses on Romantic poetry in which, as William Franke has discussed, the revelatory character of subjective experience turns the lyric subject into a prophetic voice.[19] Influenced by the Hebrew scholarship of Robert Lowth and linked to the development of higher biblical criticism, Romanticism has been associated with the secularization of prophecy, reducing it from the word of the Lord to a rhetorical discourse, but the Romantics also understood poetic

---

15. Ong, *Presence*, 9–16, 111–16; NB Derrida, *Grammatology*, 271–2, also picks up on the theological implications in his discussion of breath in Jean-Jacques Rousseau's *On the Origins of Languages* as a sign of the 'pure' and disembodied presence of God, above and behind all things.

16. This rendering of the passage appears in the Wycliffe and Geneva versions, through the King James to the NRSV. *NB* Tod Linafelt reads the direct discourse of the voice of the Lord in Hebrew prophetic poetry as a potential 'precursor of the modern "lyric I"', in *The Hebrew Bible as Literature*, 67.

17. *NB* Olson draws a similar connection between breath and being through a (rather dubious) etymology: '"Is" comes from the Aryan root, as, to breathe.' Olson, 'Projective Verse', 239–49.

18. Ong, *Presence*, 128; see Ben Quash on God as 'an all-encompassing environment – both public and intimate', in 'Wonder-Voyaging: The Pneumatological Character of David Ford's Theology', in *The Vocation of Theology Today: A Festschrift for David Ford*, ed. Tom Greggs, Rachel Muers and Simeon Zahl (Eugene, Or: Cascade, 2013), 149; David Kelsey, *Eccentric Existence: A Theological Anthropology*, 2 vols (Louisville, KY: Westminster John Knox Press, 2009), 443–6.

19. William Franke, 'Poetry, Prophecy, and Theological Revelation', in *Oxford Research Encyclopedia of Religion* (Oxford: Oxford University Press, 2016), 9–10, online, https://doi.org/10.1093/acrefore/9780199340378.013.205.

creativity as stemming from sublime if not divine inspiration.²⁰ This elevated vocation is expressed in Shelley's account of poets as prophets: 'the hierophants of an unapprehended inspiration, the mirrors of the gigantic shadows which futurity casts upon the present'.²¹ Coleridge's transcendental philosophy also provided an account of the prophetic vocation of poetry by drawing a connection between the lyric 'I am' and the divine 'I AM' in its description of self-consciousness as the way into knowledge: 'We begin with the I KNOW MYSELF, in order to end with the absolute I AM. We proceed from the SELF, in order to lose and find all self in GOD.'²² In such passages, the self-declaration of the Romantic lyric 'I' is interpreted as a prophetic whisper of the voice of the Lord.

This chapter explores the capacity of the lyric 'I' to be a prophetic 'I': truth-speaking, world-facing and open to all. It looks to the figure of the British bard which, most notably as adopted by Thomas Gray in the mid-eighteenth century, provides a lineage for the prophet as a public poet whose harp or lyre sounds against tyranny.²³ Their lyric voice, however apparently personal or private, can be heard as at once possessed by the voice of a community and infused by the breath of God. Isolated but not alone, the power of this 'voice … crying in the wilderness' is that of being at the same time the voice of the outsider and the voice of God.²⁴ Accordingly, this chapter approaches the lyric prophetic voice by looking to the margins of the canon, through the childlike lyrics of William Blake, the provincial idioms of John Clare and the hip hop style of Kae Tempest. Blake and Clare work in different ways with a pastoral tradition associated both with a flight from the world and a satirical critique of society from the marginal perspective of rural poverty. The final section of the chapter turns to Tempest's urban aesthetic as a modern counterpoint to these voices that remains rooted in Romanticism.

I love: The prophetic lyrics of Blake's Songs of Innocence and Experience

The lyric subject as a prophetic voice

The prophetic character of Romantic poetry is nowhere clearer than in Blake, not only in his overtly prophetic epics, such as *America a Prophecy*, *Europe a Prophecy*, *Milton*, *Jerusalem* and *The Four Zoas*, but also in his earlier pastoral

---

20. On Romantic prophecy as a rhetorical form, see Ian Balfour, *The Rhetoric of Romantic Prophecy* (Stanford, CA: Stanford University Press, 2002), 55–8.

21. Percy Bysshe Shelley, *A Defence of Poetry* (1821), in *Essays, Letters from Abroad, Translations and Fragments*, ed. Mary Shelley, 2 vols (London: Edward Moxon, 1840), 1: 57; on poetry as prophecy, see also, *e.g.*, S. T. Coleridge, *The Destiny of Nations* (1817); William Wordsworth, 'The Passing of the Elder Bards' (1835).

22. Coleridge, *Biographia*, chap. 12, p. 188.

23. See Thomas Gray, 'The Bard' (1757).

24. Isaiah 40.3; John 1.23.

lyrics. As discussed above, in a Romantic sensibility the voice of the Lord is heard through the testimony of the self. What Blake termed the 'Poetic Genius' was not the preserve of an artistic elite but the creative spirit within all people, manifest in the 'Spirit of Prophecy' that is its religious expression.[25] In Blake's universalizing vision, 'Every honest man is a Prophet', since prophecy concerns not the prediction of the future but a confrontation with truth and a commentary on the present.[26] Blake's famous apocalyptic poem 'Jerusalem' was glossed by a reference to Numbers 11.29: 'Would to God that all the Lord's people were Prophets.' This poem appears in the preface to *Milton*, which recounts Blake's own discovery of the spirit of prophecy and poetry within. The verse is copied half in lament and half in hope, by a poet committed to the 'Mental Fight' of bringing heaven to earth and building 'Jerusalem/ In Englands green & pleasant Land'.[27]

The prophetic honesty that Blake prized is not to be confused with straightforward speech.[28] Blake's apocalyptic, visionary, poetic-artistic creations model a highly imaginative response to the inspiration that he received. In his account of a visionary encounter with the two prophets Isaiah and Ezekiel, Blake explains the role of prophet and poet in conveying the voice of the Lord. In this 'Memorable Fancy', Isaiah recounts that he did not hear the voice of the Lord as such. Instead, he received an ineffable sense of 'the infinite in every thing' which he then translated into words.[29] The essence of this prophetic message, which recurs throughout Blake's work, is that 'every thing that lives is Holy', a message given form and beauty by the creative participation of the poet-prophet.[30]

The poetic dynamic of prophetic revelation is expressed in Blake's last great work, *Jerusalem*, which opens with a vision of Christ hovering 'over me/ Spreading his beams of love & dictating the words of this mild song'.[31] The words may be 'dictated', but the form is chosen by the poet who first 'consider'd a Monotonous

25. William Blake, All Religions Are One (circa 1788), 'Principle 5th' in Keynes, Complete Writings, 98. N.B. all quotations from Blake's works are taken from Keynes, Complete Writings.

26. Blake, 'Annotations to Watson's 'Apology for The Bible'' (1798), note to p. 14 in Keynes, *Complete Writings*, 392.

27. Blake, 'I: Preface', *Milton, a Poem in 2 Books* (1804-8), in Keynes, p. 481; for a discussion of this passage as an example of 'radical prophecy', see Christopher Rowland, *Radical Prophet: The Mystics, Subversives and Visionaries Who Strove for Heaven on Earth* (London: I.B. Tauris, 2017), 4.

28. Eliot termed honesty in Blake his capacity to 'exhibit the essential sickness or strength of the human soul', in T. S. Eliot, 'Blake', in *The Sacred Wood: Essays on Poetry and Criticism* (London: Methuen, 1920), 137-43 (137). On honesty as a virtue of radical theology, see John A. T. Robinson, *Honest to God* (London: SCM, 1963), 28, 140-1; Andrew Shanks, *Faith in Honesty: The Essential Nature of Theology* (Aldershot: Ashgate, 2005), 1-2.

29. Blake, 'A Memorable Fancy', *The Marriage of Heaven and Hell* (c. 1790-3), 153, Plates 12-13.

30. Blake, 'Chorus', *Marriage*, 160, Plates 25-7.

31. Blake, *Jerusalem*, 622, Plate 4, lines 4-5.

Cadence ... derived from the modern bondage of Rhyming ...' before deciding that '... such monotony was ... as much a bondage as rhyme itself. I therefore have produced a variety in every line, both of cadences & number of syllables.'[32] Austin Farrer famously asserted that 'the poet is a maker, the prophet is a mouthpiece'.[33] On the contrary, the creative intervention of the poetic subjectivity is crucial to Blake's prophetic poetic.[34] His idiosyncrasies of style are testament not only to Blake's radical vision but also to a consistency with the traditions of Hebrew prophecy that inspired him. The Hebrew prophets were poets too, and Lowth's famous lectures on Hebrew poetry of 1753 describe their sublime style much as Blake described his own: as 'of too ardent a spirit to be confined by rule ... [but] guided by ... the impulse of divine inspiration'.[35] No mere ventriloquist of the voice of the Lord, Blake's prophetic poetic was intimately bound up with poetic creativity and thereby with poetic subjectivity.

The testimony of Jesus in the Songs of Innocence

In *Songs of Innocence and of Experience* (1789/1794), this prophetic poetic is manifest in a pastoral style that models what Robert Alter has termed a '*rhetoric of entrapment*', a mode at once sweet and satirical that draws the reader into a confrontation with truth in spite of themselves.[36] Pastoral conventions are exploited throughout the collection, established at the start by an image of the poet as shepherd, 'Piping down the valleys wild', and reinforced by the rural settings of the first four poems: 'Introduction', 'The Shepherd', 'The Echoing Green' and 'The Lamb'.[37] The classical conventions of pastoral were not just about a withdrawal from public life into the bucolic realm of shepherds and their sheep. From Virgil and Theocritus to Milton and Andrew Marvell, pastoral was a vehicle for social critique from the wilderness of rural isolation.[38] In *The Marriage of Heaven and*

---

32. Blake, 'To the Public', *Jerusalem* (1804–20), Plate 3.

33. Ibid., 'To the Public', ibid., 621, Plate 3.

34. For a summary of Blake's position on prophetic poetry as a combination of 'inspiration' and 'craft', see Michael D. Hurley, 'William Blake: Destabilized Particulars', in *Faith in Poetry: Verse Style as a Mode of Religious Belief* (London: Bloomsbury, 2017), 9–38.

35. Robert Lowth, *Lectures on the Sacred Poetry of the Hebrews*, ed. Calvin E. Stowe, trans. G. Gregory (New York: J. Leavitt, 1829), 170. On prophecy as poetry, see James Kugel, ed., *Poetry and Prophecy: The Beginnings of a Literary Tradition* (Ithaca: Cornell University Press, 1990); Ezra Spicehandler, 'Hebrew Poetry', *PEPP* (1975), 336–43 (338).

36. Robert Alter, *The Art of Biblical Poetry*, rev. edn (New York: Basic Books, 2011), 180. See also ibid., 171–204 on his classification of Hebrew prophecy into admonition, satire and the foretelling of disaster.

37. Blake, 'Introduction', (*Innocence*), 111, line 1.

38. On Blake's 'social vision', see David Erdman, *Blake: Prophet against Empire*, 3rd edn (Princeton, NJ: Princeton University Press, 1977), xiii. See also 'The Little Black Boy' and 'London'.

Hell, Isaiah declares: 'The voice of honest indignation is the voice of God.'[39] Poems such as 'On Another's Sorrow', 'London' or 'Holy Thursday' in *Experience* convey a frank and vehement indignation against injustice, but other *Songs* employ irony and satire to catch the reader off guard. 'Holy Thursday' in *Innocence* is mostly preoccupied with praising the orphans of London, who are described as 'lambs', a symbol of innocence and sacrifice, but the poem concludes with a sudden turn to admonishment: 'Then cherish pity, lest you drive an angel from your door.'[40] The tale of 'The Chimney-Sweeper' in *Innocence* is filled with pathos; their acceptance of their unjust lot provokes pity and guilt in the reader, which is driven home by the irony, patent falsehood and implicit threat of the closing maxim: 'if all do their duty, they need not fear harm.'[41]

This work is brimming with indignation, but the tone of jolly insouciance that characterizes many of the 'happy songs' in *Innocence* is more than a satirical device. The prophetic message of these songs is that 'every thing that lives is Holy.'[42] So the infant of 'Infant Joy', for example, bears witness to their own glory, not in an egoistic assertion of the self but in a declaration of the goodness of all creation. In this poem a newborn child introduces themselves in terms that echo the great 'I am' statements of Christ.[43] These infant declarations of the self ('"I am but two days old". "I happy am"') are not overtly prophetic; they do not admonish injustice or foretell disaster, but they do speak of the joy of existence to an indifferent world that neglects and exploits its children.[44]

The nursery-rhyme simplicity of this poem is both a declaration of glory and a prophetic against tyranny, an act of resistance to the adult voices of moral instruction and control. As the poem progresses, this simple joy is accompanied by a sense of ambivalence, as the pure happiness of egoless being is spoilt by the intervention of an adult voice. The child begins with 'no name:', but in conversation with an adult they are led into undertaking the Adamic task of naming themselves:

What shall I call thee?
'I happy am,
'Joy is my name.'[45]

---

39. Blake, 'A Memorable Fancy', *Marriage*, 153–4, Plates 12–13.
40. Blake, 'Holy Thursday' (*Innocence*), 121–2, lines 7, 12; ibid., 'Holy Thursday', (*Experience*), 211–2, line 4.
41. Ibid., 'The Chimney-Sweeper' (*Innocence*), 117–18, line 24.
42. Ibid., 'Introduction' (*Innocence*), line 19; ibid., 'Chorus', *Marriage*, Plates 25–7.
43. See John 8.58; John 10.11; Revelation 22.16.
44. Blake, 'Infant Joy', 118, lines 2, 4.
45. Ibid., lines 1, 3–5.

Out of this exchange, the voice of the infant fades into silence, taken over by the song of the adult who has named and tamed them: 'Sweet joy I call thee', as the prophetic declaration 'I am' is buried under the impulses of self-assertion ('I am *x*') and categorization ('you are *y*').[46]

The lyric 'I' of 'Infant Joy' is a voice of testimony, more specifically 'the Spirit of prophecy who bears testimony to Jesus' as described in Revelation 19.10. The voice of Christ is heard throughout the *Songs of Innocence*: in the Shepherd, 'his tongue ... filled with praise', in the Lamb's 'tender voice' and the 'laughing' cherub of the 'Introduction', and in the infant, whose 'smiles are His own smiles;/ Heaven and earth to peace beguiles'.[47] The *Songs* are a self-conscious subversion of popular collections of children's verse such as Isaac Watts' *Divine Songs* (1715), but their 'mild song' also presents the testimony of Jesus as a voice of laughter and praise, gentleness and joy, an attractive prophetic vision of life and love.[48]

In Ezekiel 33.32 the Lord condemns those who treat the prophet 'like a singer of love songs ... they hear what you say, but they will not do it'. The sweetness of the song is a strength and a weakness, a mirror of the beauty of truth and a mask that conceals the message. Yet for those with ears to hear, the sweetness of the lyric can act as an intensifier of the prophetic voice: of joy in existence, anger against oppression and yearning for justice, as expressed in the poem that concludes the *Songs of Innocence* (which echoes Isaiah 49.15):

> Can I see another's woe,
> And not be in sorrow too?
> ... No, no! never can it be!
> Never, never can it be![49]

The voice of wounded love in the Songs of Experience

In the *Songs of Experience*, the voice of honest indignation which is the voice of God appears as a voice of wounded love. This theme first appears in the 'Introduction', where the cherub-muse of the 'Introduction' poem in *Innocence* is replaced by the hoary figure of the bard, declaiming the lament of 'The Holy Word' who walked

---

46. Ibid., line 9.
47. Ibid., 'The Shepherd', line 4; *cf.* John 10.14 and 10.27; Blake, 'The Lamb', line 7; ibid., 'Introduction', line 4. NB the cherub's command to the poet echoes that of Christ in Revelation 1.11 and 1.19, to 'write what you have seen'; ibid., 'A Cradle Song', lines 31–2.
48. Ibid., 'Introduction' (*Innocence*), line 19. The Christ figure of 'The Lamb' alludes to the 'Gentle Jesus, meek and mild' of Charles Wesley's hymn, in which Christ is a model for childlike devotion, but Blake's 'little child' resembles more the infant king of Isaiah's apocalyptic vision (11.6). *Cf.* Blake's 'He is meek, & he is mild; / He became a little child' and Wesley's 'Thou art gentle, meek and mild; / Thou wast once a little child'. Blake, 'The Lamb', lines 15–16; Charles Wesley, 'Gentle Jesus, Meek and Mild', stanza 2, lines 3–4.
49. Blake, 'On Another's Sorrow', lines 1–2, 11–12.

through the fallen Eden, calling out: "'O Earth, O Earth, return! … "Turn away no more;/ "Why wilt thou turn away?'"[50] These words echo a leitmotif of Hebrew prophecy, in which God speaks to Israel as a grieving husband to an unfaithful wife.[51] In Blake's hands this prophetic theme is not a tool for a condemnation of sin but a visionary window into a deeper understanding of the nature of love. The *Songs of Innocence and Experience* explore *the Contrary States of the Human Soul*, and so the theme of disappointed love is addressed from two sides.[52] The 'voice of the bard' is first challenged and undercut by 'Earth's Answer' in the following poem, which labels God's cuckolded cry a sign of a possessive and controlling love: a "'Cruel, jealous, selfish fear!'"[53] In this reply, the authority of the bard, and through them the voice of the Lord, is called into question. In the illuminations to this collection, Blake depicts the bard as white-bearded, a symbol of the bitterness of age, while the triangular shape of his harp mirrors that of Newton's compass, a symbol of narrow vision.[54] His authority is not undisputed, his voice not entirely to be trusted.

How then does the Spirit of prophecy speak through these poems? Not through the tone of admonition but most clearly through a song of love. An alternative vision of disappointed love appears in 'The Garden of Love'. This lyric is modelled on the song of the vineyard in Isaiah 5.1-7, which F. W. Dobbs-Allsopp has called one of the 'high lyrical moments' in Hebrew prophecy.[55] Blake's 'Garden' models the kind of subversive reading of the Bible advocated in *The Marriage of Heaven and Hell*.[56] Isaiah 5.1-7 is a prophecy of doom where the Lord is cast as the keeper of the vineyard of Israel, who has tended and cared for it without yielding a harvest of righteousness and who will now abandon it to the wilderness.[57] Blake's poem concerns not a vineyard – which is expected to produce fruit – but a garden – which need only be beautiful. The first-person voice of Blake's poem is that of one who played there as a child and returns to find it dreadfully changed:

50. Ibid., 'Introduction' (*Experience*), 210, lines 4, 11, 16–17.

51. Consider, *e.g.*, Hosea 1.2.

52. Blake, *Innocence and Experience*, frontispiece.

53. Blake, 'Introduction' (*Experience*), 210, line 1; ibid., 'Earth's Answer', 210–11, line 12.

54. See ibid., 'The Voice of the Ancient Bard', 126.

55. Dobbs Allsopp, *On Biblical Poetry*, 228. For an analysis of the poetics of Isaiah 5.1-7, see J. Blake Couey, *Reading the Poetry of First Isaiah: The Most Perfect Model of the Prophetic Poetry* (Oxford: Oxford University Press, 2015), chap. 3, esp. 162, 95.

56. On Blake's imaginative approach to scriptural hermeneutics, see Rowland, '"From impulse not from rules": William Blake's Apocalyptic Pedagogy', in *Radical Prophet*, 99–128; Northrop Frye, *Northrop Frye's Fearful Symmetry: A Study of William Blake*, ed. Nicholas Halmi, Collected Works of Northrop Frye 14 (Toronto: University of Toronto Press, 2004), 112–14.

57. In Lowth's translation the 'I' of verses 1–2 is that of the prophet singing of God's love, before becoming in verse 3 God's direct first-person address to Judah, Robert Lowth, *Isaiah: A New Translation* (London: J. Nichols, 1778), 5, 1–2.

> I went to the Garden of Love,
> And saw what I never had seen;
> A Chapel was built in the midst
> Where I used to play on the green.[58]

This garden has not been abandoned because of sin but has instead been choked by the trappings of religious and moral instruction. While the 'Beloved' of Isaiah lovingly provides a fence and tower to protect the vineyard, the closed chapel erected in the middle of Blake's garden is a symbol of exclusion and moral oppression, with its 'gates … shut,/ And "Thou shalt not" writ over the door'.[59] The 'briars' that choke the garden echo 'the briar and the thorn' of Isaiah 5.6, which in the Hebrew text are the fruit of Israel's unrighteousness but in Blake's lyric represent sexual repression and institutional religion.[60] There are echoes here of Lowth's 1778 translation of Isaiah, which adopts a hermeneutic of faithfulness to the text that eschews literalism in favour of a dynamic style reflective of the passion of the original.[61] Blake reproduces Lowth's anaphoric repetition of 'And' as an intensifier (opening each line of the final stanza with this word), a rhetorical device also employed in his famous prophetic lyric 'Jerusalem'. This fervent re-telling of Isaiah rejects a moralistic condemnation of humanity's ingratitude towards God's love and care, instead relating the horror of the beloved who finds their joys constrained and their love trampled upon.

The lyric 'I' of 'The Garden of Love' is quite unlike the mournful pleading and authoritarian admonition of 'The Introduction'. Its ingenuous surprise and wounded disappointment is more resonant of the 'mild songs' of *Innocence*, whose love songs are the song of Love itself, the voice of Christ. The unnamed 'I' of this poem merges the voice of Jesus with that of fallen humanity, excluded from the garden, giving a right of reply to those bowed down by the weight of moral judgement. At the same time, this prophetic poem is faithful to the heart of Isaiah 5.1-7 in its condemnation of the corruption of love and the neglect of the common good by those in authority. The prophetic power of indignation is conveyed here less through a declaration of (self) righteous judgement than by inciting a sense of revolt against the wounding of love, the tarnishing of innocent beauty and the curtailment of freedom. Heard as the 'testimony of Jesus', this voice speaks from the wilderness of a divine love that is at one with human suffering. It goes beyond lament to bear witness to 'Love, the human form divine', who embodies the hope of redemption by uniting the voices of God and humanity.[62]

---

58. Blake, 'The Garden of Love', 215, lines 1-4.
59. Ibid., lines 5-6.
60. Ibid., line 12.
61. Lowth sought to craft a unity between 'the Poetical and the Prophetical character of style and composition', arguing that 'Flatness and insipidity will generally be the consequence of deviation from the native manner of an original', Lowth, *Isaiah*, iii, xxxvi.
62. Blake, 'The Divine Image', 117, line 11.

Blake's pastoral poetry illustrates how the spirit of prophecy might be heard through the lyric declaration 'I love' when it is heard as the voice of Love itself, the voice of Christ. In a sweet song of love this phrase can be an affirmation of the beauty of being, but 'I love' can also be a defence of the loveliness of the unloved, or a rebuke against the callousness of the unloving. Each of these is a prophetic declaration that unveils what for Blake was the central inspiration of the Spirit, the holiness of everything that lives.

I am: John Clare's prophetic testimony[63]

The late Romantic 'peasant-poet' John Clare (1793–1864) has long lain on the fringes of the Romantic canon, but his very isolation provides a model for a discussion of the prophetic lyric 'I'.[64] Clare may not have been as poor or as prodigious as his first editors claimed but he does represent, perhaps better than 'great' Romantics such as Wordsworth or Blake, the 'real language of men', a voice in tune with what Adorno calls the 'collective undercurrent' through its concern with social and economic change.[65] Incarcerated for many years for mental instability, Clare's later poems often take on the persona of the suffering prophet after the model of Job or Jeremiah. Reading Clare's famous 'I am' poems in the light of his

---

63. This section is reproduced with minor adaptations from Elizabeth S. Dodd, 'John Clare's Romantic "I": A Prophetic Poetics of Testimony', in *Prophetic Witness and the Reimagining of the World: Poetry, Theology and Philosophy in Dialogue*, Power of the Word, ed. Mark S. Burrows, Hilary Davies and Josephine von Zitzewitz, vol. 5 (London: Routledge, © 2020). Reproduced by permission of Taylor & Francis Group.

64. On Clare's relationship to the Romantic movement, see Adam White, *John Clare's Romanticism* (London: Palgrave, 2017). For a previous discussion of Clare's first-person perspective that describes it not as the 'enclosed' I of Coleridgean individualism but an 'itinerant' I that provides a communal site of resistance to the present order through a nostalgic appeal to the past, see Mark Nicholson, 'The Itinerant "I": John Clare's Lyric Defiance', *English Literary History* 82 (2015): 637–69. This section develops the notion of Clare's 'I' as a site of prophetic resistance, but locates it not as the ghostly voice of godless past but rather as a participation in the divine voice through exile and suffering.

65. Wordsworth, 'Preface', *Lyrical Ballads*, para 1; Adorno, 'Lyric Poetry and Society', 344. On the social implications of Clare's use of local diction and syntax, see John Barrell, *The Idea of Landscape and the Sense of Place 1730–1840: An Approach to the Poetry of John Clare* (Cambridge: Cambridge University Press, 2010), 126–7, 159; on Clare's position at the fringes of Romanticism, see James McKusick, 'Beyond the Visionary Company: John Clare's Resistance to Romanticism', in *John Clare in Context*, ed. Geoffrey Summerfield, Hugh Haughton and Adam Phillips (Cambridge: Cambridge University Press, 1994), 221–37 (225, 228); see also Simon Kövesi and Scott McEathron, 'Introduction', in *New Essays on John Clare: Poetry, Culture and Community*, ed. Simon Kövesi and Scott McEathron (Cambridge: Cambridge University Press, 2015), 1–16 (7).

biblical paraphrases and prose letters, and informed by Adorno's lyric theory, this section argues that Clare's inescapable, expansive, diffuse and conflicted 'I' can be interpreted as a voice of prophetic witness.

Adorno's 1957 essay on 'Lyric Poetry and Society' influentially argued for the social function of lyric poetry. Adorno does not deny the subjectivity of the lyric 'I', indeed the very assertion of individuation in the lyric poem presents a challenge to the forces of totalitarianism, its uniqueness protesting the reification of modern mass culture. Following Hegel's account of lyric as socially located, Adorno defines it as 'the subjective expression of a social antagonism'.[66] The apparently solipsistic lyric sets into sharp relief the very social forces that it rejects: 'The "I" whose voice is heard in the lyric is an "I" that defines and expresses itself as something opposed to the collective, to objectivity.' Lyric thereby implicitly addresses society while it seems to ignore it, seeking for its transformation while appearing to flee in the other direction. This poetics is prophetic rather than utopian because it judges the world rather than seeking to escape it: 'The work's distance from mere existence becomes the measure of what is false and bad in the latter.' Lyric subjectivity is prophetic insofar as it gives voice to the masses who are objectified by existential constraints, but who still 'grope for the sounds in which sufferings and dreams are welded'.[67]

I and O

In March–April 1830, Clare wrote a letter to Eliza L. Emmerson to apologize for his regrettably delayed composition of 'gossip' for her entertainment. Characteristically eschewing grammar and punctuation, Clare writes the following:

> I determined to speak in parables & that in past moods & tenses for I am growing out of myself into many existences & wish to become more entertaining in other genders for that little personal pronoun 'I' is such a presumption ambitious swaggering little fellow that he thinks himself qualified for all company all places & all employments go where you will there he is swaggering & bouncing [] in the pulpit the parliment the bench aye every where even in this my letter he has intruded 5 several times already ... he is a sort of Deity over the rest of the alphabet being here there & everywhere ⟨at one & the same time⟩ he is a mighty vapour in grammer he grows into a pedantical nuisance & often an O would be a truer personification in philosophy a juggling gossip in oratory a consequential blusterer & in fashion a pretender to every thing ...[68]

---

66. On the social location of lyric, Hegel argues that the great lyric poet Schiller 'does not sing quietly to himself ... he is a bard who recites a subject-matter dignified in itself to an assembly of all the best and most prominent people', *Aesthetics*, 1147.

67. Adorno, 'Lyric Poetry and Society', 339–49.

68. John Clare, *The Letters of John Clare*, ed. Mark Storey (Oxford: Clarendon, 1985), 504.

Clare's sense of 'growing out of' himself through the past-tense and character-led perspective of narrative is an attempt to move beyond the narrow world of the lyric personal present.[69] It is indicative of a typically Romantic sense of progression towards self-actualization, but in this case this occurs through a process of diffusion rather than development into self-consciousness. In his entertainingly failed attempt to surpass the first-person pronoun, Clare complains of what Keats once called the 'egotistical sublime' of Wordsworthian poetry.[70] Clare wishes to surpass himself through the personification of other characters but seems unable to: 'he is an absolute Paul Pry —I ⟨therefore hope to get rid of his company for⟩ wish there he is agen.'[71] The 'I', for Clare, seems both ubiquitous and inescapable.

The phrase, 'he is a sort of Deity over the rest of the alphabet' flippantly refers to the 'I's frustrating omnipresence in speech. Yet the reference to the divine evokes a deeper – but perhaps equally intrusive – presence of the great 'I [AM]' behind the frivolity of parlour-game amusement. Coleridge is the great poet-philosopher of divine subjectivity. In *Biographia Literaria* he discusses the tenets of transcendental philosophy in terms consistent with his account of the poetic imagination; the great 'I AM' of divine creativity is 'one and the same thing with our own immediate self consciousness'.[72] Divine inspiration is thereby to be found in self-conscious subjectivity. Clare makes no such claim for an easy identification between (to put it in the terms of prophetic rhetoric) the voice of the Lord and human speech. Nevertheless, the voice of the Lord intrudes upon human speech in the form of the name of the Lord.

Clare concludes this passage by expressing a desire to progress from the 'I' of self-expression to the 'O' of wonder or passion. A similar progression from 'I' to 'O' is evident in one of Clare's more well-known poems. The opening stanza of 'Sighing for Retirement', printed in the *English Journal* in 1841, proceeds thus:

> *O* TAKE me from the busy crowd,
> *I* cannot bear the noise!
> For Nature's voice is never loud;
> *I* seek for quiet joys.[73]

---

69. On this passage as a reaction against 'Romantic egotism', see Simon Kövesi, *John Clare: Nature, Criticism and History* (London: Palgrave Macmillan, 2017), 88. See also Clare's 1820s poem 'The Parish' for his dislike of an egotistical concern with the 'self'.

70. John Keats, 'Letter to Richard Woodhouse, 27 October 1818', in *Life, Letters, and Literary Remains, of John Keats*, ed. Richard Monckton Milnes (London: Edward Moxon, 1848), 221–3.

71. Clare, *Letters*, 504.

72. Coleridge, *Biographia*, chap. 12, p. 183.

73. John Clare, 'Sighing for Retirement', in *The Later Poems of John Clare, 1837–1864*, ed. Eric Robinson and David Powell, 2 vols (Oxford: Clarendon, 1984), 1:19–20 (my italics).

In the opening apostrophe the 'O' takes precedence. As the poem progresses the agential and expressive phrases 'I cannot bear' and 'I seek for quiet' are replaced by a repeated reference to nature as 'The book I love', a phrase where the 'I' sits enclosed within the warm 'o's of 'book' and 'love'.

> The b*o*ok *I* l*o*ve is everywhere,
> And not in idle words;
> The b*o*ok *I* l*o*ve is known to all,
> And better lore affords.

The wide 'o' of the world is where Clare's 'I' finds both poetry and God:

> *I* found the poems in the fields,
> And *o*nly wr*o*te them d*o*wn. (my italics)

This movement from 'I' to 'O' carries layers of poetic resonance.[74] On the one hand it represents the bending of the upright 'I' from a straight line into a circle, the humbling of subjectivity through submersion in the objective world. The fact that an identical sign is used for the expressive 'O' and the numerical zero indicates this progression as one of disintegration or the loss of self. This sublimation of the self might alternatively be figured as an expansion of the line into a circle, a moving into the wideness of the world or into the great I AM. Clare's notion of the 'O' as a 'truer personification' than the 'I' thereby encompasses the paradoxical resonances of reduction and magnification, of *kenosis* and *theosis*.

The name of the Lord

The ambivalence and significance of the first-person singular in Clare's poetics is further elucidated by the translation of the phrase, 'I am', in his biblical paraphrases. Clare's major scriptural influences are commonly identified as Old Testament and apocalyptic.[75] In the wake of Lowth and Hugh Blair's interpretations of Hebrew poetics, Clare wrote poetic paraphrases of the Song of Deborah, passages from Isaiah, Lamentations and Revelation, as well as the end of the Book of Job.[76] Clare's biblical paraphrases remain quite close to the sense and syntax of the Authorised Version, but the effect of rendering it into rhyming couplets is one of relentless intensity, consistent with the 'CONCISENESS and strength' cited by Blair as one

---

74. On Clare's attentiveness to the natural world through the sound and form of words, see Stephanie Kuduk Weiner, *Clare's Lyric: John Clare and Three Modern Poets* (Oxford: Oxford University Press, 2014), 23–50.

75. See, *e.g.*, Sarah Houghton-Walker, *John Clare's Religion* (Farnham: Ashgate, 2009), 113–32.

76. Clare was probably familiar with Lowth but certainly with Hugh Blair, see Houghton-Walker, *Clare's Religion*, 116.

of the main features of Hebrew poetry.[77] In Clare's paraphrase of Isaiah 47.8. God speaks to the Chaldeans, chastising them for:

> Saying 'I am' as there was none beside
> '& know no loss of children in my pride'[78]

'I am' here is a declaration of human pride set up in competition with the great 'I AM' who is God. This is not as it appears in the Hebrew where the phrase is simply 'as there were none beside I [*ani*]'.[79] Instead it follows the Authorized Version and the Septuagint where the characteristic *ego eimi* becomes 'I am', echoing back to Exodus 3.14 and forward to the prophetic 'I am' sayings of Christ in the Gospel of John.

The phrase appears again in Clare's translation of Lamentations 3.1, which begins with a prophetic complaint:

> I am the man that affliction hath seen
> By the rod of his wrath sorely scourged have I been

Again the resonance with the 'I am' sayings is not there in the Hebrew and this time barely in the Greek, while even the Authorised Version indicates the tenuousness of the intertextual link by placing the '*am*' in italics to indicate its superfluousness to both Hebrew *ani* and Greek *ego*. Nevertheless, in Clare's translation the poetic resonances of the phrase cannot be ignored, given its status elsewhere in his corpus. There is an irony invested in the proud statement 'I am the man', as the phrase is immediately qualified by his description as a man marked out only for suffering. When the phrase is then repeated, its structure breaks down into its most concentrated and most colloquial form, 'I'm', as an expression of anguish and of the disintegration of the subject:

> I'm a mark for his arrow he bendeth his bow
> & empties his quiver to pince me with woe[80]

Jeremiah the subject is turned into an object, a man not only marked but himself a mark of suffering.

In both of these poetic translations, the resonances between the human 'I am' and the divine 'I AM' cannot be ignored. The first speaker declares 'I am' in pride, the second in anguish, but in both cases the phrase draws an implicit analogy and a comparison with the divine *ego eimi*. In both cases the phrase appears in

---

77. Hugh Blair, 'Lecture XLI: The Poetry of the Hebrews', in *Lectures on Rhetoric and Belles Lettres*, 3 vols (Dublin: Whitestone et al., 1788), 3:189–214 (197).

78. Clare, *Later Poems*, 1:142.

79. *Ani* does not echo Exodus 3.14 which in the Hebrew is *ehyeh aser ehyeh*.

80. Clare, *Later Poems*, 1:144.

the context of a passage that emphasizes the distance and difference between humanity and God. Whatever pretensions it may express, the 'I am' remains a paradoxical statement that reveals its opposite. 'I am' what I am, a human being, but in so being I am *not* God. Of course, in the Lamentations passage this irony is double layered, as a typological interpretation turns the 'I' of human anguish into the voice of Christ as the ultimate man of affliction.

It is Jeremiah's tone of suffering that resonates most with Clare, as in the following draft letter to Mary Collingwood, from his notebook of 1849–50:

> but there is no faith here so I hold my tongue—& wait the end out withou[t] attention or intention— 'I am that I am'—& done nothing Yet.[81]

Here again the 'I am' performs a paradoxical function. The ironic appropriation of the name of the all-powerful sets into relief the helplessness and inactivity of the poet: one who *is* but has no capacity to *do*. Clare takes the role of a silent prophet, God's mouthpiece refusing to speak to a faithless generation. Yet in his very recalcitrance, this silent prophet-poet quotes the name of God, and so the voice of God is still heard embedded even within a declaration of despair.

I am

This same paradox of silence and speech, of human frailty and the echo of divine power, is invested in the appearance of the phrase 'I am' in Clare's poetry. The inescapability of the 'I', the poetic expansion from 'I' to 'O' and the conflicted prophetic 'I' who at once declares 'I am' and 'I am not', are all evident in Clare's two great 'I am' poems, written after the loss of fame, family and community in Northampton Asylum between 1841 and 1864.[82] Against the background of his biblical paraphrases it is appropriate to read the poetic voice here as akin to a Jeremiah or a Job, complaining to the Lord. What is known of the circumstances of composition would suggest that the occasion for these poems is no trivial cause for lament, but a debilitating state of exile. Martin Buber has addressed the essential role of complaint in prophetic literature, pointing out that if God wishes a dialogical relationship with humanity, then God must make humanity able not only to echo but also to respond to the divine word in terms that include protest, lament, complaint and argument.[83] Nevertheless, Clare's poems tread a fine line between complaint and despair, raising the question of whether they can be considered a prophetic cry of dereliction that yet remains open to God or whether

---

81. Clare, 'To Mary Collingwood [1849–50], *Letters*, 0.

82. Clare, *Later Poems*, 1.397-99. For a discussion of this period in Clare's life, see Jonathan Bate, *John Clare: A Biography* (London: Picador, 2003), 485–506.

83. Martin Buber, *The Prophetic Faith*, ed. Jon Douglas Levenson (Princeton: Princeton University Press, 2016), 204.

their despair is such as to close off the speaker from comfort, grace or the voice of the Lord.

Are these lines anything other than expressions of self-pity inimical to the transformative rhetoric of prophetic hope?[84] There are hints of openness to transcendence that indicate the prophetic potential of these poems. The 'I am' poem begins with the lament 'I am – yet what I am none cares or knows' but concludes with a vision or a memory of 'the vaulted sky' that the speaker longs for, hinting at a yearning for the divine despite the poem's overtones of defiance, self-assertion and despair. The sonnet 'I feel I am', on the other hand, is framed and pursued by the 'I am' phrase, which reasserts itself in the second stanza and again at the end. The conclusion here is much more wearied and prosaic than the former: 'But now I only know I am, – that's all.' Both poems regret humanity's earthly exile and both contain a vision of a primal state of unity with the divine, but one ends with longing for the future, while the other concludes with a present desolation. These distinctions are too fine to designate the former as potentially open to the divine and the latter as mere solipsistic despair. They represent, as often in the Psalms, the self at different stages. Insofar as both contain references to transcendence, however brief and melancholy, so far both remain open to God even in the midst of their denial of the knowledge of God.

Clare's 'I am' poems illustrate the prophetic potential of lyric subjectivity through the persistent 'I' of Romantic expressivity, which takes centre-stage throughout, as illustrated by the opening to the sonnet: 'I *feel* I am – I only know I am' (*sentio ergo sum* as opposed to the Cartesian *cogito*).[85] As Adorno pointed out, the closer the cleaving to the 'I', the stronger the challenge to what has rejected or abandoned it, whether that is human society or a sense of rejection by God. In these poems existence itself is called into question through the repetitive re-examination of self-identity and presented as a problem and a mystery to the speaker: 'And yet I am, and live – like vapours tost.' The 'I' is problematized, diffused or self-consumed (see line 3 of 'I am', 'I am the self-consumer of my woes'), through the interplay of vowels. Close vowel sounds (*i* and *e*) appear in words that signify action and agency such as 'rise and vanish' or the desires of the spirit and the joys that have been lost such as 'my lifes esteems'. The movement from close to more open vowels, from *I* to *O*, signifies the transition of the self into nothingness, or into the wide world 'like vap*ou*rs tost'.[86]

---

84. On the character of prophetic speech as necessarily transformative and not just condemnatory, consider Walter Brueggemann, *The Prophetic Imagination*, 40th anniversary edn (Minneapolis, MN: Fortress Press, 2018), 94.

85. My italics. For a discussion of Clare's poetic submission to changing emotional impulses, see Andrew Hodgson, 'Clare's Lyric Impulse', *The Cambridge Quarterly* 45 (2016): 103–18.

86. My italics. Consider also the juxtaposition of I and O and the progression from closed to open vowels in phrases such as: 'oblivious host', 'stifled throes', 'Into the nothingness of scorn and noise, – / Into the living sea of waking dreams'.

The problematized Romantic *ego* of these poems, constantly in doubt, in search and in construction of itself, provides a model not only of an ever-intensified introspection but also of an investigation, critique and remaking of the self in relation to self, society and God. In this context the declaration, 'I am' entails a question, am I? There is more to this than the expression of self-doubt. The prophetic word is a transformative word and Clare's diffusive lyric I is inherently transfigurative. The transition from 'I' to 'O' draws attention to the way in which a poem inevitably moves not only 'Into the nothingness of scorn and noise' but also away from the individual poet towards the collectivity of the audience, simply through the act of being read. Every reader declares 'I' along with the poet, relocating, diffusing and expanding the poem's 'I' so that neither they nor it can be left untransformed.

Conclusion

From a New Testament perspective, the prophetic poetics of the phrase 'I am' in Hebrew poetry culminates in the Gospel of John where the last of the Hebrew poets, John the Baptist, declares both 'I am' and 'I am not'. Exploiting the theological connotations of *ego eimi*, John proclaims 'I am the voice' in the wilderness (John 1.23) but also 'I am not the Christ' (3.28).[87] John's prophetic first-person discourse points not towards himself but away towards the great 'I AM' who is manifest in the prophetic sayings of Christ. In a similar way, the prophetic force of Clare's poetics may be found in the disjunction between his words and their silent, divine, contradictions. By declaring 'I am', these poems point both to what the speaker is not and to what they have lost. They create a space for the 'I' to speak which might be a place not only of complaint but also of comfort, hope and restoration.

The prophetic potential of Clare's lyric 'I' is further elucidated by a Ricoeurian poetics of testimony. Paul Ricoeur defines testimony as 'words, works, actions, and lives which attest to an intention, an inspiration, an idea at the heart of experience and history which nonetheless transcend experience and history'.[88] Testimony cannot avoid history. Nor can it avoid the 'I' since it is by definition an eyewitness account. In Ricoeur's hermeneutics of testimony the anguish of the prophet-witness is an important feature of the form, as proof of their integrity and commitment to the message. Clare's poetic account of forsakenness, exile and suffering conforms to this model, attesting to the honesty of a speaker who has lost everything and so has nothing to lose.

Rebecca Chopp's feminist account of post-Holocaust poetics goes further by asserting that the prophetic speaker's authority may lie in the simple fact of

---

87. There is a good case for the Johannine influence on Clare. His poetic paraphrase of Revelation 21–22 interestingly chooses a passage which foregrounds the prophetic 'I' in dialogue with God.

88. Paul Ricoeur, 'The Hermeneutics of Testimony', in *Essays on Biblical Interpretation*, ed. Lewis S. Mudge (London: SPCK, 1981), 119–20, 123, 134–5, 139.

survival, which ensures the telling of a story that 'renders a moral claim on human existence'.[89] In more general terms, the very particularity of subjectivity – the simple assertion that 'I am' – speaks against the oppressive influence of totalizing theory, rational abstraction or social convention. This phrase is prophetic not because it is the last or only word but because it is a word that needs to be heard. Clare's bare but repeated 'I am' is the assertion of a being that is inconvenient to others, perhaps also to itself. Stripped back to bare existence by suffering, the surviving 'I' bears witness to that suffering and to the evils that have caused it.

In true lyric style, Clare's 'I' speaks most clearly to that which it appears to flee, but this is more than a cry of protest. In its simple self-assertion, Clare's declaration of individuation, his 'I am' set up *against* God is also a cry *to* God. It invokes the divine name, thus saying implicitly 'I am not', and draws God into dialogue by calling on the name of the Lord. Clare's is a Job-like prophetic in that the depths of his anguish, even to the level of despair, challenge or even provoke God to speak. Clare's 'I am' is a prophetic word of protest and of hope that bears witness to collective suffering by presenting it from an individual perspective. In his persistent, conflicted, diffusive and expansive first-person singular, a discourse that might be read as pure solipsism is shown to have a public face, and the makings of a lyric prophetic of testimony become apparent.

I feel: Kae Tempest's lyric turn

The final section of this chapter explores the lyric affirmation of affective subjectivity, 'I feel', as a prophetic declaration. It turns from the Romantics of the eighteenth and nineteenth centuries to the very different context of contemporary performance poetry, but continues to reflect on poetry in a Romantic vein through the work of Kae Tempest (1985–). Tempest is a poet and recording artist with a strong social message who has positioned their work in continuity with Jungian Romanticism and in particular with Blake's prophetic poetry.[90] Like Blake, Tempest speaks out of and into their native context of London, crafting an urban aesthetic that draws on the stories of the city. This section charts the evolving sound of Tempest's voice, from the stridency of their earlier denunciative visions towards a more lyrical connectivity with self and world. This turn from condemnation to connection is discussed in the light of a reading of Joel 2.28-9 and Acts 2.16-18 as a democratization of the prophetic voice, a pouring out of the Spirit on all people.[91]

---

89. Rebecca S. Chopp, 'Theology and the Poetics of Testimony', in *Converging on Culture: Theologians in Dialogue with Cultural Analysis and Criticism*, ed. Delwin Brown, Sheila Greeve Davaney and Kathryn Tanner (Oxford: Oxford University Press, 2001), 57.

90. *Brand New Ancients* (2012) won the Ted Hughes award, while *Everybody Down* (2014) was nominated for the Mercury Music Prize and *Let Them Eat Chaos* (2016) was nominated for both the Mercury Music Prize and the Costa poetry book award.

91. See Kae Tempest, *On Connection* (London: Faber & Faber, 2020), Kindle, chap. 1, 'Set Up'.

The pouring out of the Spirit in Let Them Eat Chaos *(2016)*

Spoken word or performance poetry might be considered an ideal form for prophetic discourse. It is often embedded in a culture of social activism, while the forum of the poetry slam is renowned for crafting a space for speaking truth to power by championing voices conventionally neglected by the literary establishment. Spoken word has represented for many a true democratization of poetry, compared to that less convincingly championed by Wordsworth and Coleridge.[92] The following discussions explore the prophetic power of spoken word poetry not just through its social agenda but through its capacity to connect people, less a democratizing than a humanizing force that can make all people prophets by establishing the bonds of love between them.

The impact of Tempest's often overtly prophetic lyrics has been intimately bound up with their stage presence, a poetic persona which, as their chosen name suggests, can be overwhelming, like a storm. Their powerful performance style relies heavily on the driving rhythms and virtuosic breath-patterns of hip hop, often performed to an electronic soundtrack that adds an extra layer of intensity. In *Let Them Eat Chaos*, this gale of words is put in service of a blunt attack on the self-protective instincts of consumerist capitalism.[93] The hour-long performance is made up of interspersed lyrics and narrative interludes that are unified by the apocalyptic conceit of an oncoming storm. The sections of the piece tell the stories of several characters who are struggling in life, but who join together at the end to revel in this unexpected deluge. The track 'Don't Fall In', which appears about half way through, evokes the voice of a building storm and its sudden downpour through a relentless vocal delivery that hits the audience with the force of a gale. Tempest invites their audience to 'Come dance in the deluge', to allow themselves to be engulfed because, as becomes clear by the end of *Let Them Eat Chaos*, this is not a storm of destruction but an outpouring of love and justice inspired by 1 John 4.18 ('perfect love casts out fear').[94]

Speaking amidst the tumult of Pentecost, Peter in Acts 2.16-18 declares that the Spirit has been poured out on all people, a fulfilment of the prophecy of Joel 2.28-29 and of Moses' desire that all God's people would be prophets (Numbers 11.29).

---

92. See Wordsworth's commitment to write poetry in 'the real language of men', Preface to the *Lyrical Ballads* (1802), para. 1. On the culture and prophetic potential of spoken word poetry, see Pete Bearder, *Stage Invasion: Poetry & the Spoken Word Renaissance* (London: Out-Spoken Press, 2019); for a more complex reflection on similar themes in an American context, see Javon Johnson, *Killing Poetry: Blackness and the Making of Slam and Spoken Word Communities* (New Brunswick, NJ: Rutgers University Press, 2017), chap. 3.

93. For a more extensive discussion of this poem, see Elizabeth S. Dodd, 'Spoken Word and Spirit's Breath: A Theopoetics of Performance Poetry', *Literature & Theology* 33, no. 3 (September 2019): 292–306.

94. Kae Tempest, 'Don't Fall In', in *Let Them Eat Chaos* (London: Picador, 2016), 41; one of the epigraphs to the work is 1 John 4.18 (unfortunately misquoted as John 4.18), and the storm occurs at 4:18 am. The other epigraph is from Blake's *Marriage of Heaven and Hell*.

The Hebrew term to 'pour out' (from *shaphak*, Joel 2.28) signifies not the trickling of oil but the deluge of a waterfall, while the connotations of the Greek *ekkhéō* (Acts 2.17) signify to pour out or shed, connecting the pouring out of the Spirit with the wine of the covenant and the shedding of sacrificial blood.[95] Tempest's carefully crafted barrage of words can be similarly overwhelming. Described as 'sermonic', at times denunciative, it can also be heard as a prophetic call to live in love without fear, drawing on the elemental sounds of wind and rain not as agents of judgement but signs of energy and life.[96]

Presence and authenticity: Voice and body in Hold Your Own *(2014)*

Spoken word entails a more literal connection between the voice of the poem and the person of the poet than is encountered in print. Although broadly in continuity with the long history of oral poetry, unlike the traditioned culture of performance and reperformance surrounding classics such as the *Mabinogion* or *Beowulf*, modern performance poetry generally involves the poet performing their own material. While the speaker may adopt a heightened poetic persona, they may also capitalize upon the appearance of expressivity that comes from speaking in one's own voice. Accent, tone, timbre, rhythm – all carry poetic significance. In this context, the question of the authenticity of the lyric 'I' takes on a particularly acute significance. Their prophetic authority may depend upon an appearance of authenticity, through which the singular 'I' onstage may take on the capacity to represent the collective 'I' of a marginalized or discontented community.

Voice is therefore deeply implicated in the prophetic power of the spoken word. In their essay collection *On Connection* (2020), Tempest reflects at length on the poetic implications of their bodily and vocal presence, as at once given and constructed, involuntary and imposed. They note the incongruity between the fierceness of their performance and the popular perception of their appearance as '"unthreatening"': 'white and young-looking' with face and hair (now cut short) described as '"angelic"'. According to Tempest, this disjunction between appearance and poetic presence gave them an audience, giving them permission to speak with a violent intensity that from others would have been received as overly aggressive.[97] They express ambivalence towards this aspect of their success, acknowledging the injustice that others equally talented or visionary may be less recognized because they do not look or sound right.

---

95. Also used for the blood that poured out of the sacrificial offering or the innocent victim of injustice, *shaphak* also carries connotations of purification, immolation and wrath. See James Strong, 'Hebrew and Chaldee Dictionary', in *Concordance*, #8210; Strong, 'Greek Dictionary', in *Concordance*, #1632.

96. Sam Wolfson, 'Kate Tempest: The Performance Poet Who Can't Be Ignored', *The Guardian* (10 April 2013), https://www.theguardian.com/books/ 2013/apr/10/kate-tempest-performance- poet-cant-be-ignored.

97. Tempest, *Connection*, chap. 3.

For the poet-prophet, the drive for respectability or for impact may risk undermining the message to cater for an audience that seeks only to be entertained by their song.[98] In Tempest's case, there is an apparent incongruity between different aspects of their poetic presence which might have undermined the authenticity of their voice, but in fact such multiplicity has proved integral to their prophetic persona. The collection *Hold your Own* draws heavily on the classical myth of Tiresias, the blind prophet whose wisdom derived from having lived as both man and woman.[99] The prophet's clear vision emerges from their position of multiplicity and estrangement: 'Born strong./ Born wrong … Born to hold the world under her tongue.'[100] Their wisdom is lost on the audience who, while he is 'sentencing their spirits … think he's rapping lyrics'.[101] The autobiographical significance of this theme emerged in August 2020 when Tempest announced their change of name from Kate to Kae (symbolizing, among other things, renascence, joy and the coming of the rain) and publicly adopted nonbinary pronouns.[102] This announcement exposed the poetic persona: part given, part imputed, part exploited and part constructed, as an extension, intensification or adaptation of personal presence integral to the poetry's prophetic message.

The presence that Tempest conveys on stage is more than a poetic persona and its prophetic message is more than a performance. The poet's life experience and sense of identity are implicated in it, contributing to a Blakean prophetic vision of a wisdom that brings contraries together.[103] Ricoeur rejected a Romantic hermeneutic that identifies the poetic voice with the subjectivity behind it, but his account of prophetic testimony as words that involve 'The total self-implication of the subject' nevertheless signals the significance of the 'I' in the event of prophetic disclosure.[104] The costly self-exposure involved in Tempest's poetry is arguably the reason why theirs remains a powerfully prophetic voice.

The lyric turn as a turn to compassion

Tempest's transition towards publicly embracing a boundary-crossing identity opened up a new phase in their writing that was marked by a turn to the lyric 'I'. Tempest concluded the announcement of their transition by writing: 'For me,

---

98. Consider the warning of Ezekiel 33.32-33, discussed above, p. 103.

99. See Kae Tempest, 'Tiresias' 'The boy Tiresias', 'The woman the boy became', 'The woman Tiresias', 'The man Tiresias' and 'The prophet Tiresias', 'Party Time' and 'Prophet', *Hold Your Own* (London: Pan Macmillan, 2014), Kindle locs 60, 736, 791, 1061, 1117, 1411, 1734, 1761.

100. Ibid., 'The woman the boy became', loc. 778.

101. Ibid., 'Party Time', loc. 1747.

102. The announcement was made on their website, https://www.kaetempest.co.uk.

103. See Blake, 'Marriage', 149 Plate 3.

104. Ricoeur, *Essays in Biblical Interpretation*, 13.

the question is no longer "when will this change" but "how far am I willing to go to meet the changes and bring them about in myself."[105] This turn from a more declamatory mode towards greater introspection is explained in *On Connection* as not a retreat into self-absorption but a growth in self-knowledge. Far from abandoning the world, it involves a movement towards the other by progressing from judgement to compassion: 'I do not want to change minds any more. I just want to connect.'[106]

The catalyst for this transformation involved a quite literal conversion of the poet's voice. In their autobiographical account, which is reminiscent of Augustine's *Confessions*, Tempest recalls their early career as marked by a driving ambition, contempt for the audience and the subsuming of the 'offstage' by the 'onstage' self. The resulting bodily strain caused nodules on the vocal cords that left them speechless. Described as a 'humbling' process of being 'reduced to' their body, the loss of their public voice enabled them to open out toward the other as they were forced not to speak but to listen.[107] This experience inspired a greater empathy towards others and towards the artist's own body, illustrating a link between a connectivity with the self and a creative connection with others that Tempest outlines through a description of the experience of walking onstage. This is a 'deafening moment' in which heavy silence the artist, excited by anticipation, becomes acutely aware of 'each pump of blood and oxygen' through their veins, in preparation for the 'formidable undertaking' of 'meeting the room'.[108] Tempest outlines the connection between inner and outer self, and between self and others, through Carl Jung's distinction between 'the spirit of the depths' and 'the spirit of the times'.[109] For Tempest, the poet-prophet is not only a voice 'of' or even 'for' the times but one that must, if it is to survive and thrive, draw on 'the spirit of the depths'.[110]

Tempest's more mature work involves a lyric turn that is a turn not to isolation but to connection. To perform on stage, for Tempest, is about connection with others, as it is through connection that transformation can occur. Listening to the minutiae of what goes on within their own body, the artist becomes open to hear the sympathetic resonances between bodies. Out of this communal experience of onstage performance a prophetic voice can emerge that is not after all the voice of the individual poet but a joining with the cries of all people. The onstage voice can be a prophetic voice in the wilderness (Isaiah 40.3), not a cry *out of* the wilderness

---

105. Reproduced in Ben Beaumont-Thomas, 'Kate Tempest Announces They Are Non-binary, Changes Name to Kae', *The Guardian*, 6 August 2020, https://www.theguardian.com/music/2020/aug/06/kate-tempest-announces-they-are-non-binary-changes-name-to-kae.

106. Tempest, *Connection*, chap. 3.

107. Ibid., chap. 6.

108. Ibid., chap. 6.

109. Ibid., chap. 4, which is headed by Blake, 'Without Contraries is no progresssion', *Marriage*, Plate 3.

110. Ibid., chap 6.

alone, of separation or distinction, but a transformative imagination, an attractive as well as a challenging vision, that calls people *into* the wilderness with the poet to prepare the way of justice and love.[111]

Feelings and faces: The Book of Traps and Lessons *(2019)*

The Book of Traps and Lessons provides a helpful illustration of Tempest's transformed approach to prophetic poetics. It was recorded in a single take, bringing it close to the organic experience of live performance. Not an extended narrative like some of their previous works, this album is a lyric sequence in two parts, with numerous resonances between tracks that draw them into a kind of unity.[112] The two parts of the album correspond to a dual focus on the personal and the political. Many of the tracks retain the sermonic first-person plural 'we' and the didactic tone of direct address evident in earlier works such as *Let Them Eat Chaos*, while the cover image, an outline map of the UK and Ireland, signals an ongoing geopolitical concern. As with Blake, who finds in Jerusalem a spiritual counterpart to the earthly London, Tempest's outward-facing themes are accompanied by an exploration of the inner world. The 'peace' referenced in 'Thirsty', 'Holy Elixir' and 'People's Faces', for example, speaks both to an inner peace and an anti-war agenda, a peace either way found through human interconnection.[113]

In *Traps and Lessons*, the storm that was always a deluge of love is felt as a softer rain of compassion, through what Tempest terms 'The passionate [lyric] declaration of, "I have seen. I have heard. I have felt. And it's for you that I am moved to speak."'[114] The album culminates in 'People's Faces', a track which Tempest has described as 'the moment when the clouds lift' and there is a 'shocking feeling of connectedness'.[115] This concluding 'spark of hope' turns the album as a whole from a litany of doom into a prophetic word.[116] It is a word of hope in the form of a lyric love song, addressed not to an individual but the collective 'you' of the audience and beyond. The love it expresses is grounded in a concrete encounter with the body, specifically the faces of the audience. The line 'I can see your faces' is habitually reinforced in performance by gestures towards the audience,

---

111. See, *e.g.*, John 1.23.

112. The collection opens with the first-person phrase, 'I came to' and ends with 'I love people's faces'. Kae Tempest, 'Thirsty', 'People's Faces', *The Book of Tracks and Lessons* (Republic Records, 2019), tracks 1 and 11. Repeated motifs include the phrase 'Keep Moving Don't Move' (track 2), while the last line of the first two tracks links directly into the first line of the next.

113. Tempest, *Book of Traps*, tracks 1, 10, 11.

114. Tempest, *Connection*, chap. 7; *cf.* Bob Dylan's 'A Hard Rain's a-Gonna Fall', which is referenced in the refrain to Tempest, 'Don't Fall In', *Chaos*, 40.

115. Tempest, *Connection*, chap. 7.

116. Ibid. See Brueggemann, *Prophetic Imagination*, 94, as discussed above, p. 112, n. 84.

drawing attention to the face as that through which the presence of the other can be discerned, the uniqueness of the other acknowledged and empathy with the other can be communicated.[117] Tempest describes being onstage as a 'feeling of landing in the present tense', a connection with the here and now through which performance can become performative, as audience and artists are 'really there, all in this together, feeling something happening'.[118] In the refrain to 'People's Faces', the intimacy of this encounter (signalled by romantic lyrics like 'I can feel your heart racing') is expressed in terms that evoke a more global sense of hope ('I can feel things changing') and might be taken as a spur to action.[119]

The prophetic tone of this track is enhanced by a half-chanted tremolo reminiscent of surviving recordings of W. B. Yeats, an incantatory delivery that expresses an outpouring of affectivity. Such half-steps towards music convey a poetic of transcendence that enhances the rhetorical power of the refrain. The line 'I can feel things changing' is half-sung to the three-note ostinato of the acoustic piano, which continues throughout the piece, undergirding lyrics that acknowledge the grinding struggle of modern life with a subtle but building sense of hope and purpose.[120] Through such poetic devices, the classic expression of lyric sensibility 'I feel' becomes a means of connection: with the individual, with a community and with a global sense of progress, in service of a prophetic vision that inspires the audience to strive for the good.

According to Tempest, their most popular and powerful tracks are not their strident social critiques but those, like 'People's Faces', that adopt a gentler lyricism.[121] Through the lyric turn the impersonal voice of the gale, of invective and exhortation, has become a song of love and encouragement that is no less candid or visionary but is more relational. The prophetic 'I' onstage is not an 'I' alone, as their being-there depends upon the presence of the audience. In this context, the 'I' of 'I feel' emerges not as a solipsistic concern with the self but as an empathetic movement towards the other through a recognition of mutual subjectivity. This kind of poetic 'connection', embodied in tracks such as 'People's Faces', could be interpreted as a response to the Mosaic/Blakean hope and to the promise of Joel 2.28-29 and Acts 2.16-18, through which the poet invites the audience to share in their vision of a world transformed and become prophets themselves.

---

117. Tempest, 'People's Faces', *Book of Traps*, track 11; consider Tempest's performances of the track at Glastonbury Festival, the Park Stage (29 June 2019), and at the BBC 6 Music Festival, The Roundhouse (8 March 2020).

118. Tempest, *Connection*, chap. 1, 'Set Up'.

119. The phrase also gestures back to the line in 'Brown Eyed Man', 'I can feel you shaking', Ibid., *Book of Traps*, track 3.

120. This track, like much of Tempest's work, discusses the everyday challenges and injustice of life, such as low wages, high rents and overwork, which weigh people down and allow oppression to flourish.

121. Tempest, *Connection*, chap. 7, 'Feeling It Happen'.

Grace as a prophetic word

In Tempest's prophetic poetry, the lyric cry, 'I love', 'I am' or 'I feel', is a word from within that connects with others, a word that insists on being heard.[122] The concluding track of Tempest's following album, *The Line Is a Curve* (2022), illustrates this through a quotation from the noncanonical words of Jesus in the Gospel of Thomas, saying seventy. This is a moving rereading of Matthew 15.11, 25.29 or Mark 7.15, which declares that we are saved by speaking forth the words that are within us. In the track 'Grace', this cry is revealed as, at its heart, not just a voice of testimony but a voice of praise, bearing witness to the goodness of creation. 'Grace' crafts a moment of hope and transcendence at the end of the album by describing a sunset swim as an epiphany of the beauty of the world and the glory of life. This revelation is presented as a prophetic testimony, a word that must be spoken ('There are things I must record, must praise').[123] In 'Grace', as in the rest of Tempest's prophetic lyric, the first-person 'I' is not simply a reflection of a modern Western preoccupation with the self but echoes the prophetic cry '*myself*' that belongs to all creation: the cry '*Whát I dó is me: for that I came*' upon which claims to dignity and justice are founded.[124]

'Would that all the Lord's People were Prophets': *The lyric voice in public theology*

By exploring the social, embodied and performative features of the lyric first-person in prophetic Romantic poetry, this chapter makes a case for the importance of the 'I' in public discourse to, for and about God. This lyric 'I' is not isolated but actively related to others through the declaration 'I love' and integrated with the material world through the corporeal confession 'I feel'. Even the naked 'I am', as discussed by Buber and von Balthasar, is a being-in-relation to the 'Thou' who is addressed.[125] Despite the dangers of egotism and individualism, the 'I' remains not only inescapable but indispensable to a public theology that is humble in acknowledging the narrow scope of its knowledge, joyful in its celebration of the particularity of human life and prophetic in its willingness to challenge convention from the perspective of subjectivity.

---

122. On God's word as one that 'insists', as opposed to merely 'existing', see John Caputo, *The Insistence of God: A Theology of Perhaps* (Bloomington: Indiana University Press, 2013).

123. Kae Tempest, 'Grace', in *The Line Is a Curve* (New York: Republic Records, 2022), audio, track 12.

124. Gerard Manley Hopkins, 'As Kingfishers Catch Fire' (1877), line 8.

125. On prophecy as 'Human speech on God's behalf' and as characterized by the relationship between 'I' and 'Thou', see R. W. L. Moberly, who discusses Buber and von Balthasar in *Prophecy and Discernment* (Cambridge: Cambridge University Press, 2006), 4, 36–9.

Public theologians concerned with questions of speaking about God in and for the public have expressed understandable hesitancy towards the lyric 'I'. Seen as indicative of the privatization or over-emotionalization of religious language in the modern Western church, the first-person perspective has been viewed as a threat to theological engagement with the public sphere.[126] Duncan Forrester has defined public theology as interested not in 'individual subjectivity' but the common good, a position that owes much to a South African critique of over-spiritualized 'church theology' and defence of the 'prophetic witness' to which the church is called in imitation of Christ.[127] A major concern of theologians such as John Hull and Elaine Graham has been that public theology should address issues of justice and peace rather than the expansion or survival of the church.[128] These discussions carry an implicit critique of the 'I' of lyrical discourse, not only of the dangers of over-introspection or self-interest but of an underlying liberal epistemology that assumes a universality of human experience upon which Christian theology can rely to be relevant to the wider world, without translation or contextualization.[129]

At the same time, a shifting sociocultural landscape has had a profound effect on public theology in the West. As Forrester and Graham have described it, the so-called 'public sphere' of nineteenth-century liberalism: a neutral space of rational, secular discourse, has been replaced in a post-9/11, post-Christendom and post-secular context with a much more fluid mélange of public and private exemplified by the world of social media.[130] In order to listen and respond well to society in this context, and to translate the claims of Christian theology into terms that are more widely comprehensible and persuasive, theologians must draw on wider and more imaginative forms of communication that transgress the boundaries of public and private. The importance of the arts to this prophetic discourse has been well established through the influence of Walter Brueggemann, who has highlighted the role of 'lyrical thought' in presenting an alternative vision to the status quo.[131]

There is a space for lyric in this changed environment for public theology, through what Graham calls 'personal testimony'.[132] As discussed above, the power

---

126. See David Tracy, 'The Role of Theology in Public Life: Some Reflections', *Word and World* 4, no. 3 (1984): 230, cited in Elaine Graham, *Between a Rock and a Hard Place: Public Theology in a Post-Secular Age* (London: SCM, 2013), 82; John Hull, *Towards the Prophetic Church: A Study of Christian Mission* (London: SCM, 2014), 231.

127. Duncan Forrester, 'The Scope of Public Theology', *Studies in Christian Ethics* 17, no. 2 (2004): 6; John de Gruchy, '*Kairos* Moments and Prophetic Witness: Towards a Prophetic Ecclesiology', *Hervormde Teologiese Studies* 72, no. 4 (2016), https://doi.org/10.4102/hts.v72i4.3414.

128. Graham, *Rock and a Hard Place*, 223; Hull, *Prophetic Church*, 235.

129. See Forrester, 'Public Theology', 7–8.

130. Forrester, 'Public Theology', 16; Graham, *Rock and a Hard Place*, 223.

131. Brueggemann, *Prophetic Imagination*, 40; see also Andrew Davidson, 'Introduction', in *Imaginative Apologetics: Theology, Philosophy and the Catholic Tradition*, ed. Andrew Davidson (London: SCM, 2011); Graham, *Rock and a Hard Place*, 54.

132. Graham, *Rock and a Hard Place*, 206–7, 229–30.

of testimony lies not only in the narrative that it tells but in the invocation of the lyric 'I' in solidarity with marginalized others. In Graham's dialogical, persuasive and performative model of public theology as 'prophetic advocacy', there is room for the 'I' of the one who speaks truth to power with and for the oppressed. Anna Rowlands further endorses the contribution of a lyric poetics of testimony to public theology in her argument for an imaginative Christian discourse of the common good. She recounts an exercise conducted in schools where participants were asked to write a poem in which each line begins with 'I am'. Rowlands speaks of this experience as 'stimulat[ing] the restoration of something vital that had been beaten down, stripped away or simply unawakened by her pupils' life experience'.[133] In a context where personhood or individuation is diminished or neglected, the lyric 'I' becomes not only a valid but necessary starting point for discussion and action for the common good. To begin with the 'I' is not only to expose the supposed neutrality of rational secular discourse as an illusion but to validate the role of the affections in public life, exploring 'how it *feels to inhabit* ... a metaphysics as embodied social practice'.[134] To say 'I am' in a social context is less a personal confession than a public affirmation through which all are invited to share in the celebration of the individual as part of the building of communion.

The themes of this chapter have the potential to both affirm and expand understandings of the prophetic power of the lyric 'I' in public theology. The Kairos-Palestine document of 2009 speaks of the church's prophetic mission 'to speak the Word of God courageously, honestly and lovingly'.[135] John Clare's declaration 'I am' is an affirmation of selfhood that is courageous in its vulnerability, exposing the 'I' to scrutiny. Tempest's 'I feel' is honest in its turn from judgement towards self-examination. Rooted in bodily presence, this voice acknowledges that it can only speak of and for itself while at the same time seeking a connection that will enable it to speak also for the sake of others. Blake's pastoral lyrics incorporate what Bernard Youngman called the 'gentle persuasion of love', hearing in the voice of Jesus meek and mild also the voice of Jesus the prophet, enemy of injustice and advocate for the poor.[136]

---

133. Anna Rowlands, 'The Language of the Common Good', in *Together for the Common Good: Towards a National Conversation*, ed. Nicholas Sagovsky and Peter McGrail (London: SCM, 2015), 4. On the liberative power of the 'I' for those to whom the recognition of personhood has been denied, see also Mary Grey, *A Cry for Dignity: Religion, Violence and the Struggle of Dalit Women in India* (London: Routledge, 2014), 105. Grey discusses the 'Self-Respect' movement among Dalit women, which helps them transition 'from "subaltern consciousness" to a sense of self-esteem'. See also Graham, *Rock and a Hard Place*, 215–17 on Gustavo Gutiérrez's liberation theology for the 'nonperson'.

134. Rowlands, 'Common Good', 5.

135. Kairos-Palestine, *A Moment of Truth: A Word of Faith, Hope and Love from the Heart of Palestinian Suffering* (2009), http://www.kairospalestine.ps, cited in de Gruchy, 'Prophetic Witness', 6.

136. Bernard Youngman, cited in Hull, *Prophetic Church*, 48.

These three lyric poets embody the voice in the wilderness, not as a cry of isolation alone but as a transformative imagination that is both challenging and alluring. In Isaiah 40.3 (and the accounts of John the Baptist's ministry that draw on it) the voice in the wilderness not only calls people *from* the wilderness but calls them *into* the wilderness to prepare the Lord's way.[137] Tempest's track 'Holy Elixir' similarly describes the prophetic wilderness not as a place of escape but of transformation, with a voice speaking out of the desert: '*This* is the garden/ Now you better start sowing or there won't be a harvest.'[138] A lyric prophetic of hope and transformation is heard in Blake's satirical song: resisting social mores, courting derision and revelling in subversion. It is heard in Clare's voice of suffering and rejection, which defends a beauty that is under threat, and in Tempest's voice that seeks for human connection in a context of desolation. Not confined to the individual poetic genius but poured out on all flesh, the Spirit of justice, hope and liberation is manifest in the word performed, made present in body, breath and voice. The Spirit who speaks from the wilderness is a presence into which people are invited to come, a voice in which, through the universality and multiplicity of the lyric 'I', all are invited to share.

---

137. See, *e.g.*, John 1.23.

138. Kae Tempest, *Book of Traps*', track 10 (my italics).

Chapter 4

THE SOUND OF THE WIND – FRAGMENTATION AND ABUNDANCE IN THE POETIC LINE

Introduction

This final chapter takes as its starting point a conventional definition of lyric poetry that is straightforward but unhelpfully generic: that a lyric is a short poem. Does the shortness of the lyric do more than distinguish it from an epic or dramatic poem, which both tend towards length? Does it simply signify a humility of scope or ambition far removed from the great project of a *Divine Comedy* or an *Oedipus Rex*? Edgar Allen Poe described the true poem as necessarily brief, since the sublime elevation it achieves can only be sustained across a short span.[1] His argument resists the equation of shortness with diminution, granting a paradoxical grandeur to the short poem and asserting the relevance of shortness to poetic meaning-making.

This chapter approaches shortness through the lens of the fragment, a concept with currency in post-Romantic poetics that also has significance for theological discourse in a late-modern context.[2] The definition of the fragment adopted here is threefold. Firstly, the fragment is understood as something small and beautiful, a self-contained unit of meaning-making like the lyric fragments of the Romantic period. Secondly, the fragment is defined as something broken, like the disintegrated manuscripts of Sappho's poetry, of which only tantalizing fragments remain. Thirdly, the fragment is defined as part of a whole, drawing on David Tracy's apology for a theology constructed out of fragments. The poetic fragment is addressed in this chapter through a focus on the line, which in modern literature is largely what distinguishes poetry from prose. The chapter addresses three features of the line which correspond to the three aspects of

---

1. Edgar Allen Poe, 'The Poetic Principle', cited in Jackson, 'Lyric', *PEPP*, 461.

2. On literary fragments, see A. Slessarev, 'Fragment', *PEPP*. On postmodern theology as constructed out of fragments, see Kevin Vanhoozer, 'Preface' and 'Scripture and Tradition', in *The Cambridge Companion to Postmodern Theology*, ed. Kevin Vanhoozer (Cambridge: Cambridge University Press, 2003), xiv–v, 149–69 (157).

fragmentation just described. Firstly, the line gives the poem form by restricting the length of a phrase. Secondly, it fragments the flow of words in a way that shapes meaning. Thirdly, the poem hangs together on the intangible connections between lines.

The three aspects of the line-as-fragment just outlined structure a discussion of how constraint and brokenness can contribute to the formation of lyric coherence. The theme of constraint or curtailment is addressed through two contrary characteristics of poetic language: sparsity and density, as seen in Gillian Allnutt's reticent poetic and Geoffrey Hill's highly condensed style. Fragmentation as brokenness or disruption is addressed through the gaps between lines, which in Allnutt's apophatic poetic are the space in which the Spirit moves, but in Hill signify the end of breath, a place close to death. The fragmentary coherence of lyric is described as a product of parataxis, a poetic grammar that draws connections between one thought and the next not through logical discourse but through apposition and association. After discussing the fragment as a window into lyric intelligibility, the chapter concludes by introducing an alternative model of lyric coherence through the episodic poetry of Warsan Shire.

According to Charles Olson, the poetic line is measured by the length of a breath.[3] This detail sets up the theological theme of this chapter, which addresses the relationship between the poetic word and the breath-between-lines as a metaphor for human participation with the Spirit of God. It draws on the scriptural imagery of the Spirit as breath or wind in John 3.1-8, Luke 4.1-4 and Ezekiel 37.1-14, key passages that reimagine the *ruach* of Genesis 1.2 as a Spirit of rebirth, renewal and re-creation. Through a reflection on these passages, this chapter asks how a lyric grammar might seek to discern the presence of the Spirit of creation: of freedom, power and abundance, in human contexts of fragmentation: of limitation, brokenness and death.

This final chapter draws out a recurrent theme of this book: the need for a lyric theology that takes proper account of post-Romantic critiques of lyric and the modern transmutations of the genre. The first feature of lyricism to have come under scrutiny in this period is what Ezra Pound called *melopoeia*: the straightforward equivalence between beauty and truth or the music of language and its meaning. The second is the authority of the self-expressive 'I'.[4] In the discussions below, revisionist perspectives on lyric musicality and lyric expressivity are applied to the question of what a lyric theology might look like in and for a late-modern context. Accordingly, the poets discussed below are not unambiguously lyric poets. Allnutt has been classed among the modern 'expansions' and 'explosions' of

---

3. See Olson, 'Projective Verse', 242.

4. Geoffrey Hill discusses the loss of lyric *melopoeia* in 'Envoi (1919)', in *Collected Critical Writings*, ed. Kenneth Haynes (Oxford: Oxford University Press, 2009), 565–80 (567–8) [hereafter *CCW*], 249.

English lyric tradition, while Hill's work is often overtly anti-lyrical.[5] Shire adopts a more straightforwardly expressive voice, but her work stretches lyric conventions in other ways through its embeddedness in social and audio-visual media.

These poets' often ambivalent relationship to lyric tradition is in many ways characteristic of the transformations of the English lyric in the twentieth century. The status of the English lyric in modernity has been one of fragmentation, disrupted by the anti-lyric reactions of modernism and the avant-garde.[6] These developments have been associated in the popular imagination with the effects of the First World War. While anti-lyricism predates this event, it is nevertheless appropriately interpreted as a poetics of trauma, rupture and fragmentation.[7] This chapter engages with the continuities and disruptions of English lyric tradition in a late modern context, exploring how the fragmentations of lyric might shed light on a theological grammar that can do poetic justice to the dissolution of certainty, the senselessness of suffering and the traumas of experience.

'The wind bloweth ...': Reticence and spaciousness in Gillian Allnutt's lyric fragments

Gillian Allnutt (b. 1949) is a feminist spiritual poet who characterizes her own work as short, difficult and fragmented.[8] Her poems reflect the influence of modernist and radical poetics in their collage of voices, their partial quotations and obscure allusions. Her work also conveys a sometimes intensely personal lyric voice concerned with the inner lives of ordinary people, alongside an unconventional musicality that has been described as a kind of avant-garde lyricism.[9] This section focusses on the strikingly short lines and exaggerated gaps and spaces in two of Allnutt's later collections: *Indwelling* (2013) and *Wake* (2018). It examines the

---

5. On Allnutt, see Fiona Sampson, *Beyond the Lyric: A Map of Contemporary British Poetry* (London: Chatto & Windus, 2012), chap. 4. On Allnutt's adaptations of lyric tradition, see, *e.g.*, Gillian Allnutt, 'Lullaby', in *Indwelling* (Hexham: Bloodaxe, 2013), 50, which echoes the medieval lullaby carol, or 'Abut', in ibid., 24, which is a Shakespearean sonnet. On Hill's critical relationship with lyric tradition, see Andrew Michael Roberts, 'Introduction', in *Strangeness and Power: Essays on the Poetry of Geoffrey Hill*, ed. Andrew Michael Roberts (Swindon: Shearsman, 2020), 7–15 (13).

6. On modernism as an anti-lyric reaction, a theory promoted by Olson and Adorno, see P. Nicholls, 'Modernism', *PEPP*, 890–4 (especially 891 on the dissolution of the lyric 'I', 892 on the fragmentary and paratactic construction of poetry and 893 on poetic 'difficulty').

7. See Andrew Palmer and Sally Minogue, 'Modernism and First World War Poetry: Alternative Lines', in *The Cambridge Companion To Modernist Poetry*, ed. Alex Davis and Lee M. Jenkins (Cambridge: Cambridge University Press, 2015), 227–52.

8. Gllian Allnutt, interview by Geoff Hattersley, *Writers Aloud* (Royal Literary Fund, 13.09.2018), episode 185, audio, https://www.rlf.org.uk/showcase/wa_episode185/.

9. Sampson, *Beyond Lyric*, 269.

reticent poetic and the resulting spaciousness of Allnutt's fragmentary lyrics, as a model of lyric invocation, a site for discernment of the indwelling and interrupting wind of the Spirit and a picture of human participation in God.[10]

Reticence: Making space for breath

Allnutt's poetry is characterized by reticence or a holding-back of words. Her poetic process involves contemplative practices that engender a poetry which emerges *out of* silence, but this poetry also leans back *into* silence. The poems 'infather' and '"love to burn him down like belsen"', for example, have lines that progressively decrease in length down to a single word.[11] The poem 'silence' in *Wake* is made up of only one line and three words. In this poem, the religious term 'discalceate' (which usually refers to a barefoot friar) seems to describe silence as poetry stripped of all accessories, the height of the poetic vocation.[12] In these short lines and short poems, silence appears not only as the origin but the essence of poetry.

In many of Allnutt's poems, the excision of extraneous words is so acute that what remains is ungrammatical English. The poem 'Abut', for example, opens with the short and apparently nonsensical line 'Am but'.[13] The only way this line could make grammatical sense is as expanded into the phrase 'I am, but …'. As the poem proceeds, it becomes apparent that the 'I' has been cut out of the poem completely. The verb forms continue in the first-person singular, with half of the lines beginning with the word 'Am', but the pronoun is consistently omitted. The omission of the 'I' models a kind of apophatic poetic whereby the essence of the poem lies outside of the words. The reader cannot help but hold the absent yet grammatically essential 'I' in the mind's eye, or in the act of inhalation at the beginning of each line.[14] The absent 'I' is not a denial of subjectivity; instead it is held in the silence out of which the words proceed. The words on the page consequently appear like apophatic statements: contradictions and equivocations that gesture beyond themselves. Through this device the poem draws the reader ever further into the realms of the unknown and the unspoken, encapsulated in the question: '[who] am [I]'?

In this poem, the shortness of the line does not narrow down interpretation but opens up space around the words, through which silence can speak. The words

---

10. The term 'Spirit' is capitalized here in acknowledgement of its capitalization in the two epigraphs for *Indwelling*, but her work should not be read through a solely Christian lens. Allnutt has commented on the range of spiritual influences on her work, including Catholicism, Anglicanism, the Baptist church, Quakerism, Buddhism and shamanism. See Allnutt, interview, *Writers Aloud*.

11. Allnutt, *Indwelling*, 65–6.

12. Ibid., 'silence', *Wake* (Hexham: Bloodaxe, 2018), 41.

13. Ibid., 'Abut', *Indwelling*, 24, line 1.

14. On the inescapability of the I, see the discussion of Clare above, pp. 107–8.

that remain on the page appear like the kernel of a thought, a smallness that may be unfurled in the reader's imagination. In the case of 'Abut', a world of reflection is opened up by the two-word, two-syllable, ungrammatical statement 'Am but'. This could, for example, be an allusion to Clare's famous oxymoronic self-declarations: the first line of 'I am' ('I am – yet what I am none cares or knows') or the last line of the sonnet 'I feel I am' ('But now I only know I am – that's all').[15] Like Clare's 'I feel I am', Allnutt's poem is a sonnet of sorts, in fourteen lines, and both Allnutt and Clare appear to define the self through contradiction, but while Clare's 'I am' poems rest upon the sole assurance of the individual's existence, in Allnutt's poem, existence is no sure foundation for self-knowledge. Where Clare ends with a kind of hope, or at least desire, for an 'untroubled' solitary existence, Allnutt's poem concludes with the same brief contradictory self-denial: 'Am, but'.[16] Set against Clare's lonely Romantic vision, Allnutt's poem appears to do away with the lyric 'I' in favour of a late modern account of an unstable and uncertain subjectivity.[17]

The relationship between word and silence in these poems models a poetic invocation that does not call out, importuning the muse to speak, but instead draws back, crafting a space in which the sound of the Spirit may be heard. The poem 'prayer' provides a striking example of this poetic at work. This poem could be read like Herbert's 'Prayer (I)' as a series of descriptions of prayer. The first three lines, 'impromptu/ of the hour/ the heart', certainly could be read in this way, although the rest of the poem is more obscurely allusive.[18] These lines are brief and intense, unlike Herbert's measured iambic pentameter, with most only one or two words long. The extreme fragmentation of the language contrasts with the poem's seven lines, a number that often symbolizes fullness or completeness. There is a divergence between the highly reticent lines and the plenitude suggested by the poem's overall form. This creates a space around the poem through which the reader might be drawn into a space of contemplation, so that the poem becomes itself a prayer.

Like the hazelnut of Julian of Norwich's vision, which contains all of creation, Allnutt's fragments are vaster than they appear.[19] The reticence embodied in Allnutt's short lines creates spaciousness: an ambivalent space of ambiguity, an apophatic space of unknowing or a space into which the Spirit is invited to speak. To read these brief utterances as poetic invocations provides a counterpoint to a masculine or colonialist language of the poetic word as probing or even 'raiding' the silence of God.[20] Invocation as in-breathing models a creative engagement with

---

15. Clare, 'I am', line 1; ibid., 'I feel I am', line 14.

16. Ibid., 'I am', line 17; Allnutt, 'Abut', line 14.

17. On the postmodern deconstruction of the concept of a single and stable 'self', see John Webster, 'The Human Person', in *Postmodern Theology*, ed. Vanhoozer, 222–3.

18. Allnutt, 'prayer', *Wake*, 42, lines 1–3.

19. Julian of Norwich is a key influence on Allnutt, cited in several poems in *Indwelling* and *Wake*, including 'the child', 'Shore', *Indwelling*, 21, 35, 'The Word Quire', *Wake*, 44.

20. See the discussion of Mark S. Burrows above, p. 19.

the in-spiring Spirit that is not an assertion of agency or an attempt to control, nor is it merely a drawing back into silence, but an intentional making of space like the expansion of the chest in the act of breathing, confident in the coming presence of the Spirit who is invoked.

'So is every one that is born ...': The Spirit within the words

Allnutt's short lines in *Indwelling* and *Wake* draw attention to the spaces around and within the poem as spaces in which the Spirit moves, an interpretation supported by the recurring imagery of the wind in these collections. For example, the Hebrew term for wind or spirit, '*ruach*', is used as the opening line of the poem 'music'.[21] With reference to the driving gales of the Northumbrian coast, 'lindisfarne: the roughs' describes both 'priory' and 'prayer' as spaces that 'the wind blows through'.[22] In '"the wind like glass"', the wind takes on an epiphanic quality, conveying a fleeting 'clarity/ which too will pass'.[23] A guiding hermeneutic for these passages is provided by the opening epigraph to *Indwelling*, which cites the Authorised Version of John 3.8. This reference to the 'wind [that] bloweth where it listeth', an uncontainable and unpredictable force, provides a counterpoint to the title, which in its literal sense of *In-dwelling* is suggestive of the interior life and the domestic sphere. The Spirit of this collection is the irrepressible Spirit of life who dwells in the human being, a power and freedom also evoked in the second epigraph from Naomi Littlebear's 'You Can't Kill the Spirit', a feminist anthem notably used in the Greenham Common protests in the 1980s.[24]

In *Indwelling*, this infinite Spirit, this unappreciated freedom and power found within the narrow space of a life, is explored through poems about the interiors of mundane objects. *Indwelling* reflects on a range of everyday insides that possess a significance well beyond their ordinary uses. The title of the section 'Stoup', for example, could be a reference to an ordinary jar or cup or a basin for holy water, or to the act of bending in work or prayer, oppression or humility.[25] The poem 'his cello' associates the 'abyss, embodied' of the musical instrument with the creative darkness of the womb. The allusion in the following line ('who would not have been abhorred by it') to the carol 'O Come All Ye Faithful' ('Lo, he abhors not the virgin's womb') connects the enfleshment of the human soul or spirit with the Christological theme of the incarnation.[26] 'Elspeth' draws on the myth that 'a saint came out of an egg' to imagine the soul as a 'laid' egg. This poem asks whether the

---

21. Allnutt, 'music', *Wake*, 34, line 1.
22. Ibid., *Wake*, 13, line 21.
23. Ibid., 'the wind like glass', *Indwelling*, 69, lines 3–4. The line comes from Joseph Ceravolo's brief poem, 'Non-Spatial', in *Collected Poems*, ed. Rosemary Ceravolo and Parker Smathers (Middletown, CT: Wesleyan University Press, 2013), 251.
24. See Anon., *The Greenham Song Book*, online, www.yourgreenham.co.uk, 4.
25. Allnutt, *Indwelling*, 33.
26. Ibid., 67, lines 5–6; *cf.* Frederick Oakeley, 'O Come All Ye Faithful' (1841), verse 2.

soul might be painted, suggesting perhaps that, like an egg, the substance of the human being is hidden inside, not available to view.[27]

This imagery addresses feminist themes of liberation and empowerment, particularly in poems about the home. The poem 'stoup' combines allusions to female domestic labour ('the worn towel on a woman's arm') with suggestions of a rich interior life (a 'heart, whole, hollowed').[28] 'The Quiet Parisian' describes the vase of flowers in the painting 'A Corner of the Artist's Room in Paris', by Gwen John, as 'summer in a jamjar', evoking a feminine space of light and warmth.[29] This ostensibly commonplace, sweet image conveys a sense of expansiveness, just as a posy might invoke the summer, or a glass jar magnify the sunlight. The imagery in these poems celebrates the strength, beauty and power contained in the small and quotidian, affirming by extension the hidden magnitude of underappreciated lives.[30]

These poems evoke a Spirit who not only dwells in the expanse around the lines but invests the words with a magnitude that is all the greater for their smallness on the page. This effect is enhanced by a consistent use of double spacing, which gives weight to the words visually, by widening the gaps between lines and expanding the poem to take up more space on the page, and aurally, by slowing down the pace of reading. This effect is of particular importance in poems about the home, where the expanded space between lines becomes a material representation of an interior world as-it-were exploded and made open to view. This effect can be seen in the three-line poem 'drawing', where the opening reference to a 'little saucepan set' evokes a homely scene that then opens out into a meditation on the nature of love.[31] The poem 'her dwelling' similarly imagines the home of the woman depicted in the painting *La Femme au Chapelet* by Paul Cézanne, as a window into her interior life: 'the sill as conscience clear'.[32] Both of these poems invest the mundane with significance, their sparse lines given weight by the expanse of space around them.

Space inhabits these poems as Spirit indwells the body. They are, like Lindisfarne Priory, or like the name of Paul Cézanne's house alluded to in one poem, a 'habitation of the wind'.[33] The significance of this imagery becomes apparent in the second poem called 'prayer' in *Wake*. This poem is a prayer of repentance, which seeks a transformation of 'the tent or tabernacle of the heart'. It concludes with a prayer that the heart might have 'only the wind/ for wall'.[34] Alluding in

---

27. Allnutt, *Indwelling*, 11, lines 1, 6.
28. Ibid., 46, lines 2, 4.
29. Ibid., 'The Quiet Parisian', *Indwelling*, 12, line 9. See also 'Morning Room', 'drawing', 'her dwelling' and 'stoup' in ibid., 13, 24, 36, 46.
30. Consider also, *e.g.*, 'Conversation with a Woman from the Orthodox Jewish Community', 'Her Stroke' and 'Daft Sister' in ibid., 15, 18, 25.
31. Allnutt, 'drawing', *Indwelling*, 14, line 1.
32. Ibid., 'her dwelling', ibid., 36, lines 1–2.
33. Ibid., 'the one', ibid., 68, line 3; ibid., 'lindisfarne: the roughs', *Wake*, 13.
34. Ibid., 'prayer', *Wake*, 49, lines 5, 7–8. See also the note in ibid., 71.

the previous line to the situation of asylum seekers in Calais, who live 'À l'abri [de rien]' (sheltered by nothing) this is an appeal for a love without borders or boundaries. The poem challenges the reader to aspire to a more spacious existence that is open to others and to the world. The final line tails off swiftly into silence as if the words are carried away by the wind, the boundaries between poem, world and Spirit already dissolved, the prayer already answered.

Allnutt's creative engagement with the white page in *Indwelling* models a poetic spaciousness: a breaking-open of words and a breaking-apart of lines through which the infinity of space is incorporated into the poem, the circumambient air infused into the gaps. In his commentary on the Gospel of John, David F. Ford describes the Spirit of John 3.8 as 'pervasive and surprising as the wind', as 'abundance' and 'uncontainability'.[35] Allnutt's fragmented lyrics present a picture of such freedom, extensity and abundance present amid the constraints of life. As such, the fragmentations of her poetry are not so much an acknowledgement of the limits of words as transformative spaces that foster silence for contemplation, room for interpretation, food for imagination and scope for transformation, open to the possibilities of creative participation with the wind beyond words.

'You hear the sound of it': The Spirit between lines

Through this creative interplay of word and wind, a poem is constructed out of lines, a whole out of fragments. This is seen perhaps most clearly in the paratactic structure that shapes the transitions between lines.[36] Parataxis is a grammar, often used in poetry, whereby the connection between one thought and the next is left implicit. Standard definitions illustrate parataxis through a succession of short and distinct, yet interconnected, phrases such as '*veni, vidi, vici*'.[37] Without conjunctions such as 'so', 'but' or 'if' to build a logical argument, phrase is piled on top of phrase, line on top of line. Sense is made instead through the resonances between distinct but interconnected segments – what Olson, following Aristotle, called 'the way beads are strung on a string one bead and thread after another'.[38]

In Allnutt's fragmentary poems, the transitions between lines are sometimes marked by an em-dash (—) that could almost be read as a visible representation of the string that connects the beads.[39] Used at the end of a fragmentary phrase,

---

35. David F. Ford, *The Gospel of John: A Theological Commentary* (Ada, MI: Baker Academic, 2021), 7, 90.

36. Heffelfinger has described parataxis in Hebrew poetry as a paradoxical way of constructing unity out of fragments, an alternative to narrative chronology and discursive logic, in *I Am Large, I Contain Multitudes*, 32, 43.

37. J. Burt, 'Hypotaxis and Parataxis', *PEPP*, 650–1.

38. Olson, 'The Projective, in Poetry and in Thought and the Paratactic' (1965), cited in *Collected Prose*, 424.

39. Sometimes the em-dash is the sole punctuation mark in a poem. This is true of 'Mother', 'Grief' and 'The Word *Quire*' discussed below.

the em-dash not only bridges the gap between lines but draws attention to the incompleteness of the line and gestures toward the space in between lines.[40] In the poem 'Mother', which contains a fragmentary account of the Annunciation, the em-dashes at the end of lines mark the transition from one half-formed thought to another. They mark out space on the page, inscribing the gulf between lines as a sound of wonder ('his wings, his grandeur —' (referring to Gabriel)), of memory ('whilom, whilom —') and of regret ('what was lost to her —').[41] The poem hangs together on these resonating silences, which evoke the overshadowing Spirit through a drawing-out of substance from the space between lines.

In 'The Word *Quire*', the transitional space between lines similarly evokes the creative abyss behind and between words as a space through which the sound of the Spirit might be heard. This poem is an invocatory prayer for inspiration, its title referring to a blank piece of parchment, ready to be written upon. Its opening appeal to the Spirit to 'come ... from I know not where —' cuts off with an em-dash that appears to inscribe the force of the poet's desire. It is followed by a fragmentary quotation from John 3.8 that reads almost like a reply. This concludes with the same word '*where* —', evoking a sense of mystery.[42] The shifting voice in this stanza crafts a kind of call-and-response between poet and Spirit, woven into a poetic unity that incorporates the silences of yearning and of possibility into the substance of the poem.

In some cases, Allnutt uses an em-dash to cut short a cliché, appearing to choose silence over the banality of convention, but also opening a path for a thought to go in a new direction. In the poem 'Earth', in the line 'Hard of —', the em-dash fragments the cliché 'hard of hearing'. It redirects the poem towards the following lines, which describe a mind that is deaf to the sounds of the earth: 'The lucid talk of stones' and the roaring of the sea. Exploding the deafening 'helmet' of conventional language, the em-dash that fragments the cliché jolts the reader out of the stupor of expectation to really listen for the sounds of creation, the witness of the earth.[43]

There is a similar use of the em-dash in the poem 'Grief' in *Wake*.[44] This poem imitates the faltering of a grief-stricken voice with brief stanzas made up of one or two lines. It begins with the poetic subject having stopped their car, 'blinded by —'. This sentence does not need to be completed, since the reader already knows how it might end. The subject of the poem may be blinded by grief, by tears or by the light of oncoming headlights. In leaving the sentence unfinished, all these interpretations may be valid. At the same time, each of these possible endings is a cliché that the poet might wish to avoid. The use of the em-dash simultaneously

---

40. Consider also the use of the em dash at the end of lines in 'my mother, her brother' and 'Shore', *Indwelling*, 19, 35.
41. Allnutt, 'Mother', *Indwellng*, 20, lines 6, 9–10.
42. Ibid., *Wake*, 44, lines 2, 4.
43. Ibid., 'Earth', *Indwelling*, 34, lines 2, 4, 3. Line 4 is an allusion to Luke 19.40.
44. Ibid., *Wake*, 15.

evokes these meanings and leaves them unspoken. Implicitly highlighting the inadequacy of words, and perhaps calling for a new vocabulary of grief, this line-ending unveils the space between lines as a space of multiplicity and of creative possibility.

The em-dash in line 1 evokes a sense of disconnection from the world, but it also connects to the following line, which continues in a similar vein. 'Worlds in their otherness thundered by —' presumably refers to the other cars on the road. In this line, the dash inscribes a pause, amplifying the silence into a white noise that enhances the distance between the speaker and the other worlds contained within each car as it passes. This sense of isolation contrasts with the line 'by one another' in the next stanza, which for the first time forms a complete phrase out of the word 'by'. This line is the first suggestion that the subject of the poem is not alone; an intimation confirmed in the final line where the plural form of the verb '[we] were' is used instead of the singular '[I] was'. Despite the distancing effect of the line-breaks, the grief of the poem is, it turns out, a grief shared. By the end of the poem this sharing appears to have led the speaker out of a state of paralysis and back on to the road. The em-dashes in 'Grief' give substance to the unspeakable and weave difficult silences into the fabric of the poem. These line-endings are signs of brokenness, disconnection and distress, but they also help to lead the poem towards its resolution. By incorporating the silence-between-lines into the body of the poem, like the string on which the beads are strung, this poem forms a whole out of fragments, bridging the gap between the spoken and the unspeakable through the mysterious grammar of parataxis.

In Allnutt's later poetry the shortness of the line, the large gaps and ineffable connections between lines, all confront the relationship between the poetic word and the space that surrounds it. Modern theological poetics has engaged with this space as a silence out of which poetry comes and to which it might aspire, in Karl Rahner's terms the 'abyss … in which all possible sounds are still gathered up'.[45] Silence has a long theological history, in the mysticism of apophasis, but George Steiner has described the *poetic* appeal to silence as a peculiarly modern phenomenon, which finds in the negation of the word the sublimity of the inexpressible, the unsaying of the unspeakable and a resistance to the tyranny of the prosaic.[46] There is much to be gleaned from a theological poetic of word and silence, but the theo-lyric reflection explored here invites instead a consideration

---

45. Karl Rahner, 'Poetry and the Christian', in *Theological Investigations*, vol. 4 (New York: Crossroad, 1974), 358–9. See also Oliver Davies, 'Soundings: Towards a Theological Poetics of Silence', in *Silence and the Word: Negative Theology and Incarnation*, ed. Oliver Davies and Denys Turner (Cambridge: Cambridge University Press, 2002), 201–22; Rachel Muers, *Keeping God's Silence: Towards a Theological Ethics of Communication* (Oxford: Blackwell, 2004).

46. George Steiner, 'Silence and the Poet [1966]', in *Language and Silence: Essays 1958–1966* (London: Faber & Faber, 2010), 57–77 (69–71, 77–8, 80).

of the dynamic coinherence of word and breath in the fragmented lyric.[47] Unlike the dualism of word and silence, the lyric partnership of word and breath reads the space around the line not as an absence of words but as a movement of breath, a sign of presence and a vital component of the voice. The plenitude of the space around the line becomes a part of the poem, both affirming and expanding the materiality of the word.

Fragmentation in Allnutt's poetry is not only a sign of a retreat into silence but also a model of the creative participation of word with Spirit. Allnutt's poems make space for breath, working intentionally with the broken edges of words and creatively with the space that surrounds them, weaving the fragments of existence together to make a whole without a false or forced unity, just as a poem can be made of lines, or a life out of breaths. The wind that is breathed into the lungs, absorbed as oxygen in the blood (which Allnutt describes as "umbilical" breath) and expelled through the voice, is both other to and one with the body.[48] Even so, the wind of the Spirit might be imagined as woven into the fabric of the word while remaining transcendent to it.[49] This theo-lyric of the Spirit-as-breath might inform a grammar of participation with the Spirit that acknowledges the indwelling of the expansive Spirit in mundane and difficult realities and explores the transformative possibilities of the Spirit-inspired life.

'Can these bones live?'[50] Density, parataxis and breathturn in Geoffrey Hill

Geoffrey Hill (1932–2016) has often been hailed one of the greatest English poets of his time.[51] He represents the evolution of religious poetry in the generation after T. S. Eliot, demonstrating an often-ambivalent relationship to Christianity that is perhaps most faithful when it addresses its difficulties with faith.[52] Hill adopted a rigorous ethical stance towards language, reflected in a 'difficult' style that makes his poetry, for some, virtually unreadable.[53] For a poet who grew up during the

---

47. On Charles Williams' notion of the coinherence between human beings, and between humanity and God, see Paul S. Fiddes, *Charles Williams and C.S. Lewis: Friends in Co-Inherence* (Oxford: Oxford University Press, 2021), chaps 4, 5 and 15. On the creative partnership of word and breath in the act of creation, see above, pp. 18–19.

48. Allnutt, 'music', *Wake*, 34.

49. On the proximity of the imagery of Word and Spirit in the Gospel of John, see Ford, *John*, 50.

50. Ezekiel 37.3.

51. See, *e.g.*, Christopher Ricks, 'Geoffrey Hill and 'The Tongue's Atrocities', *The Times Literary Supplement*, no. 3978 (30 June 1978): 743; Harold Bloom, 'The Survival of Strong Poetry (on Geoffrey Hill): Introduction to Somewhere Is Such a Kingdom', *The American Poetry Review* 4, no. 4 (July/August 1975): 18.

52. Ibid., 19.

53. On Hill's three kinds of difficulty, see Roberts, *Strangeness and Power*, 14.

Second World War, this difficulty provided a way of coming to terms not just with the horrors of this period but with its aftermath, interrogating the complex ethics that surround the memorialization of war in poetry.

Hill's poetry reveals a complex engagement with lyricism that, like Allnutt's, illustrates the transmutations of the religious lyric to meet a changing sociopolitical and ecclesial-theological context. Inspired by the modernism of Eliot, W. B. Yeats and Ezra Pound, Hill is known for an impersonal style, a multi-layered, unreliable and frequently self-sabotaged poetic voice.[54] A resistance to lyric is alluded to in poems such as 'Doctor Faustus', which rejects the 'innocent' or 'overheard' voice, in reference to John Stuart Mill's famous characterization of lyric poetry.[55] Hill's critique of expressive poetry could be caustic, his resistance to the 'lyric cry' sometimes entertainingly overstated, as in the scathing lines, 'Lyric cry lyric cry lyric cry, I'll/ give them lyric cry!' from poem 'XXX' in *The Orchards of Syon*, where repetition creates a nonsensical, though pleasingly musical almost-palindrome.[56] While there is a strong prejudice against lyric expressivity in his work, there also appears an inability to move conclusively beyond the lyric voice.[57] Hill worked closely with lyric forms such as the elegy, sonnet, song and pastoral. Adapting these genres to a new context, he embraced the constraints of form as, in Yeats' terms, the 'plough' that forces the writer deeper, turning over the hard soil of language to produce a harvest.[58] Hill engaged with the issue of lyric subjectivity in his famous essay 'Poetry as "Menace" and "Atonement"', where he conceded that:

> However much and however rightly we protest against the vanity of supposing [poetry] to be merely the 'spontaneous overflow of powerful feelings', poetic utterance is nonetheless an utterance of the self, the self demanding to be loved …

Hill goes on to discuss how poetry that is thus painfully aware of itself may be a means of the atonement of language, defined as a literal 'at-one-ment', whereby 'selfhood may be made at-one with itself'.[59]

---

54. Ibid., 9.

55. Hill, 'Doctor Faustus', *For the Unfallen*, 31. All citations from the poetry of Geoffrey Hill are taken from *Broken Hierarchies: Poems 1952–2012*, ed. Kenneth Haynes (Oxford: Oxford University Press, 2013).

56. Ibid., 'XXX', *The Orchards of Syon*, 380, lines 18–19.

57. See, *e.g.*, Hill's lecture as Oxford Professor of Poetry, 'Poetry and "the Democracy of the Dead"' (Oxford University, 3 December 2013), audio, http://media.podcasts.ox.ac.uk/engfac/general/mt13-hill-lecture.mp3, 0:00-10:00.

58. Ibid., 'A Postscript on Modernist Poetics', *CCW*, 565–80 (567–8). On Hill as a modern 'formal' poet, see Jon Silkin, 'The Poetry of Geoffrey Hill', *The Iowa Review* 3, no. 3 (Summer 1972): 108–28.

59. Geoffrey Hill, 'Poetry as "Menace" and "Atonement"', *CCW*, 3–20 (15–17, 19).

This section discusses Hill's poetry not as a rejection but rather an atonement of lyric, asking what resources it might provide for a lyric theology that seeks to address the traumas of history. Turning first to his elegies on the Second World War in *For the Unfallen* (1959) and *King Log* (1968), and then to the much later collection *The Orchards of Syon* (2002), it examines three features of Hill's poetry that engage with the limits of the poetic line: 'density' within the line, parataxis between lines and *atemwende* or the turn of breath at the end of the line. It finds in Hill's dense style, his heaping up of words and his embracing of breathlessness a resistance to and transformation of the natural rhythms of breath that have been defined throughout this book as a rule of lyric form. The motif of the Spirit as breath or wind is likewise re-examined through engagement with Hill's dense, anti-lyric poetic, which appears to pursue breathlessness, crying 'Against the burly air' of the Spirit of Genesis 1.2 and finding solidarity underground with 'The bones that cannot bear the light'.[60] Through a reflection on the miracle of the dry bones in Ezekiel 37.1-14, the section concludes with an exploration of how a poetry that is invested in the materiality of words – in body, blood and soil, and which embraces the proximity of life to death – might provide an alternative grammar for the discernment of the Spirit of life – of creation, re-creation, transformation, resurrection or rebirth – in contexts of fragmentation, failure and death.

Density: Poetry as memorial for the dead

One of the most frequently mentioned features of Hill's poetry is that it is 'difficult'.[61] Hill embraced the term, which for him did not signify elitism or obscurantism, but an ethical approach to poetry inspired by modernism. Hill was a post-war poet who took seriously Adorno's famous declaration that 'to write lyric poetry after Auschwitz is barbaric'.[62] He maintained that 'tyranny requires simplification', seeing 'difficult' poetry as a moral as well as an aesthetic choice.[63] According to Eliot, poetic difficulty 'dislocates' language so that it can address the 'complexities' of modern life.[64] In taking up this challenge, Hill sought to do poetic justice not just to modernity but to life in general, explaining in one notable interview that:

---

60. Ibid., 'Genesis', *For the Unfallen*, lines 1, 46. On Hill's investment in materiality, see Bloom, 'Strong Poetry', 19–20.

61. On the charge of obscurantism in Hill, see, *e.g.*, William Wootten, *The Alvarez Generation: Thom Gunn, Geoffrey Hill, Ted Hughes, Sylvia Plath, and Peter Porter* (Liverpool: Liverpool University Press, 2020), 197–8.

62. Theodor Adorno, *Prisms* (Cambridge, MA: MIT Press, 1981), 28.

63. Geoffrey Hill, 'The Art of Poetry No. 80', interview by Carl Phillips, *The Paris Review* 154 (Spring 2000), online, https://www.theparisreview.org/interviews/730/the-art-of-poetry-no-80-geoffrey-hill.

64. See ibid., 'Envoi (1919)', *CCW*, 258–9; T. S. Eliot, 'The Metaphysical Poets', in *Selected Essays*, 3rd edn (London: Faber & Faber, 1951), 289.

> Human beings are difficult. We're difficult to ourselves, we're difficult to each other. And we are mysteries to ourselves, we are mysteries to each other. One encounters in any ordinary day far more real difficulty than one confronts in the most "intellectual" piece of work.[65]

One of the ways in which poetry might do justice to the difficulty of life is through what Hill termed 'density'. In simple terms, density is a consequence of the constraints of poetic form. The limitations of the line compress language, resulting in a conciseness that exploits the multiplicity of meaning in a word. By condensing language, density can unearth a surprising depth and magnitude in the short poem, opening-up layers of ambiguity and levels of meaning.

Hill advocated density as not only a poetic device but an ethical and theological concept. His account of density in 'Poetry as "Menace" and "Atonement"' drew on Karl Barth and Simone Weil's notion of sin as gravity. He described 'the density of the medium' of language as the sedimented layers of meaning that words take on over time, a history not only of change but of corruption.[66] Density signifies the original sin of language but, according to Hill, 'it is at the heart of this "heaviness" that poetry must do its atoning work, this heaviness which is simultaneously the "density" of language and the "specific gravity of human nature"'. Poetry that 'goes deep' into the morass of language might atone for its debasement and misuse by bringing the past into conversation with the present, recovering forgotten senses of a word, or uniting its various and even conflicting senses.[67] Take, for example, Hill's first collection, *For the Unfallen*. The title is a play on Laurence Binyon's nationalistic elegy 'For the Fallen', written at the start of the First World War in 1914. The term 'unfallen' satirizes the elegiac function of poetry, perhaps suggesting that the survivors of war also need commemorating or implying that 'fallen' is not an appropriate term to refer to the dead.[68] The theological roots of this word, as a reference to a prelapsarian or even a redeemed state, raise parallel questions about who, if anyone, might be found innocent in the context of war. These various connotations are drawn together in a phrase designed to disrupt convention and challenge lazy conviction, as a way of highlighting, and in some sense atoning for, the failings of the poetry of war.

In a discussion of Charles Williams, Hill argued that poetry requires not only '"intensity"' but '"density", if necessary as heavy as lead'.[69] Lead was often used in the

---

65. Hill, 'Art of Poetry'.

66. Hill was a particular admirer of the *Oxford English Dictionary*'s lists of the historical uses of terms. See 'Common Weal, Common Woe', *CCW*, 265–6.

67. Ibid., '"Menace" and "Atonement"', 15–17. On Hill's theology of language, see Matthew Sperling, 'The Theology of Language I: Sin and Fall', in *Visionary Philology: Geoffrey Hill and the Study of Words* (Oxford: Oxford University Press, 2014), chap. 5.

68. See also the final poem of the sequence, 'To the (Supposed) Patron', ibid., *For the Unfallen*, 35, line 17.

69. Ibid., 'Postscript on Modernist Poetics', *CCW*, 572.

lettering on war memorials, and Hill adopted a similarly dense poetic medium to simultaneously craft and critique the memorialization of war.[70] The double sonnet 'Two Formal Elegies: *For the Jews in Europe*' is one example: both an elegy and a critique of poetry about the Holocaust.[71] There is a heaviness to this poem, with its convoluted prose-like iambic pentameter, its imagery of bodies 'Subdued under rubble … In clenched cinders' and its diction stilted by a heavy use of alliteration.[72] The highly condensed and contradictory lines at the centre of the first sonnet get to the heart of this poem's critique of the poetry of war, describing the ambivalent power of elegy as a song that 'The wilderness revives,/ Deceives with sweetness harshness'.[73] In these lines, the exaggerated alliteration on the sibilants and the strong internal rhymes appear a deliberate overdoing of *melopoeia*, a cloying conjunction that parodies elegiac lyricism. The thought turns mid-sentence across the line, which is also a stanza-break between the sonnet's octave and sestet. The double space that spans the gap between the half-rhyming words 'revives' and 'deceives' draws attention to the two contradictory impulses of the elegy, whose song has life-giving power, but in its self-regarding prettiness also glosses over the horrors that it relates.

In the ironically titled 'A Pastoral', density not only delves into the depths of language but overturns the settled ground of the poem-as-memorial to judge the poet who may be more concerned with their own glorification than with doing justice to or for the dead.[74] The displacement of words begins with the title, which alludes to the rural idyll of the classical lyric genre, but here describes a field which is a field of battle, a place of horror. This is not a poem about the battlefield, but about the war poets who appear to traverse the remains of war like nurses, not caring for but 'assessing' the wounded, categorizing the horrors that they relate and 'cleansing' or sanitizing them 'with a kind of artistry'.[75] The war poets are represented in this poem by the figure of 'The Pities'. Hill's use of the term 'pity' here exemplifies his understanding of poetic density, which can be both wide-ranging and precise, relying not on 'random association' but on the poet's judicious selection and exclusion of the appropriate connotations of a word.[76] 'The Pities' in

---

70. On the use of lead on war memorials, see https://historicengland.org.uk/images-books/publications/conserving-war-memorials-inscriptions/heag274-conserving-war-memorials-inscriptions/. For a different analogy of Hill's poetic density, using stone not lead, *cf.* David Isaacs, 'Unfinished to Perfection: Geoffrey Hill, Revision, and the Poetics of Stone', *Textual Practice* (13 April 2021), https://doi.org/10.1080/0950236X.2021.1900377.

71. Hill, 'Two Formal Elegies', *For the Unfallen*, 16.

72. Ibid., lines 2–3. There is a similar overdoing of alliteration in the phrases 'Arrogant acceptance' and 'bedded with … blood' lines 6, 7.

73. Ibid., lines 8–9.

74. Ibid., 'A Pastoral', *For the Unfallen*, 32.

75. Ibid., lines 3–4. For a summary of this poem as a critique of war poetry, see Vincent Sherry, *The Uncommon Tongue: The Poetry and Criticism of Geoffrey Hill* (Ann Arbor: University of Michigan Press, 1987), 75–7.

76. Ibid., '"Menace" and "Atonement"', 16.

this poem are an allusion to Wilfred Owen's famous description of war poetry: 'the Poetry is in the pity'.[77] Hill, like Blake, disliked the virtue of pity, seeing it as a cold and detached piety that does not recognize its own complicity in evil, and so the Pities' work appears to be pitiless, a probing of the dead that is compared in line 2 to Doubting Thomas' finger in Christ's side.[78] The range of classical allusions in the poem, such as the 'Furies' of the following stanza who act as a counterpart to the 'Pities', suggests that this term may also be interpreted in its Aristotelian sense, as a feeling of sorrow that requires a degree of emotional distance.[79] A further classical allusion appears in the final lines as the scene shifts to a graveyard where laurel, whose wreaths crowned the great classical poets, 'darkens' the effigies of the dead.[80] There is a suggestion here that the commemoration of the war dead glorifies not them but the poet who writes about them, if anything obscuring rather than celebrating the fallen.

The densities of Hill's poetry of memorial have been described here as a means of critiquing the very poetic medium that he is working with. Read as a descriptor for commemorative poetry, density can also be seen in more constructive terms, as a disturbance of the past that opens up the hope of renewal. Density might involve digging into history as in the act of burial, a mining of material out of which to construct a memorial or an exhumation, turning over the soil of language to disrupt settled meanings and bring new ones to light. In Hill's early collections, the poetry of memorial is also described as a kind of resurrection, 'unearthing' Lazarus as it were 'from among the speechless dead'.[81] The power of this poetry is an ambivalent one. The elegy gives the dead breath and a voice, but just as a monument both makes the dead visible and buries them out of sight, so poetry has power to bring them to life while betraying their memory. 'Funeral Music' no. 8, for example, ventriloquizes the ghosts of the past who speak 'Not as we are but as we must appear', forced to conform to the poem's requirements.[82] Another poem in this collection reminds the reader that with resurrection comes judgement: 'we/resurrect and the judges come'.[83] The elegist who sets themselves up to judge the dead may also be judged *by* the dead.

Density in Hill serves difficulty, contributing to an equivocal elegiac that consistently emphasizes the limitations of poetry, which can never fully do justice to or for the dead. This dense poetic resists *melopoeia*, the sweetness that results

---

77. Wilfred Owen, 'Preface', *Poems* (2018/1918, Outlook Verlag), 3.

78. Hill, 'A Pastoral', lines 1–2; see Blake, 'The Human Abstract', *Songs of Experience*, line 1; Rowan Williams, 'The Standing of Poetry: Geoffrey Hill's Quartet', in *Geoffrey Hill: Essays on His Later Work*, ed. John Lyon and Peter McDonald (Oxford: Oxford University Press, 2012), 55–69 (60).

79. Aristotle, *Rhetoric* 2.8.2-14.

80. Hill, 'A Pastoral', line 17.

81. Ibid., 'History as Poetry', *King Log*, 61.

82. Ibid., 'Funeral Music' 8, *King Log*, 54, line 1.

83. Ibid., 'Domaine Public', *King Log*, 57, lines 14–15.

from an easy consonance of beauty and truth, music and meaning. It is not, however, a poetic that abandons beauty or truth. The beauty of a dense poetic is the 'difficult' beauty described by Pound and Yeats: complicated, multifaceted and hard-won.[84] It is a beauty perhaps alluded to in 'Coplas' no. 4, which describes poetry as crafted out of 'fragments': tears of grief hardened into 'semi-precious' jewels, that 'kindle[] ... into the light of appraisal' or poetic judgement.[85] Similar imagery is employed in poem 'XXX' in *Orchards*, where the speaker appears to be riding in a car, their tears refracting the light of streetlights and headlights into 'flowerets, faceted clusters' of colour, turning a singular brightness into a fragmentary, multifaceted beauty and a deeper truth, a 'Blurring [that] sharpens'.[86] Just so, the poet can take a simple word and unfurl its varied meanings, revealing a breadth and depth to language that is both truer and more beautiful than its conventional use.

Hill's poetic of density provides a counterpoint to the lyric poetic of breath that has dominated this study so far. Not an anti-lyricism so much as a chastened lyricism that works with the fragmentations of language in late modernity, it serves as a reminder that the resurrecting power of the Spirit is encountered first in the place of the dead. The Spirit of beauty and truth who is, in Tom Greggs' words, 'multiply intensely present within the creation', may yet be discerned by the one who digs into the compacted depths of history, language, sin and the self.[87] The Spirit is encountered here as the one who indwells the dense fragments of existence like the light that kindles the brilliance of a jewel, or that reveals the rainbow beauty even in a tear.

Parataxis as a heaping up of words

In 'Poetry as "Menace" and "Atonement"', Hill declares: 'the proof of a poet's craft is precisely the ability to effect an at-one-ment between the "local vividness" [of the line] and the "overall shape" [of the poem]'.[88] As introduced above, parataxis is one way in which the fragments of lines are drawn together into a poem. Parataxis leaves the connections between these fragments implicit, avoiding the conjunctions essential to the logic of prose. Instead, parataxis builds a poem a phrase at a time through devices of resonance, intensification and contrast. In a notable essay on the later poetry of Friedrich Hölderlin, Adorno describes the capacity of parataxis to 'connect things that are remote and unconnected', in a

---

84. See Pound's 'Pisan Cantos' and Yeats' 'The Tragic Generation', as cited in Hill, 'Envoi (1919)', 258–9.

85. Hill, 'Coplas' no. 4, *King Log*, 72, lines 5–6. A Copla is a Spanish love song popular in the 1930s–1940s, often addressing themes of illicit passion. The term 'appraisal' evokes both the valuation of jewels and poetry as an epideictic act of judgement on the past.

86. Ibid., 'XXX', lines 1, 2.

87. Greggs, cited in Ford, *John*, 89.

88. Hill, '"Menace" and "Atonement"', 12.

manner that stresses the holding together of difference over the construction of unity.[89] For Adorno, parataxis represents an epistemological humility that acknowledges the gaps between the fragments of human knowledge, 'as though it were hubris to fix the relationship [between things] … in propositional form'. This resistance to the smooth logic of prose is also a reaction against the idea of the poet as judge, somehow able to stand apart from events. Parataxis 'puts explication without deduction in the place of a so-called train of thought', rejecting the idea of poetry as an expression of the poet's mind. It foregrounds the materiality of words, favouring a reading of the poem that focusses not on (hidden) meaning but on (manifest) content and form. The result is a sense-making that Adorno describes as 'musiclike': not a sweet lyricism but an irregular music that is a 'rebellion against harmony. What is lined up in sequence, unconnected, is as harsh as it is flowing'.[90]

The disjunctive music of parataxis takes on particularly intriguing forms in Hill's much-anthologized lyric 'September Song', an elegy for a child killed in the Holocaust.[91] This is a poem made up of fragments, whose paratactic structure foregrounds the brokenness of the poetic voice. In the first two stanzas in particular, sense emerges through the cumulative resonances that develop as line proceeds line. The poem begins by addressing the dead child: 'Undesirable you may have been, untouchable/ you were not. Not forgotten/ or passed over'.[92] The first line hangs together on the resonance between the opening word 'Undesirable' and the closing word 'untouchable'. As the line turns, this resonance becomes a contrast, as it becomes clear that the child who was supposedly undesirable was only untouchable in a metaphorical and not a literal sense. The phrase 'Not forgotten' reads at first like an honouring of the dead, resonant of the cliché that someone may be gone, but not forgotten. The sense shifts with the phrase 'passed over' in the following line, as it becomes apparent that 'not forgotten' means that the child was not overlooked when people were rounded up to be sent to the concentration camps. Hill makes particular use of the line-breaks to convey this sense of a meaning that shifts under the reader's feet. Line-breaks can also convey the brokenness of language; the words 'patented/ terror', for example, use the line-break to highlight the oxymoronic nature of the phrase, which is both an accurate description of the business-like processes of the concentration camps and an evocation of the horror of programmatic genocide.[93]

---

89. Theodor Adorno, 'Parataxis: On Hölderlin's Late Poetry', in *Notes to Literature, European Perspectives: A Series in Social Thought and Cultural Criticism* (New York: Columbia University Press, 2019), 401.

90. Ibid., 396–7.

91. Geoffrey Hill, 'September Song', *King Log*, 44. For a discussion of this poem that emphasizes its subversion of the lyric I and its continuity with the elegiac tradition, see Kevin Hart, *Poetry and Revelation: For a Phenomenology of Religious Poetry* (London: Bloomsbury, 2017), 80–1, 84–6.

92. Hill, 'September Song', lines 1–3.

93. Ibid., lines 6–7.

This is a poem that seeks atonement. It is a sonnet of sorts, in fourteen irregular lines divided into five stanzas of differing lengths. The tone shifts with each stanza, as the poem attempts to produce a dirge appropriate to its subject. The first two stanzas, as illustrated above, are pithy and impersonal, conveying a self-critiquing voice that weighs every word. The lyric fragment of stanza 3 – '(I have made/ an elegy for myself it/ is true)' – interrupts this flow with a moment of apparent introspection that questions the whole project of the poem. The tone shifts again in the fourth stanza, towards an elegiac sweetness that conforms more closely to the easy lyricism of the title 'September Song'. It turns to the allusive autumnal imagery of ripening grapes, fading roses and autumn bonfires, along with a (more than subtly ironic) reference to the popular song 'Smoke Gets In Your Eyes'. The fifth stanza concludes the poem with a brief exclamatory declaration: 'This is more than enough', after which it descends abruptly into silence.[94] These shifts in tone are not unlike the *voltas* of the sonnet form, which follows the twists and turns of the speaker's mind, but there is no singular mind or voice, and no final resolution here.[95] The fragmented voices of this poem remain disconnected, but there is a kind of atonement in the very representation of the impossibility of speaking well about the Holocaust.

The poem turns on the intriguingly parenthetical third stanza.[96] The poem's subtitle, '*born 19.6.32 – deported 24.9.42*', is a kind of epitaph for the unnamed child, which reveals that they were born the day after Hill. The phrase 'I have made/ an elegy for myself', suggests that the self-regarding poet has noticed this fact, and has written the poem with themselves in mind. This passage also resonates with another poem about autumn, Gerard Manley Hopkins' 'Spring and Fall', which addresses a child (Margaret) who is grieving for the falling leaves, and concludes with the observation 'It is Margaret you mourn for'.[97] Hill's moment of apparent lyric self-examination encapsulates the implicit self-questioning of the poetic voice that persists throughout the poem, prompting the reader to question their own collusion in the self-pitying memorialization of the dead. This interpolated stanza is more than a hiatus, after which the sonnet might resume unaffected; it is an interruption that alters the trajectory of the poem.[98] This fragment is held together with the other stanzas, not in a unity but an at-one-ment, a holding-together

---

94. Hart has noted that this final phrase of 'September Song' could be a mantra for much of Hill's early poetry, in *Phenomenology*, 121.

95. There is also an echo of the traditional sonnet form in the structure of the stanzas, which are not divided into three quatrains and a coda, but three stanzas of 3 or 4 lines, with the three-line lyric aside, 'I have made/ an elegy for myself', interpolated into the gap between the second and third stanzas, and the final couplet replaced by a concluding single-line stanza divided into two sentences.

96. Hill, 'September Song', lines 8–10.

97. Gerard Manley Hopkins, 'Spring and Fall' (1880), line 15.

98. On a theology of interruption, see Lieven Boeve, *God Interrupts History: Theology in a Time of Upheaval* (New York: Continuum, 2007), 48, 103.

capable of incorporating even those voices, including the lyric 'I', that have been rejected. The result is a 'harsh' and difficult music, but one that seeks to do poetic justice to history and to the present.[99]

The structure of parataxis can flow smoothly like a stream, crafting a musical resonance that is held together through invisible bonds of association. In 'September Song', it is more like a piling up of line upon contradictory line. In an essay on Robert Burton, Hill cites an early-modern mistranslation of the Psalms that renders the title not as 'The booke of Praise' but 'The book of Heapes'.[100] Elegy might involve a heaping up of praise upon the dead, but it has been discussed here as more like a heaping up of earth, a construction of memory that conceals, reveals and recreates. 'At-one-ment' occurs in this equivocal space through the holding-together of disjointed fragments. Donald M. MacKinnon (1913–94), an important influence of Hill, modelled a fragmentary theological methodology that has been described, Like Hill's poetry, as 'difficult' and 'dense'.[101] MacKinnon described the at-one-ment of theology, the systematic work of 'synthesis', as not the task of the theologian but 'an act of God, a putting together of fragmentary lives and efforts in the resurrection of the dead'.[102] The grammar of parataxis can evoke the resonances between things, but can also provide a medium in which theology might hold together disjunction, difficulty and contradiction, without reaching for a false unity or premature synthesis. It is a discourse capable of acknowledging the limitations of human speech, while remaining open to the hope of resurrectio by which all things will be drawn together.

Atemwende: *The Spirit at the end of breath*

A collection of seventy-two 24-line poems in blank verse, *The Orchards of Syon* belongs to what is commonly seen as Hill's later period, which has been associated with a turn to a more pastoral lyricism and a more confessional, albeit self-satirizing, style.[103] Throughout this collection, Hill experiments with a word coined

---

99. Adorno, 'Parataxis', 396–7.

100. Hill, 'Keeping to the Middle Way', *CCW*, 297–315 (315).

101. John C. McDowell, 'Editor's Introduction: Donald Mackinnon: Extraordinary Theologian of the Ordinary', in *Philosophy and the Burden of Theological Honesty: A Donald MacKinnon Reader*, ed. John C. McDowell (London: Bloomsbury, 2011), vii–xvii (vii–x, xii). Andrew Bowyer describes difficulty in MacKinnon as a 'therapeutic' tool for opening up the complexity of difficult issues, *Donald MacKinnon's Theology: To Perceive Tragedy without the Loss of Hope* (London: Bloomsbury, 2021), 8–10. On MacKinnon's influence on Hill, see, *e.g.*, Hill, '"Menace" and "Atonement"', 8, 15.

102. Donald MacKinnon, 'Some Reflections on the Summer School' (1945), cited in Bowyer, *MacKinnon's Theology*, 6.

103. For an introduction to *Orchards*, see Stephen Romer, 'Laus et Vituperatio: *The Triumph of Love* (1998); *Speech! Speech!* (2000); *The Orchards of Syon* (2002)', *Études Anglaises* 71, no. 2 (2018): 191–206.

by the German-speaking Jewish poet Paul Celan: *atemwende* or 'turn-of-breath', which Celan describes as the essence of poetry. *Atemwende* might be interpreted as the transition between inhalation and exhalation – a moment of possibility – or of exhalation and inhalation – the point where the voice breaks or tails off at the end of a line.[104] As Celan described it in his 1960 speech 'The Meridian', *atemwende* is a silence that modern poetry reaches towards, not in a mystical or apophatic gesture but as part of a poetics of resistance, a kind of silent protest against the corruption of language.[105] *Atemwende* was the title of Celan's 1967 collection, marking a new phase in his poetry as it turned from beauty to truth, from lyricism to a more reticent, radical style that confronted the inadequacies of conventional poetry after the Holocaust.[106] *Atemwende* is the 'abyss' of silence out of which the true poem might emerge, a creative medium akin to the chaos of Genesis 1.2.[107]

Hill's poetry and criticism resonate with Celan's critique of conventional speech and his search for poetic justice. He experiments with a number of translations of *atemwende* in *Orchards* but, rather than a space of possibility or an act of resistance, his uses of the term cohere around a sense of breathturn as a faltering or failing of breath.[108] '[C]atch-breath', for example, gives a sense not of the plenitude of the primal abyss but of an exhausted mind at the end of itself, 'congested and vacant'.[109] Poem 'XXVIII' contains a particularly illuminating passage:

... *Atemwende*,
Celan almost at last gasp, *atemwende*, breath-glitch, say;[110]

Celan's 'last gasp', a reference to his apparent suicide in the Seine, raises the thought that the end of every exhalation might be a kind of dress rehearsal for death. The phrase 'breath-glitch, say' seems a performance of this end-of-breath,

---

104. Cf. Edmund de Waal's interpretation of breathturn as 'the strange moment of pause between breathing in and breathing out, when your sense of self is suspended and you are open to everything', in *The White Road: A Pilgrimage of Sorts* (London: Chatto & Windus, 2015), 388. For a fuller account of breathturn in Celan, see Antti Salminen, 'On Breathroutes: Paul Celan's Poetics of Breathing', *Partial Answers: Journal of Literature and the History of Ideas* 12, no. 1 (2014): 107–26.

105. Paul Celan, 'The Meridian', trans. Jerry Glenn, *Chicago Review* 29, no. 3 (1978): 29–40 (35–6).

106. See Pierre Joris, 'Introduction', in *Breathturn*, by Paul Celan, trans. Pierre Joris (Los Angeles: Sun & Moon Press, 1995), 15–17.

107. Celan, 'Meridian', 35–6.

108. Hill also translates the term as 'breath-ply', which could suggest density (*i.e.* 'ply' as a measure of thickness), extension as in to 'ply' a route or craft as in to 'ply' a trade, Hill 'XXXI', *Orchards*, 381, line 16.

109. Ibid., lines 16, 19.

110. Hill, 'XXVIII', 378, lines 16–18.

voicing a catch in the throat in the 'gl' of 'glitch' that suggests gagging or choking. The hyphenation of '*atem-/wende*' across the line creates a similar vocal glitch, a miniature fracturing of language. The use of enjambment here resists the natural pause to which the line aspires, drawing the breath out to its fullest degree by extending it into the following line. In this passage, *atemwende* seems a space not of possibility but of brokenness and vulnerability, the interruption or ending of breath. Celan describes it as a 'turn', evocative of the dance-like movement of the Greek chorus, but in this poem *atemwende* is more a moment of 'stasis' or 'Frozen/irresolution', evocative perhaps of the periods of writer's block that inhibited Hill's poetic output in earlier years.[111]

This poem presents a very different model of the relationship between word and breath to that found in Allnutt, one in which the poem might emerge as much out of the emptiness of expiration as the plenitude of inspiration. In the act of breathing, the pause between exhalation and inhalation might be felt in the body as a stillness, holding or tension, as tranquillity, anticipation or dread. Hill's use of *atemwende* in *Orchards* seems to point to this turn-of-breath as a space of fragility. It confronts the fear that the end of each exhalation could be not just the end of this breath but the end of all breaths and the end of a life. This is a space of weakness but also of power, out of which a poem can arise.

To do theology at this point, where the voice winds down at the end of the line, might mean to inhabit a similarly fragile space, embracing proximity to death as a place in which, too, the Spirit may be found. In MacKinnon's account of Luke 4.1-4, the Spirit appears as a driving wind that impels Jesus into the desert. MacKinnon wrote in relation to this passage that the Spirit is at work precisely in and through Christ's 'acceptance' of 'the sort of fragmentation of effort, curtailment of design, interruption of purpose, distraction of resolve that belongs to temporal experience'.[112] Rachel Muers draws on the same passage as part of a theological response to the climate crisis, interpreting the driving Spirit as a 'leading … into chaos and fragmentation, a summons towards death'.[113] Karen O'Donnell's account of the hope and hopelessness held together in the body of the miscarrying person similarly describes a breathing-with the Spirit who inhabits the womb, as the one who is both 'the Spirit of creation' and 'the Spirit of death'.[114] These theologies listen for the Spirit in the wind that, if only for a moment, takes one's breath away, accepting the realities of chaos, death, even despair, but also finding in these contexts a reason to hope.

---

111. Ibid., lines 21-2.

112. Donald Mackinnon, 'Incarnation and Trinity', 162-3, 154, cited in Rogers, *After the Spirit*, 163-8.

113. Rachel Muers, 'The Holy Spirit, the Voices of Nature and Environmental Prophecy', *Scottish Journal of Theology* 67, no. 3 (2014): 323-39 (336-7).

114. Karen O'Donnell, *The Dark Womb: Re-Conceiving Theology through Reproductive Loss* (London: SCM, 2022), 129, 189.

Soil, body, breath and breathlessness: Resurrection and the Spirit of life

This chapter has described Hill's poetry of memorial as an exhumation – delving into the soil of history, a re-membering – bringing fragments together, and a kind of resurrection – giving breath and voice to the dead.[115] Committed to the materiality of words, of soil, body and blood, and to confronting the realities of failure and death in language and history, Hill's chastened elegies model a poetic of resurrection that, brought into dialogue with Ezekiel 37.1-14, has important implications for a theo-lyric of the Spirit as the breath of life.

In Ezekiel 37.1-14, the breath of life is breathed into a multitude of the dead, as a sign of the returning of God's Spirit to God's people in exile (vv. 5-6, 9-10, 14). Despite the prominence of the imagery of breath, wind or s/Spirit in this passage, this is not a miracle of breath alone but of the body and the soil. It begins with the drawing together of fragments: of bones, sinews, flesh and skin, to form whole bodies (vv.6-8). In an otherwise sparse text, there is a strikingly sensory evocation of the sound of the dry bones rattling as they come together, a tumultuous noise like that of an earthquake or the rattling of weapons in battle (vv. 2, 7).[116] The vision concludes with the promise that the people of Israel will be brought up from their graves and returned to the land of Israel (vv. 12-13). There is no life without breath, but the rebuilding of broken bodies and the restoration of the land is more than a preface to the miracle of rebirth, it is a vital part of it.[117] This is a vision of resurrection that affirms body and soil, hoping for something more than a spiritual transformation.

There is a moment in this narrative when the prophet has invoked the Spirit to come and revive the dry bones, and the bodies of the slain have come back together, but there is still no breath in them (v. 8). This pause, when the prophet has called and the breath has not come, is a moment that confronts the finality of death and the fear of failure. This passage can be read as a moment of breathlessness, the end of the exhalation, at which point it is unclear whether another breath will be taken. It is swiftly revealed to be not the end of the story but only the end of the line, as the prophet calls again and the breath arrives. This is a moment that confronts the fear of death while remaining open to hope: the hope of the coming of another breath, a faith that ultimately there is more to be said. As a grammar for late modern theology, it models a discourse that addresses the unspeakable and goes to the limits of human experience, in Rowan Williams' terms, 'struggl[ing] towards a vision of the wholeness of the contradictory world'.[118]

---

115. In a discussion of the word 'disremembering', Hill describes the forgetting of the past in graphic terms as 'dismembering the memory'. Hill, 'Common Weal, Common Woe', *CCW*, 265–79 (266).

116. See Strong, 'raash', *Concordance*, #7494.

117. For a discussion of the theological significance of the land, see Willie James Jennings, *The Christian Imagination: Theology and the Origins of Race* (New Haven, CT: Yale University Press, 2010).

118. Williams, 'Poetic and Religious Imagination', 179, 185.

Poetry and theology in fragments: Introducing the episode

The fragment has a rich heritage in literature and theology, with a capacity to convey the peculiar beauty of the small and fragile, to lament or celebrate the disintegration of form and meaning, and to engender new kinds of coherence. The classical lyric inherited by modern Western culture largely survives in fragments of manuscripts. The lyrics of Sappho, most notably, consist only of tantalizing clusters of lines, half-lines and isolated words. The Romantics received such remnants as symbols of a golden age that they attempted to recreate by constructing literary fragments of their own. Like the follies that adorned the gothic landscapes of the time, Romantic aphorisms, epigrams and notes were not simply partial or incomplete works. As Schlegel described them, such fragments recreate a lost unity in 'miniature', crafting a reality 'entirely isolated from the surrounding world and perfect in itself'.[119] Coming to grips with a modern world that seemed to be disintegrating around him, Eliot described such fragments as 'shored against [the] ruins' of Western culture.[120] Modern Christian theology has been similarly concerned with the fragmentations of the moral and epistemological landscape.[121] Fragmentary theological methodologies not only reflect these realities of modern life, but acknowledge the limitations of a theological response to them.[122] Nicola Slee has described this epistemological humility as symptomatic of a distinctively British sensibility, which 'favours the small-scale, the incidental, the narrative and metaphorical' over the systematic.[123]

The significance of fragments lies not just in the disintegration of form, structure and meaning but in the way that fragments brought together breed new forms of coherence. One of the most influential voices in the field, American theologian David Tracy, has addressed fragmentation through the lens of liberation. According to Tracy, fragments are like shockwaves that 'shatter or fragment any false whole', tearing down the pretensions of totalizing systems and enabling the voices of the so-called marginalized or disenfranchised to be heard.[124] In his theological vision, fragments take on an eschatological significance as a sign of hope, not for a

---

119. Friedrich Schlegel, Athenaeum Fragment #206, *Philosophical Fragments*, trans. Peter Firchow (Minneapolis, Minnesota: University of Minnesota Press, 1991), 45. See also Athenaeum Fragment #24, p. 21.

120. T. S. Eliot, 'The Waste Land', section V, line 110, from *Collected Poems: 1909–1962* (London: Faber & Faber, 2020).

121. See, *e.g.*, Zygmunt Bauman, *Life in Fragments: Essays in Postmodern Morality* (Oxford: Blackwell, 1995).

122. See, *e.g.*, Duncan B. Forrester, *Theology in Fragments: Explorations in Unsystematic Theology* (London: T&T Clark, 2005), 1.

123. Nicola Slee, *Fragments for Fractures Times: What Feminist Practical Theology Brings to the Table* (London: SCM, 2020), 3.

124. David Tracy, 'Introduction', in *Fragments: The Existential Situation of Our Time: Selected Essays*, vol. 1 (Chicago: University of Chicago Press, 2020), 1–16 (9).

simple restoration of what has been lost but for an, as yet, unimagined and greater wholeness.

For all its advantages, the terminology of fragmentation is rooted in materiality in a manner not necessarily conducive to the kind of hope that Tracy outlines. As with Sappho's lost manuscripts, textual fragments demonstrate the vulnerability of matter to neglect, destruction or decay, evoking the irrevocable progression of history towards dissolution. Forrester describes the fragments out of which theology is made as jewels that must be 'quarried' from the ground or sustenance retrieved like crumbs under a table. They are easily lost or forgotten in the darkness, abandoned or cast aside.[125] The materiality of fragments also sits uneasily for a postmodern theology that understands reality more as 'event' (which is historical and subjective) than as 'substance' (which is ostensibly fixed and objective). Consequently, Tracy has coined the term 'frag-event' to describe the liberative and life-giving fragments (like Sappho's poems, treasure in the earth or crumbs under the table) that are the ingredients of theology.[126]

A more straightforward term for the fragment-as-event in the context of a lyric theology would be 'episode'. This is a term with lyric roots, which refers to the sections of a Greek tragedy in which the characters speak for themselves, interrupting the third-person narrative delivered by the chorus with a first-person lyric voice.[127] There is both an interpretive and an interruptive quality to this part of the drama, as a moment in which the lyric 'I' might express a personal response to or assert their role within the events of a wider narrative. There is a similar dynamic at play in the so-called lyric passages in the histories of Hebrew Bible, such as the songs of Moses, Miriam or Hannah, which also give weight to individual voices within the larger story and cast a personal perspective on events.[128]

The interruptive quality of the episode is reinforced by its popular and medical use to refer to a life event, mental health crisis, or period of illness.[129] Carrying connotations of digression, transience or atypicality, an episode that interrupts the narrative of a life may not only disrupt events but send the story in a different direction.[130] The episodic character of lyric has proved useful in therapeutic contexts, as it resists the requirement to make sense out of senseless events by

---

125. Forrester, *Theology in Fragments*, 16–18.
126. Tracy, *Fragments*, 31.
127. 'Episode (epeisodion)', in *The Oxford Companion to Classical Literature*, ed. M. C. Howatson, 3rd edn (Oxford: Oxford University, Press, 2011).
128. See, *e.g.*, Exodus 15.1-21; 1 Samuel 2.1-10; 2 Samuel 22. See Linafelt, *Hebrew Bible as Literature*, 5.
129. 'Episode', in *A Dictionary of Public Health*, 2nd edn, ed. Miquel Porta and John M. Last (Oxford: Oxford University Press, 2018), https://www.oxfordreference.com/display/10.1093/acref/9780191844386.001.0001/acref-9780191844386-e-1353?rskey=4BIfJK&result=5.
130. Consider, *e.g.*, Ruth's lyric response to Naomi in Ruth 1.16-17, which affects the course of their lives and through them the history of Israel.

turning them into a coherent narrative.[131] As an episodic form of meaning-making, lyric is capable of holding gaps and inconsistencies, and of foregrounding feelings over events, in a manner that reflects the way that traumatic experiences are often remembered.[132] In the episodic lyric, the gaps and aporias typical of the traumatized memory can remain not as a sign of deficiency or inconsistency but as testament to the impact of the experience.[133]

More fundamentally, the episodic structure of lyric has implications for the construction of identity. Analytic philosopher Galen Strawson has taken up the episode as a lyric hermeneutic of experience, free from the pressure to construct a broader narrative out of discrete iterations of a non-unitary self.[134] This position is more than implicitly anti-theological. Targeting the narrative theologies of Paul Ricoeur, Charles Taylor and Alasdair Macintyre, Strawson argues that a diachronic sense of self as subsisting across time is necessary neither for the construction of personhood (through a sense of stable identity) nor for living an ethical life (based on the assumption that moral responsibility relies upon taking responsibility for past actions).[135] Strawson defends the episodic construction of identity as free from the constraints of a wider narrative, able to focus on the present moment rather than ruminating on the past or anxiously anticipating the future. What Strawson casts in anti-narrative and anti-theological terms is treated here as consistent with lyric traditions of theological discourse, which may work not against but in concert with narrative. The interruptive quality of the lyric episode, its therapeutic uses and its role in the construction of identity are explored here through the poetry of Warsan Shire (1988–).

---

131. See, *e.g.*, Donald Capps, *The Poet's Gift: Toward the Renewal of Pastoral Care* (Louisville, KY: Westminster/John Knox Press, 1993), 2. For another study of, largely lyric, poetry from a pastoral theological perspective, see Mark Pryce, *Poetry, Practical Theology and Reflective Practice* (Abingdon: Routledge, 2019).

132. See, *e.g.*, Ananaya Jahanara Kabir, 'Affect, Body, Place: Trauma Theory in the World', in *The Future of Trauma Theory: Contemporary Literary and Cultural Criticism*, ed. Gert Buelens, Sam Durrant and Robert Eaglestone (London: Routledge, 2014), 64–6.

133. These features of traumatized memories are now widely recognized and influence the treatment of, *e.g.*, witnesses in court. See Crown Prosecution Service, 'Psychological Evidence Toolkit – A Guide for Crown Prosecutors', *Prosecution Guidance* (11 September 2019), https://www.cps.gov.uk/legal-guidance/psychological-evidence-toolkit-guide-crown-prosecutors.

134. *Cf.* John Swinton's assessment of episodic memory in his pastoral response to dementia. In neuroscience, episodic memory refers to the capacity to recall events as personal experiences. Swinton acknowledges the importance of episodic memory in the construction of identity, while critiquing the overreliance of modern medicine on episodic memory as a sign of personhood, in *Dementia: Living in the Memories of God* (London: SCM, 2012), chaps 3, 4, 8 and 9, especially 204–5.

135. Galen Strawson, 'Against Narrativity' and 'Episodic Ethics', in *Real Materialism: And Other Essays* (Oxford: Oxford University Press, 2008), 189–208, 209–32.

Fragment as event: The episode in the poetry of Warsan Shire

The modernist poet Archibald Macleish famously wrote that 'A poem should not mean/ But be'.[136] To treat the lyric fragment as an episode is to read it not as an interpretation of events but as an event in itself. It is this performative quality that gives lyric the power not merely to express the brokenness caused by traumatic experiences but to work towards healing. This characteristic of the episodic lyric is particularly prominent in what Patricia Smith calls Warsan Shire's 'stuttered lyric'.[137] A Somali-British poet born in Kenya, Shire's poems address themes of racism, sexual abuse, memories of war and experiences of displacement. Shire represents the poets of the social media generation who have re-popularized the lyric with an activist poetry often characterized by a pithy and rhetorical style.[138] An expressive poet of the kind that Hill professed to despise, her poetry is an opening of the self to the world which she has described as living 'like an open wound'.[139] However, her work goes well beyond expressivity and catharsis, towards poetry as a means of healing and transformation.

There is an episodic quality to the treatment of traumatic memories and experiences in Shire's first full-length poetry collection, *Bless the Daughter Raised by a Voice in Her Head* (2022). Many of these poems adopt a cinematic style in which the scene shifts from one line or stanza to the next like a series of shots in a film or music video.[140] The resulting brief, visually evocative stanzas can read like the transcription of a vision or a fragmented memory. 'Bless the Ghost', for example, depicts the memory of war as a creature that clings to the speaker's mother, described in a series of short vignettes that see it with her at the doctor's,

---

136. Archibald Macleish, 'Ars Poetica', in *Collected Poems 1917–1952* (Boston, MA: Houghton Mifflin Harcourt, 1952), lines 23–4.

137. Patricia Smith, 'Praise for *Bless the Daughter Raised by a Voice in Her Head*', in Warsan Shire, *Bless the Daughter Raised by a Voice in Her Head* (London: Chatto & Windus, 2022).

138. This is not to downplay Shire's academic training, the publishing of her work by prominent publishers or her formal recognition by the Royal Society of Literature. Nevertheless, her work was first disseminated through Tumblr, spread through the sharing of quotes on sites such as Instagram and Twitter and subsequently popularized through collaboration on Beyoncé Knowles' *Lemonade* (Parkwood Entertainment, premiered on HBO, 23 April 2016), audio-visual. See, *e.g.*, track #2, which quotes from Warsan Shire, 'For Women Who Are Difficult to Love'. For a summary of Shire's work up until the publication of her first full collection in 2022, see Alexis Okeowo, 'Warsan Shire's Portraits of Somalis in Exile', *New Yorker* (7 February 2022), https://www.newyorker.com/magazine/2022/02/14/warsan-shires-portraits-of-somalis-in-exile.

139. Warsan Shire, tweet cited in Kameelah Janan Rasheed, 'To Be Vulnerable and Fearless: An Interview with Writer Warsan Shire' (November 2012), http://wellandoftenpress.com/reader/to-be-vulnerable-and-fearless-an-interview-with-writer-warsan-shire/.

140. Shire has explained that she writes her much of poetry to music or film, and that her poems appear first as filmic images in her mind, see ibid.

while she is reading, in bed, even 'In the shower, [where] it lathers her back'.[141] In 'Photographs of Hooyo (HARLESDEN, 1990–2000)', every stanza is headed by a year, which covers the decade up to the millennium. Each of these stanzas is a snapshot, capturing a moment in time that, put together, charts the evolution of a Somali woman in exile from her home. They move from grief ('exiting her/bedroom' in tears in 1990) to homesickness, cultural integration (singing Tracy Chapman 'wearing a banana print diraac' in 1994) and the forgetting of painful memories (looking at photographic negatives in the year 2000, 'names of the dead thrown behind her').[142]

The episodic features of these poems not only evoke the fragmentary nature of traumatic memories but also have a therapeutic quality. 'Backwards' explores the transformative power of the lyric episode by describing a series of traumatic childhood events in reverse: a father leaving, a nose being broken, a mother falling down the stairs.[143] The depictions of these events are vivid and a little disturbing, like the rewinding of a film. A nosebleed in reverse looks like ants running into their nest, while the reader is also invited to imagine what it might look like to see a person grow backwards through puberty and into infancy.[144] There is a strict chiastic structure to this poem, in which the second half repeats the lines from the first half in reverse order. The poem makes as much sense backwards as forwards, giving the hopeful sense that perhaps a life might be similarly rewound and rewritten. However, the repeated promises by the speaker to undo a life through poetry draw attention to the fact that these transformations only happen within the world of the poem. The offhand cliché in the line 'I can make us loved, just say the word' is a double-entendre, both a literal assertion of the power of words and a quip that highlights the absurdity of this promise.[145]

This is a poem about the power and powerlessness of poetry to rewrite history, but even in the face of the limitations of language, it carries a tangible hope of the healing power of words. In performance, Shire takes a long pause between each line, creating space for the audience to imagine the strange reversals that the poem describes.[146] These gaps between lines reinforce the illocutionary force of the words, making good the poem's claim to recreate reality, if only in the hearer's mind. The first stanza is read in a dejected tone that conveys grief, regret or anger, but the second stanza recapitulates the lines in a more hopeful, expectant key. The turning point is the centre of the poem, where the final sentence of the first stanza

---

141. Warsan Shire, 'Bless the Ghost', *Daughter*, 13–14, lines 2, 12.

142. Ibid., 'Photographs of Hooyo (Harlesden, 1990–2000)', in ibid., 25–6, lines 2–3, 19, 35.

143. Ibid., 'Backwards', in ibid., 36–7, lines 1–4, 11, 20, 28–30.

144. Ibid., lines 4–6, 25–7.

145. Ibid., lines 7, 24.

146. Warsan Shire, reading at the launch of the Bloodaxe anthology, *The Complete Works II*, Purcell Room, Southbank Centre, London (6 October 2014), audiovisual, https://www.youtube.com/watch?v=q75bOz-7B9o.

is immediately repeated in the second. The force of the lines 'I'll rewrite this whole life and this time there'll be so much love,/ you won't be able to see beyond it' is strengthened and expanded by repetition. These two phrases surround a silence, marked in print by a double-spaced gap, that reads like the peak of a crescendo in a musical score. The hearer, primed by the first stanza to imagine a series of concrete images, is drawn here into an indescribable sense of plenitude that casts a lustre over the revisited memories in the second stanza, turning them from a song of regret into an anthem in praise of love.

These poems are performative of the healing of identities as well as of memories. The blessing referred to in the title is conferred upon people who may have been considered cursed, through poems about the child born a girl, the girl born with dark skin, refugees, migrants and people with cancer. The imperative tone of titles such as 'Bless the Qumayo', 'Bless Your Ugly Daughter', 'Bless the Real Housewife' and 'Bless our Blue Bodies' conveys an insistence that is close to defiance.[147] Through the honouring of these memories and the telling of these stories, speaking blessing over stories of neglect, abuse and trauma, these poems demonstrate the richness of lives often narrated in two-dimensional terms, either as victims or as problems. 'Bless This House' applies this blessing to female sexuality. Beginning with the statement 'Mother says there are locked rooms inside all women', the poem proceeds through a series of brief, disconnected episodes – memories, visions and maxims – that explore the conceit of the female body as a house that men try to break into.[148] A version of this poem was previously published as 'The House'. The clichéd blessing of the revised title turns what was a poem about trauma into a poem of empowerment. This is illustrated by the final line; where the earlier version concludes, 'Everyone laughs, they think I'm joking', in the revised version the speaker points towards their body and tells people, '*This is where men come to die.*'[149] In these poems, blessing is spoken over the episodic stories of people who have been neglected, oppressed or undervalued. The result is not coherence but a kind of healing that preserves the strangenesses of lives that do not conform to the dominant narrative. By resisting the impulse to draw these stories together into a neat or pleasing unity, these poems affirm the integrity of fragmented lives, conferring beauty on people considered ugly, glory on people treated as insignificant and value on stories that some would rather be forgotten.

---

147. Ibid., *Daughter*, 16, 19, 38, 59; see also 'Extreme Girlhood', 'Assimilation' and 'My Loneliness Is Killing Me', in ibid., 3–7. See also 'Bless Maymuun's Mind', 'Dahabshiil Sends Blessings', 'Bless the Bulimic', 'Bless the Ghost', ibid., 10–14.

148. Ibid., 'Bless This House', in ibid., 50–1, line 1.

149. Ibid., 'The House' (2014), https://www.poetryfoundation.org/poems/90733/the-house-57daba5625f32; ibid., 'Bless This House', line 36.

Conclusion

What kind of lyric theology might address the challenges of a late modern context? The answer that this chapter has proposed is: a fragmentary theology. Experiences of fragmentation take many forms. This chapter was written in the fragments of time available while caring for young children. It knows something of the frustration of constraint and the fear that a thought half-begun may be left unfinished. Trauma has a particularly acute fragmenting effect on the understanding, as the brain struggles to process events that explode its frames of reference. A fragmentary lyric theology may similarly take many forms. It may be a chastened lyric theology, one that acknowledges the deficiencies of a discourse that seeks truth through the balance and beauty of 'the lyric weave', or that places an implicit trust in the testimony of the 'I'.[150] This can result not only in a sceptical deconstructionism but in an epistemological humility that embraces the partial nature of any interpretive perspective and leaves space for the wisdom that breathes through the gaps between words. A fragmentary lyric theology is not merely fragmented, a collection of broken artefacts. It affirms the beauty and value of particularity: of the small, the fragile or the overlooked. Through a paratactic structure it can craft new forms of coherence. Through its episodic features it can become a transformative event in language, a site of healing, restoration or renewal.

The pneumatological reflections of this chapter have centred on the Spirit as a Spirit of creativity, creation and re-creation. The lyric voice that sings creation into being is, as intimated in Genesis 1.2, Psalm 33.6 and John 3.8, not monological but made up of the coinherence of Word and Breath. As suggested above, this imagery not only has Christological implications but is also significant for an imagination of human participation in and with the Spirit. The creative relationality of Word and Breath generates abundance by combining the constraints of form with the freedom of possibility. At the same time, to listen for the 'voice' of the 'Spirit' in the 'sound' of the 'wind' is not only to discern transcendence in immanence but also to seek after the Spirit of transformation in contexts of insecurity and disruption, in the wind that takes one's breath away.[151]

---

150. Paterson, *The Poem*, 88–93.

151. Ford notes that the 'sound' (*phōnē*) of the 'wind' (*pneuma*) in John 3.8 could also be read as the 'voice' of the 'Spirit'. Ford, *John*, 90.

EPILOGUE: THE LYRIC VOICE IN ENGLISH THEOLOGY

> When he had said this, he breathed on them and said to them, 'Receive the Holy Spirit.'
>
> (John 20.22)

This is not the book that it might have been. The original conception was a theoretical treatise in von Balthasarian theological aesthetics that might offer a step beyond the current vogue for theological dramatic theory, which has superseded in its own way the prior dominance of narrative theology. It quickly became apparent that this was not an appropriate methodology for a study of lyric, which is not theoretical or systematic but deeply affective and wonderfully particular. The standard definition of lyric in theologies influenced by von Balthasar has proved reliant on a classical or post-Romantic reading out of step with key insights from recent literary criticism. More importantly, these theological accounts of lyric seemed so bound up with negative stereotypes of modern individualism and affective pietism that a different methodological route was necessary to pursue a more nuanced and constructive analysis of the theological lyric voice.

The first major change was therefore the decision to focus not on theological texts about poetry but on the poetry of a particular culture and tradition: the English lyric. The second involved engagement with the current revival in lyric theory and criticism. The third major shift was informed both by deeper engagement with contemporary lyric poetry and by my participation in the learning communities of Sarum College and the Oxford Centre for Religion and Culture. These challenged me to look again at the canon from which I was drawing, to allow engagement with a more diverse range of texts to critique, inform and transform some of the categories with which I was working and to consider more explicitly the constructive implications of the arguments. The result is a less tidy project, but one with hopefully greater relevance to contemporary concerns in theology and culture, and with greater applicability to the constructive tasks of theology in practice.

This book has gone well beyond an exhortation to recognize the contribution of lyric texts to the development of theological discourse. Instead, guided by the insights of contemporary lyric theory, it has sought to trace the contours of a lyric theology through the history of the English spiritual lyric. Centred on the lyric as 'voice', it has developed a picture of lyric rooted in music and manifest in performance, a song infused with the breath of life and encompassed by the wind of the Spirit. Consequently, the major theological questions of this book have been: what might a theology that seeks to breathe with the Spirit, as the Spirit breathes through us, sound like? What are the grammars of its discourse, or rather the rhythms of its song?[1] How might theology better acknowledge the dynamics of beauty and power in meditation of the truth of the Spirit? Key to these discussions has been the difficult question of how the interrelationship between the human and the divine might be best expressed: in worship and prayer, in prophetic discourse and pastoral encounter. Taking as its starting point Lampe's notion of 'theandric operations' and Sonderegger's description of the Spirit as 'mixed' up in human experience, the book has found through lyric a way of speaking of the melding of Voice with voice, Spirit with spirit, inspired by the prayer of Roman 8.16 and the song of Revelation 22.17.[2] In consequence, much of the argument has run towards and not away from multiplicity and ambiguity, at times addressing difficult themes to do with the power and corruptibility of language, in service of the discernment of spirits.

The central chapters have illustrated the kinds of theological moves facilitated by a lyric lens. Chapter 1 developed a theo-lyric of praise as joy in sound, which undergirds the music of speech. Informed by Frye's lyric theory, it brought together the medieval theme of *melos* as an echo of heavenly song with the idea of xenoglossia as babble illumined by the Spirit, through a focus on nonsense-lyrics, macaronic and code-switching poetry. It also waded into the murkier ambivalences of poetic sound, probing the fine line between delight and derision, the complex dynamics of power and vulnerability in language, and the capacity of words to liberate and oppress, pointing towards an ethic of the music of words.

Chapter 2 explored the implications of lyric address for understandings of the loving relationality of prayer, as an intimate and seemingly private discourse that incorporates the community of faith and the cries of the world and participates in the Trinitarian life. Attentive to the sighs and groans of the Spirit, it focussed on the vocative ejaculation 'O' as a sign of lyric apostrophe that combines the expressivity of spontaneous passion with the persuasiveness of rhetorical speech and the formality of liturgical invocation. This argument presented an account of the lyricism of prayer that seeks to cross confessional divides, demonstrating the common threads between different traditions of liturgical discourse.

Chapter 3 addressed lyric as prophetic discourse, hearing a whisper of the voice of the Lord in the lyric 'I' of 'I love', 'I am' and 'I feel'. This discussion of Romantic lyric subjectivity concerned not just the public orientation of apparently private discourse but also the creative participation of the prophet in sounding the name

---

1. On rhythm as a theological category, see Lexi Eikelboom, *Rhythm: A Theological Category* (Oxford: Oxford University Press, 2018).

2. See above, p. 22.

of the Lord. It explored speech as a manifestation of presence, drawing on practices of poetic performance as well as on Romantic theories of language. The voice of the Lord in the prophetic lyric 'I' was discussed not as the preserve of a poetic elite but as belonging to all. Through a reading of Joel 2.28-29, the call to speak against situations of oppression was interpreted as a call to all and to each to speak in their own voice.

Chapter 4 examined the theme of the lyric fragment, drawing on theological notions of the fragment to think about the poetic line as something short, even constrained, but beautiful, and out of which new and surprising visions of the whole can emerge. This chapter imagined the gaps between lines as in-breathed by the wind of the Spirit, the intensity of constricted words as infused with the 'umbilical' breath of the Spirit and the event of the lyric episode as enlivened by the Spirit's life-giving power. Through a focus on the modern transmutations of lyric, this chapter tested and stretched the scriptural theme of the Spirit as breath, exploring the disruptive quality of the wind and finding a place for expiration as well as inspiration in a theology that breathes with the Spirit. This chapter addressed the traumas of late modernity, but its conclusions might be applied more generally to the uses of lyric in pastoral care.

This book's approach to its subject has turned up foundational theological questions to do with the work of the Spirit, the imagination of the Trinity and human participation in God. It has advocated a refined Balthasarian aesthetics of epic, lyric and drama, suggesting a Trinitarian structure for future reflection in this area. Such a methodology would need to take care to avoid a tritheistic over-identification of epic, drama and lyric with the three persons of Father, Son and Spirit, a danger not entirely averted by this lyric study's focus on the Spirit. Through a perichoretic perspective on the relationship between the theological voices, theology might be envisaged as a hybrid genre. A systematic theology on this model might be better able to incorporate whichever of the poetic voices is currently out of vogue. By avoiding the dialectical structure of a Hegelian aesthetics in which drama both surpasses and supersedes the other genres, such an approach might better recognize, for example, the lyric musicality that pervades all discourse, or the multiple ways in which parts may be made into epic wholes. The kaleidoscopic frame suggested here might contribute to more nuanced and charitable discussions of issues that have often been addressed along the fault lines between these three theological modes, such as the role of individual and community in the search for wisdom. Required not only to reckon with but to incorporate a range of voices, such a Trinitarian theological aesthetic might creatively bring these three theological voices into a harmonious unity that responds to the shifting sands of culture.

The critical landscape that supports this study ought to provoke a reassessment of some of the conventional significations of 'lyric' in theological discourse. Rather than calling any theology with a pleasing style 'lyrical', one might look for more defined norms for a lyric theological aesthetic. The sweetness of lyricism might be considered, for example, as more than prettiness, conveying an intensity of delight that carries important theological resonances. As explored in Chapter 2, lyricism might also encompass the rougher music of culturally inflected discourse, welcoming the disruptions of discordance as a conduit of grace and finding here, too, an echo of the song of the Spirit.

Out of the conceit of the lyric voice has emerged several qualities of a theology that seeks to breathe with the Spirit. Theology-as-voice is the sound of air mediated through vocal cords, the Spirit its source and life. Abandoning the search for a 'still point' at the heart 'of the turning world', lyric theology moves in the creative space that comprehends both the intimacy of divine inter-breathing and the expansive exhalation of the wind breathed upon creation.[3] Its way of knowing embraces interiority and exteriority, its way of speaking both gentleness and power. Its meter is the motion of inspiration and expiration governed by the beat of the heart, its substance the intermingling of air and body, breath and blood, spirit and matter. In the rhythms of praise and prayer, prophecy or preaching, is found a freedom to work creatively with these constants to address the needs of the moment, to comfort, challenge or enlighten. Measured by the length of a breath, the humility of the lyric voice is not that of an enforced self-attenuation but a working-with the span of human life. The energy of a lyric theology is world-facing. It may say 'I' not as end point or goal but as a starting point for reflection, with its own acknowledged limitations and its own peculiar beauty. As a performance, lyric theology is not a private soliloquy but even when singular and apparently alone is spoken with and for others. It is a ritual discourse with an enduring message designed for reperformance, a rhetorical mode whose gentle persuasiveness is energized by the charm of beauty, rooted not in violence but in love. These features are not confined to a particular genre of theological discourse. They indicate a timbre of speech that might be discerned in a range of theological forms, seeded into the epic projects of systematic theology and the drama of occasional and practical theologies.

This book has also confronted contentious issues in theological methodology, particularly the merits and risks of affective, subjective and rhetorical language, not as a poetic counterpoint to systematic thought but as fundamental to theological discourse. The definition of lyricism as musicality has entailed a concern with lyric sound. Making sense through bodily vibrations, sound is indicative of the affective core of communication. In his essay on 'Poetry and the Christian', Rahner describes poetry as a language of the heart in a manner that stresses the corporeality as opposed to the sentimentality of the metaphor.[4] This book has not abandoned an affective-expressive definition of lyric, but its defence of affectivity in theological discourse has focussed on the corporeal grammar of lyric emotion.

The vexed question of poetic subjectivity remains unresolved, but this book has noted the now widely acknowledged complexity and multiplicity of the lyric 'I', focussing on the public orientation of apparently private self-expression. Just as Rahner's theology has been shown to be susceptible to a reading of the self in the accusative as well as the nominative sense, as the 'hearer' of the divine address

---

3. T. S. Eliot, 'Burnt Norton', *The Four Quartets* II, line 16, in *Collected Poems*.
4. Rahner 'Poetry and the Christian', 360–2.

and not just the initiator of its own religious experience, so also developments in lyric studies have shown the lyric 'I' to be interpretable as a multifaceted, culturally constructed and socially located subjectivity.[5] Informed by contemporary lyric criticism, theological lyric theory might provide a grammar for the personal or affective voice in theology that interrogates its weaknesses and refines its capacity to be reasonable, faithful and creative.

The issue of rhetoric is relevant to theological engagement with culture and to intra-theological debates between rhetorical and anti-rhetorical modes of theological discourse. While 'rhetorical' has become a synonym for questionable in some contemporary theological debates, early Christian theology was deeply rooted in the rhetorical arts: from the musical prose of Augustine, to Boethius' popular *Consolation of Philosophy*, the 'silver tongued' theology of John Chrysostom or the theology-in-verse of Gregory of Nazianzus.[6] To describe such texts as 'lyrical' ought to be not only to admire the beauty of the language but to consider how their rhetoric contributes to their theology.[7] Boethius' prosody, for example, has been described as a 'therapeutic' metre that provides the very consolation the work discusses.[8] The sweet Ionian mode of Gregory's hexameter verse used a rhetorical poetic as both truth-telling and persuasion: to communicate the beauty of divine grace and to persuade the young to act virtuously. In describing poetic measure as a guard against 'measurelessness', Gregory was speaking both of moral instruction and of the order and harmony of words, which reflects that of God's creation.[9]

This book has consistently asserted the inescapability of the rhetorical component of language as embedded in the sound of words, the vibrations of vocalization and the bodily rhythms of blood and breath. The theme of *melos* has revealed rhetoric as not just a tool of persuasion but an aspect of poetic beauty and power. Attentiveness to the music of words can be a feature of theologies alert to culture, difference, contextuality and tradition. The activist theologies of such as James Cone, Emilie Townes and Azariah France-Williams embrace a rhetorical

---

5. Michael Purcell, 'Rahner amid Modernity and Post-Modernity', in *The Cambridge Companion to Karl Rahner*, ed. Declan Marmion and Mary E. Hines (Cambridge: Cambridge University Press, 2005), 195–2010 (200–1).

6. It is notable that critiques of radical orthodoxy have targeted its 'rhetoric', as language that seeks to persuade irrespective of facts, reason or truth. See, *e.g.*, Wayne J. Hankey and Douglas Hedley, eds, *Deconstructing Radical Orthodoxy: Postmodern Theology, Rhetoric and Truth* (Aldershot: Ashgate, 2005), 3; Paul Hedges, 'The Rhetoric and Reception of John Milbank's Radical Orthodoxy: Privileging Prejudice in Theology?', *Open Theology* 1, no. 1 (19 January 2014): 24–44.

7. See, *e.g.*, Morwenna Ludlow, *Art, Craft and Theology in Fourth-Century Christian Authors* (Oxford: Oxford University Press, 2020), 241.

8. See Blackwood, *Consolation*, 235.

9. See Gregory, 'On His Verses', *Carmina* II.1.39 (lines 34–57), as cited in Čelica Milovanović-Barham, 'Gregory of Nazianzus: Ars Poetica (In Suos Versus: Carmen 2.1.39)', *Journal of Early Christian Studies* 5, no. 4 (1997): 500.

poetic not in a cynical attempt to manipulate the reader but as a reflection of what is at stake in the writing of theology. To employ lyricism as a 'weapon' of resistance as Cone does is to weigh the performative power of language.[10] Townes's employment of poetic lineation instils a pace and rhythm of reading that establishes a respect for words and unlocks their transformative possibilities.[11] Such poetic theologies aspire to, In France-Williams's words, 'the liberation of our collective imagination', while recognizing the danger of words that oppress.[12] From this perspective, rhetoric proves not only unavoidable but indispensable to a theology conscious of both its materiality and its transformative potential.

There are several important avenues that could not be explored in a study of this length. This book has covered a representative range of texts from English lyric tradition, including lyrics set to music, lyric sequences, sonnets, prayer-poems, pastorals, the lyric fragment and the spoken word. It has addressed the modes of praise and prayer, love-song and lament. It has spanned Anglo-Saxon poetry, through the medieval lyric, the Renaissance and Romanticism to modernist and postmodernist lyrics. Space would not permit a thorough epistemological account of these different forms beyond some brief suggestive comments. There are some glaring omissions from the canon of the English spiritual lyric, from Shakespeare's sonnets to the hymns of Isaac Watts and Charles Wesley, the works of Wordsworth and Coleridge, the spiritual poetry of Elizabeth Barrett Browning, Gerard Manley Hopkins, W. H. Auden, Charles Williams and Elizabeth Jennings. The theological contribution of contemporary spiritual poets and poet-theologians has also been neglected, such as Rachel Mann, Micheal O'Siadhail, Michael Symmons Roberts, Nicola Slee and Rowan Williams. This is before the lyricism of other cultures is taken into account, or lyricism in other genres: from Augustine's *Confessions* to Walt Whitman's *Song of Myself* or Raine Maria Rilke's *Sonnets to Orpheus*. The features of a lyric theology drawn here from a study of English lyric tradition may be generalizable but not universal, prompting the question of what a lyric theology built on other poetic texts and traditions might look like.

One important feature only touched upon in this book is the lyric sequence. This book has been something like a lyric sequence, with repeated and overlapping themes and motifs. A more thorough reflection on this theme might extend the previous discussions on fragmentation and the episodic lyric to consider the shape of systematic theology in a lyric mode, or to outline the contours of a lyric theology of providence.

The lyric present is perhaps the most significant of the underexplored themes of this book. Not often used in colloquial speech, the simple present tense 'I do' is often seen as an indicator of (perhaps overstylized) poetry. This is a poetic tense

---

10. James Cone, *The Cross and the Lynching Tree* (Maryknoll, NY: Orbis, 2011), 13.

11. Emilie M. Townes, 'Women's Wisdom: On Solidarity and Differences (On Not Rescuing the Killers)', *Union Seminary Quarterly Review* 53, nos 3–4 (1999): 158–9, 161.

12. Azariah France-Williams, *Ghost Ship: Institutional Racism and the Church of England* (London: SCM, 2020), xvi.

that encapsulates ambiguity. Lord Byron's 'She walks in beauty like the night' could be read as 'she is walking' now or 'she [habitually] walks'.[13] This is not just a poetic device but has also been read as a ritual or liturgical tense, a kind of eternal present that stands outside of history, providing a vantage point from which words of enduring value can be spoken. The lyric present is also evoked in Wordsworth's account of the 'spots of time' that form the basis of the poem, memories recalled through poetry that are capable of bringing a wandering soul home to forgotten truths.[14] Culler avoids the fixity of the eternal present by speaking instead of a '"floating now"', a moment that can be called into being with each re-reading, capable of enunciating 'iterable' truths.[15] Such a ritual or performative reading of the lyric present might be used to address the power of words to bring the past into the present, through a eucharistic interpretation of *anamnesis*.

Lyric poems in this book have been treated as theological voices in their own right and not as mere additions or adornments to the main task.[16] These are texts that have made their own theological contribution, as well as, it has been suggested, contributing to the development of an English theological sensibility. It is hoped that this perspective might open the way to a broader acknowledgement of the contribution of lyric to English theology in particular and Christian theology in general. A largely unacknowledged lyricism is evident, for example, in Nicola Slee's poetic theology rooted in experience and Heather Walton's creative use of autoethnography. Walton's method privileges a lyric particularity of the 'small' and the 'personal', while Slee's feminist poetics of prayer is an episodic construct made up of fragments of experience, moments which 'express[] in miniature something of the larger journey'.[17] Despite the intimately subjective character of this work, it contains a notable absence of any mention of lyric.[18] For Slee and Walton, poetry incorporates affective and bodily ways of knowing in an often-dialectical relationship with rational or systematic discursivity.[19] This book has drawn on feminist perspectives on breath and body to overcome the phallocentric connotations of the egotistical lyric 'I', paving the way for the reclamation of a

---

13. Lord Byron, 'She Walks in Beauty' (1814), line 1.

14. William Wordsworth, 'The Prelude' (1805), XII, lines 208, 219.

15. Culler, *Lyric*, 287–8, 294–5.

16. Theological engagement with literature has long since moved away from an instrumentalization of poetry as a purely illustrative tool towards, in David Jasper's words, an 'understanding of the nature of theology *through* literature, or even theology itself *as* a poetry of faith', in *Handbook of English Literature and Theology*, 24.

17. Heather Walton, *Writing Methods in Theological Reflection* (London: SCM), xxvii, xvii; Slee, *Praying*, 5.

18. Slee interestingly notes that lyric poetry, more than epic or narrative, 'compresses' language and experience in a way that can be termed 'sacramental', creating 'a place where grace and truth are compressed and encountered', '(W)riting like a Woman: In Search of a Feminist Theological Poetics', in *Making Nothing Happen*, D'Costa et al., 9–48 (13 n3).

19. See, e.g., Walton, *Writing Methods*, 134–5; Slee, *Praying*, 6.

feminine/feminist lyric voice. Future moves towards acknowledging the integral role of lyric in theological discourse might also build on the theology of hymns, the rehabilitation of the Hebrew lyric and the rich field of literature and theology, of which Thomas Gardner's *Lyric Theology: Art and the Doctrine of Creation*, published just before submission of this manuscript, is a prime example.[20] It is hoped that this book will take its place alongside works such as these, to prompt future conversations on lyric theology.

Some of the energy of this project has come from a desire to defend lyric against previous theological critiques. At its heart, though, is a consideration of how lyric in its various forms has shaped theological discourse – from praise to prayer, prophetic speech to pastoral care. This book has been concerned ultimately not only with theological methodology or theological aesthetics but with a theology of human participation in God through the Spirit. Defining lyric theology as one that seeks to breathe with the Spirit, it has explored how participation in the Spirit touches upon the most intimate aspects of human experience, its breadths and depths, its intensities and extensities. Lyric as a creative engagement with the breath facilitates an understanding of relationship with the Spirit that goes well beyond the reception of inspiration. It sees the Spirit present also in the exhalations of existence, the holdings and turnings of life, the voicings of the body and the circumambient circulation of the wind.

---

20. On hymns, see Kimbrough, *Lyrical Theology*; F. W. Dobbs-Allsopp is at the forefront of attempts to rehabilitate lyric as a category for the interpretation of biblical poetry. She goes so far as to suggest that a lyric reading helps to make better sense than narrative of the form and tone of the Hebrew scriptures. See Dobbs-Allsopp, *Biblical Poetry*, 178, 213. See also Thomas Gardner, *Lyric Theology: Art and the Doctrine of Creation* (Waco, TX: Baylor University Press, 2022). Gardner's focus on the doctrine of creation provides an interesting counterpoint to this book's pneumatological lens. Like this author, Gardner foregrounds lyric as song, particularly in relation to the vocation to praise.

WORKS CITED

Abrams, M. H., 'Lyric', in *A Glossary of Literary Terms*, 4th edition (New York: Holt, Rinehart & Winston, 1981).
Adcock, Rachel, Sara Read and Anna Ziomek, eds, *Flesh and Spirit: An Anthology of Seventeenth-Century Women's Writing* (Manchester: Manchester University Press, 2014).
Adlington, Hugh, 'John Donne', in *The Oxford Handbook of Early Modern English Literature and Religion*, edited by Andrew Hiscock and Helen Wilcox (Oxford: Oxford University Press, 2017), www.oxfordhandbooks.com.
Adorno, Theodor, 'On Lyric Poetry and Society (1957; translated 1991)', in *The Lyric Theory Reader: A Critical Anthology*, edited by Virginia Jackson and Yopie Prins (Baltimore, MA: Johns Hopkins University Press, 2014), 339–49.
Adorno, Theodor, 'Parataxis: On Hölderlin's Late Poetry', in *Notes to Literature, European Perspectives: A Series in Social Thought and Cultural Criticism* (New York: Columbia University Press, 2019), 376–411.
Adorno, Theodor, *Prisms* (Cambridge, MA: MIT Press, 1981).
Albin, Andrew, 'Listening for Canor in Richard Rolle's Melos Amoris', in *Voice and Voicelessness in Medieval Europe: The New Middle Ages*, edited by I. R. Kleiman (New York: Palgrave Macmillan, 2015), 177–97.
Albright, Daniel, *Lyricality in English Literature* (Lincoln: University of Nebraska Press, 1985).
Allen, Rosamund S., *Richard Rolle: The English Writings* (New York: Paulist Press, 1988).
Allnutt, Gllian, 'Gillian Allnutt Talks to Emily Berry' (The Poetry Society, 2017). Audio. https://soundcloud.com/poetrysociety/emily-berry-in-conversation-with-gillian-allnut.
Allnutt, Gllian, *Indwelling* (Hexham: Bloodaxe, 2013).
Allnutt, Gllian, interview by Geoff Hattersley, *Writers Aloud* (Royal Literary Fund, 13 September 2018), episode 185. Audio. https://www.rlf.org.uk/showcase/wa_episode185/.
Allnutt, Gllian, *Wake* (Hexham: Bloodaxe, 2018).
Alpers, Paul, 'Apostrophe and the Rhetoric of Renaissance Lyric', *Representations* 122, no. 1 (Spring 2013): 1–22.
Alter, Robert, *The Art of Biblical Poetry*, revised edition (New York: Basic Books, 2011).
Archibald, Elizabeth, 'Macaronic Poetry', in *A Companion to Medieval Poetry*, edited by Corinne Saunders (Hoboken, NJ: Wiley-Blackwell, 2010), 277–88.
Auden, W. H., 'In Memory of W.B. Yeats', in *Selected Poems* (New York: Vintage Books, 1979).
Augustine, *Expositions on the Book of Psalms*, translated by J. H. Parker, volume 1 (Oxford: F. and J. Rivington, 1847).
Bacon, Hannah, *What's Right with the Trinity? Conversations in Feminist Theology* (London: Routledge, 2016).

Balfour, Ian, *The Rhetoric of Romantic Prophecy* (Stanford, CA: Stanford University Press, 2002).
Balfour, Ian, 'Subjecticity (On Kant and the Texture of Romanticism)', in *Romanticism and the Insistence of the Aesthetic*, edited by Forest Pyle (College Park, Maryland: University of Maryland, 2005). Online. https://romantic-circles.org/praxis/aesthetic/balfour/balfour.html.
Balthasar, Hans Urs von, *Explorations in Theology: The Word Made Flesh*, translated by A. V. Littledale and Alexander Dru, volume 1, 2nd edition (San Francisco: Ignatius Press, 1989).
Balthasar, Hans Urs von, *The Glory of the Lord: A Theological Aesthetics*, translated by John Kenneth Riches, 7 volumes (Edinburgh: T&T Clark, 1982–9).
Balthasar, Hans Urs von, *Prayer* (San Francisco: Ignatius, 1986).
Balthasar, Hans Urs von, *Theo-Drama: Theological Dramatic Theory*, 5 volumes (San Francisco: Ignatius Press, 1989–98).
Barbour, Douglas, *Lyric, Anti-Lyric: Essays on Contemporary Poetry* (Edmonton, AB: NeWest Publishers, Limited, 2001).
Barrell, John, *The Idea of Landscape and the Sense of Place 1730–1840: An Approach to the Poetry of John Clare* (Cambridge: Cambridge University Press, 2010).
Barrett Jr., Robert W., 'Languages Low and High: Translation and the Creation of Community in the Chester Pentecost Play', in *Translating the Middle Ages*, edited by Karen L. Fresco and Charles D. Wright (London: Routledge, 2012), 65–82.
Bate, Jonathan, *John Clare: A Biography* (London: Picador, 2003).
Bauman, Zygmunt, *Life in Fragments: Essays in Postmodern Morality* (Oxford: Blackwell, 1995).
Bearder, Pete, *Stage Invasion: Poetry & the Spoken Word Renaissance* (London: Out-Spoken Press, 2019).
Beaumont-Thomas, Ben, 'Kate Tempest Announces They Are Non-binary, Changes Name to Kae', *The Guardian*, 6 August 2020. https://www.theguardian.com/music/2020/aug/06/kate-tempest-announces-they-are-non-binary-changes-name-to-kae.
Beckford, Robert, *Jesus Dub: Theology, Music and Social Change* (London: Routledge, 2006).
Bede, *Ecclesiastical History of the English People*, in the *Moore Bede* (Cambridge University Library MS. Kk 5.16, fol. 128v).
Bede, *Ecclesiastical History* (Old English version), translated by Benjamin Slade (2005), https://heorot.dk/bede-caedmon.html.
Bede, *On Genesis*, translated by Calvin B. Kendall (Liverpool: Liverpool University Press, 2007).
Bede, *Venerabilis Opera; pars 4, opera rhythmica*, edited by J. Fraipont, CCSL 122 (Turnhout: Brepols, 1955).
Begbie, Jeremy, *Theology, Music and Time* (Cambridge: Cambridge University Press, 2000).
Bennett, Louise, *Jamaica Labrish: Jamaica Dialect Poems* (Jamaica: Sangster's, 1966).
Bernard, Jay, *Surge* (London: Penguin, 2019). Kindle.
Bhabha, Homi, *The Location of Culture*, 2nd edition (London: Routledge, 2004).
Binyon, Laurence, 'The English Lyric', *Journal of the Royal Society of Arts* 89, no. 4600 (November 1941): 786–96.
Blackwood, Stephen, *The Consolation of Boethius as Poetic Liturgy* (Oxford: Oxford University Press, 2015).
Blair, Hugh, *Lectures on Rhetoric and Belles Lettres*, 3 volumes (Dublin: Whitestone *et al.*, 1788).

Blake, William, *Blake: Complete Writings*, edited by Geoffrey Keynes (Oxford: Oxford University Press, 1969).
Blasing, Mutlu Konuk, *Lyric Poetry: The Pain and the Pleasure of Words* (Princeton, N.J: Princeton University Press, 2007).
Blevins, Jacob, editor, *Dialogism and Lyric Self-Fashioning: Bakhtin and the Voices of a Genre* (Selinsgrove, PA: Susquehanna University Press, 2008).
Bloom, Harold, 'The Survival of Strong Poetry (on Geoffrey Hill): Introduction to Somewhere Is Such a Kingdom', *The American Poetry Review* 4, no. 4 (July/August 1975): 17–20.
Boeve, Lieven, *God Interrupts History: Theology in a Time of Upheaval* (New York: Continuum, 2007).
Bowyer, Andrew, *Donald MacKinnon's Theology: To Perceive Tragedy without the Loss of Hope* (London: Bloomsbury, 2021).
Brathwaite, Edward Kamau, *History of the Voice: The Development of Nation Language in Anglophone Caribbean Poetry* (London: New Beacon Books, 1984).
Breeze, Jean 'Binta', in *Third World Girl* (London: Bloodaxe, 2011).
Brewster, Scott, *Lyric* (London: Routledge, 2009).
Brown, Carleton, *Religious Lyrics of the XVth Century* (Oxford: Clarendon, 1939).
Brown, David, *God and Mystery in Words: Experience through Metaphor and Drama* (Oxford: Oxford University Press, 2008).
Brown, Frank Burch, *Good Taste, Bad Taste, and Christian Taste: Aesthetics in Religious Life* (Oxford: Oxford University Press, 2000).
Brueggemann, Walter, *Genesis: Interpretation* (Atlanta: John Knox, 1982).
Brueggemann, Walter, *The Prophetic Imagination*, 40th anniversary edition (Minneapolis, MN: Fortress Press, 2018).
Buber, Martin, *The Prophetic Faith*, edited by Jon Douglas Levenson (Princeton: Princeton University Press, 2016).
Burrows, Mark S., '"Raiding the Inarticulate": Mysticism, Poetics, and the Unlanguageable', *Spiritus: A Journal of Christian Spirituality* 4, no. 2 (Autumn 2004): 173–94.
Burrus, Virginia, 'The Gospel of Luke and the Acts of the Apostles', in *A Postcolonial Commentary on the New Testament Writings*, edited by Fernando Segova and R. S. Sugirtharajah (London: T&T Clark, 2009), 133–55.
Burt, Stephen, 'What Is This Thing Called Lyric?', *Modern Philology* 113, no. 3 (February 2016): 422–40. https://doi.org/10.1086/684097.
Butterfield, Ardis, 'Why Medieval Lyric?', *ELH* 82, no. 2 (Summer 2015): 319–43.
Calvin, John, *Commentary on the Book of Psalms*, translated by James Anderson, volume 1 (Edinburgh: Calvin Translation Society, 1845).
Campbell, Jackson Justice, *The Advent Lyrics of the Exeter Book* (Princeton, NJ: Princeton University Press, 1959).
Capps, Donald, *The Poet's Gift: Toward the Renewal of Pastoral Care* (Louisville, KY: Westminster/John Knox Press, 1993).
Caputo, John, *The Insistence of God: A Theology of Perhaps* (Bloomington: Indiana University Press, 2013).
Carey, Mary, *Lady Carey's Meditations, & Poetry* (Bodl. Oxf., MS Rawl. D. 1308).
Carpenter, Anne M., *Theo-Poetics: Hans Urs von Balthasar and the Risk of Art and Being* (Notre Dame, IN: University of Notre Dame Press, 2015).
Cavill, Paul, 'The Manuscripts of Cædmon's Hymn', *Anglia* 118 (2000): 499–530.
Celan, Paul, *Breathturn*, translated by Pierre Joris (Los Angeles: Sun & Moon Press, 1995).

Celan, Paul, 'The Meridian', translated by Jerry Glenn, *Chicago Review* 29, no. 3 (1978): 29–40.
Ceravolo, Joseph, *Collected Poems*, edited by Rosemary Ceravolo and Parker Smathers (Middletown, CT: Wesleyan University Press, 2013).
Certeau, Michel De, 'Vocal Utopias: Glossolalias', *Representations* 56 (Autumn 1996): 29–47.
Chopp, Rebecca S., 'Theology and the Poetics of Testimony', in *Converging on Culture: Theologians in Dialogue with Cultural Analysis and Criticism*, edited by Delwin Brown, Sheila Greeve Davaney and Kathryn Tanner (Oxford: Oxford University Press, 2001), 56–70.
Clare, John, *The Later Poems of John Clare, 1837–1864*, edited by Eric Robinson and David Powell, 2 volumes (Oxford: Clarendon, 1984).
Clare, John, *The Letters of John Clare*, edited by Mark Storey (Oxford: Clarendon, 1985).
Classen, Albrecht, editor, *Multilingualism in the Middle Ages and Early Modern Age: Communication and Miscommunication in the Premodern World* (Berlin: De Gruyter, 2016).
Coakley, Sarah, editor, *Faith, Rationality and the Passions* (Oxford: Wiley-Blackwell, 2012).
Coakley, Sarah, *God, Sexuality and the Self: An Essay 'on the Trinity'* (Cambridge: Cambridge University Press, 2013).
Coakley, Sarah, *The New Asceticism: Sexuality, Gender and the Quest for God* (London: Bloomsbury, 2015).
Coleridge, Samuel Taylor, *Biographia Literaria*, edited by Adam Roberts (Edinburgh: Edinburgh University Press, 2014). https://ebookcentral.proquest.com/lib/oxford/detail.action?docID=4462445.
Colman, Andrew M., 'Babbling', in *A Dictionary of Psychology*, 4th edition (Oxford: Oxford University Press, 2015). https://www.oxfordreference.com/view/10.1093/acref/9780199657681.001.0001/acref-9780199657681-e-855?rskey=AeWbKO&result=3.
Cone, James, *The Cross and the Lynching Tree* (Maryknoll, NY: Orbis, 2011).
Cooper, Carolyn, *Noises in the Blood: Orality, Genre and the 'Vulgar' Body of Jamaican Popular Culture* (London: Macmillan, 1993).
Cooper Rompato, Christine, 'Xenoglossia and Multilingualism in Middle English Sermons on Pentecost', in *Multilingualism in the Middle Ages and the Early Modern Age: Communication and Miscommunication in the Premodern World*, edited by Albrecht Classen (Berlin: De Gruyter, 2016), 233–48.
Cope, Gilbert, 'Posture', in *A New Dictionary of Liturgy and Worship*, edited by J. G. Davies (London: SCM, 1986), 437–40.
Corns, Thomas N., editor, *The Cambridge Companion to English Poetry, Donne to Marvell* (Cambridge: Cambridge University Press, 1993).
Couey, J. Blake, *Reading the Poetry of First Isaiah: The Most Perfect Model of the Prophetic Poetry* (Oxford: Oxford University Press, 2015).
Countryman, Louis William, *The Poetic Imagination: An Anglican Tradition* (Maryknoll, NY: Orbis Books, 1999).
Crown Prosecution Service, 'Psychological Evidence Toolkit–A Guide for Crown Prosecutors', *Prosecution Guidance* (11 September 2019), https://www.cps.gov.uk/legal-guidance/psychological-evidence-toolkit-guide-crown-prosecutors.
Culler, Jonathan, 'Comparative Literature and the Pieties', *Profession* (1986): 30–2.
Culler, Jonathan, *Theory of the Lyric* (Cambridge, MA: Harvard University Press, 2015).

Cummings, Brian, *The Literary Culture of the Reformation: Grammar and Grace* (Oxford: Oxford University Press, 2002). Kindle.
Curran, Stuart, 'Romantic Poetry: The I Altered', in *Romantic Writings*, edited by Stephen Bygrave (Maidenhead, Berks: Open University, 1996).
Daniel, Samuel, *A Defence of Ryme* (London: Edward Blount, 1603).
Davidson, Andrew, editor, *Imaginative Apologetics: Theology, Philosophy and the Catholic Tradition* (London: SCM, 2011).
Davie, Donald, editor, *The New Oxford Book of Christian Verse* (Oxford: Oxford University Press, 1981).
Davies, Oliver, 'Soundings: Towards a Theological Poetics of Silence', in *Silence and the Word: Negative Theology and Incarnation*, edited by Oliver Davies and Denys Turner (Cambridge: Cambridge University Press, 2002), 201–22.
Dawes, Kwame, 'Black British Poetry, Some Considerations', *Wasafiri* 18, no. 38 (2003): 44–8.
Day-Lewis, Cecil, *The Lyric Impulse* (Harvard: UMI, 1965).
D'Costa, Gavin, Eleanor Nesbitt, Mark Pryce, Ruth Shelton and Nicola Slee, *Making Nothing Happen: Five Poets Explore Faith and Spirituality* (Farnham: Ashgate, 2014).
Dekker, Kees, 'Pentecost and Linguistic Self-Consciousness in Anglo-Saxon England: Bede and Ælfric', *The Journal of English and Germanic Philology* 104, no. 3 (July 2005): 345–72.
Department of Health and Social Care, UK Government, 'New Campaign to Prevent Spread of Coronavirus Indoors This Winter' (9 September 2020). https://www.gov.uk/government/news/new-campaign-to-prevent-spread-of-coronavirus-indoors-this-winter.
Derrida, Jacques, *Of Grammatology: On Orality and Literacy*, translated by Gayatri Chakravorty Spivak (Baltimore: Johns Hopkins University Press, 1976).
Detweiler, Robert, 'Vexing the Text: The Politics of Literary-Religious Interpretation', *Christianity and Literature* 41, no. 1 (1991): 61–70.
Dobbs-Allsopp, F. W., *On Biblical Poetry* (Oxford: Oxford University Press, 2015).
Dodd, Elizabeth S., 'John Clare's Romantic "I": A Prophetic Poetics of Testimony', in *Prophetic Witness and the Reimagining of the World: Poetry, Theology and Philosophy in Dialogue*, edited by Mark S. Burrows, Hilary Davies and Josephine von Zitzewitz, Power of the Word, volume 5 (London: Routledge, 2020).
Dodd, Elizabeth S., 'Silence, Breath, Body, Cry: Poetry and Prayer', in *T&T Clark Handbook of Christian Prayer*, edited by Ashley Cocksworth and John C. McDowell (London: T&T Clark, 2021), 583–600.
Dodd, Elizabeth S., 'The Spirit of the Religious Lyric: Towards Further Conversations between Literature and Theology', *Scintilla: The Journal of the Vaughan Association* 20 (2017): 66–78.
Dodd, Elizabeth S., 'Spoken Word and Spirit's Breath: A Theopoetics of Performance Poetry', *Literature & Theology* 33, no. 3 (September 2019): 292–306.
Dodd, Elizabeth S., 'Why Lyric? A Theological Perspective', in *T&T Clark Handbook of Theology and the Arts*, edited by Imogen Adkins and Stephen M. Garrett (London: T&T Clark, forthcoming).
Donne, John, *The Variorum Edition of the Poetry of John Donne*, volume 7 part 1, edited by Gary A. Stringer and Paul A. Parrish *et al.* (Bloomington, IN: Indiana University Press, 2005).

Donne, John, *The Works of John Donne*, volume 2, edited by George R. Potter and Evelyn M. Simpson (London: University of California Press, 1953–62).
Drury, John, *Music at Midnight: The Life and Poetry of George Herbert* (London: Penguin, 2013).
Du Bois, W. E. B., *The Souls of Black Folk*, edited by Brent Hayes Edwards (Oxford: Oxford University Press, 2007).
Dubrow, Heather, *The Challenges of Orpheus: Lyric Poetry and Early Modern England* (Baltimore, MD: Johns Hopkins University Press, 2008).
Duncan, Thomas G., editor, *Medieval English Lyrics and Carols* (Cambridge: D.S. Brewer, 2013).
Eikelboom, Lexi, *Rhythm: A Theological Category* (Oxford: Oxford University Press, 2018).
Eliot, T. S., *Collected Poems: 1909–1962* (London: Faber & Faber, 2020).
Eliot, T. S., *George Herbert* (Tavistock: Liverpool University Press, 2018).
Eliot, T. S., *The Sacred Wood: Essays on Poetry and Criticism* (London: Methuen, 1920).
Eliot, T. S., *Selected Essays*, 3rd edition (London: Faber & Faber, 1951).
Eliot, T. S., 'The Three Voices of Poetry', in *The Complete Prose of T.S. Eliot: The Critical Edition: A European Society, 1947–1953*, edited by Iman Javadi and Ronald Schuchard (Baltimore, MD: Johns Hopkins University Press, 2018).
Eliot, T. S., 'Tradition and the Individual Talent', *The Egoist* (1919). https://www.poetryfoundation.org/articles/69400/tradition-and-the-individual-talent.
Erdman, David, *Blake: Prophet against Empire*, 3rd edition (Princeton, NJ: Princeton University Press, 1977).
Farrer, Austin, *The Glass of Vision (Bampton Lectures for 1948)* (London: Dacre Press, 1948).
Fatsis, Lambros, 'Policing the Beats: The Criminalisation of UK Drill and Grime Music by the London Metropolitan Police', *The Sociological Review* 67, no. 6 (2019): 1300–16.
Fiddes, Paul S., *Charles Williams and C.S. Lewis: Friends in Co-Inherence* (Oxford: Oxford University Press, 2021).
Fish, Stanley, 'Masculine Persuasive Force: Donne and Verbal Power', in *Soliciting Interpretation: Literary Theory and Seventeenth-Century English Poetry*, edited by Elizabeth D. Harvey and Katharine Eisaman Maus (Chicago: University of Chicago Press, 1990), 223–52.
Ford, David F., *Christian Wisdom: Desiring Freedom and Learning in Love* (Cambridge: Cambridge University Press, 2007).
Ford, David F., *The Drama of Living: Becoming Wise in the Spirit* (Grand Rapids, MI: Brazos Press, 2014).
Ford, David F., *The Gospel of John: A Theological Commentary* (Ada, MI: Baker Academic, 2021).
Ford, David F. and Rachel Muers, eds, *The Modern Theologians: An Introduction to Christian Theology since 1918*, 3rd edition (Oxford: Blackwell, 2005).
Forrester, Duncan, 'The Scope of Public Theology', *Studies in Christian Ethics* 17, no. 2 (2004): 5–19.
Forrester, Duncan, *Theology in Fragments: Explorations in Unsystematic Theology* (London: T&T Clark, 2005).
Fowler, Alastair, *Kinds of Literature: An Introduction to the Theory of Genres and Modes* (Oxford: Clarendon, 1982).
France-Williams, Azariah, *Ghost Ship: Institutional Racism and the Church of England* (London: SCM, 2020).

Franke, William, 'Poetry, Prophecy, and Theological Revelation', in *Oxford Research Encyclopedia of Religion* (Oxford: Oxford University Press, 2016). Online. https://doi.org/10.1093/acrefore/9780199340378.013.205.
Freedman, David Noel, 'Pottery, Poetry, and Prophecy: An Essay on Biblical Poetry', *Journal of Biblical Literature* 96, no. 1 (1977): 5–26.
Frei, Hans W., *The Eclipse of Biblical Narrative: A Study in Eighteenth and Nineteenth Century Hermeneutics* (New Haven: Yale University Press, 1974).
Frye, Northrop, *Anatomy of Criticism: Four Essays* (Princeton: Princeton University Press, 1957).
Frye, Northrop, *Northrop Frye's Fearful Symmetry: A Study of William Blake*, edited by Nicholas Halmi, Collected Works of Northrop Frye 14 (Toronto: University of Toronto Press, 2004).
Fuller, David, 'Lyrics, Sacred and Secular', in *A Companion to Medieval Poetry*, edited by Corinne Saunders (London: Wiley-Blackwell, 2010), 258–76.
Gardner, Helen, editor, *The Faber Book of Religious Verse* (London: Faber, 1971).
Gardner, Thomas, *Lyric Theology: Art and the Doctrine of Creation* (Waco, TX: Baylor University Press, 2022).
George the Poet, 'Have You Heard George's Podcast?' (BBC, 2019). Audio.
Gilmour, Rachel, 'Doing Voices: Reading Language as Craft in Black British Poetry', *The Journal of Commonwealth Literature* 49, no. 3 (2014): 343–57.
Graham, Elaine, *Between a Rock and a Hard Place: Public Theology in a Post-Secular Age* (London: SCM, 2013).
Gray, Douglas, editor, *English Medieval Religious Lyrics*, 2nd edition (Liverpool: Liverpool University Press, 1992).
Gray, Douglas, *Themes and Images in the Medieval English Religious Lyric* (London: Routledge, 1972).
Greene, Richard Leighton, *Early English Carols*, 2nd edition (Oxford: Oxford University Press, 1977).
Greene, Roland, *Post-Petrarchism: Origins and Innovations of the Western Lyric Sequence* (Princeton, CA: Princeton University Press, 1991).
Greene, Roland, and Stephen Cushman, eds, *The Princeton Encyclopedia of Poetry and Poetics* (Princeton: Princeton University Press, 2017). https://doi.org/10.1093/acref/9780190681173.001.0001.
Greene, Thomas M., 'Poetry as Invocation', *New Literary History* 24, no. 3 (Summer 1993): 495–517.
The Greenham Song Book. Online. www.yourgreenham.co.uk.
Grey, Mary, 'The Core of Our Desire: Reimagining the Trinity', *Theology* 93 (1990): 362–72.
Grey, Mary, *A Cry for Dignity: Religion, Violence and the Struggle of Dalit Women in India* (London: Routledge, 2014).
Gruchy, John de, 'Kairos Moments and Prophetic Witness: Towards a Prophetic Ecclesiology', *Hervormde Teologiese Studies* 72, no. 4 (2016). https://doi.org/10.4102/hts.v72i4.3414.
Guite, Malcolm, *After Prayer: New Sonnets and Other Poems* (Norwich: Canterbury Press 2019).
Hamlin, Hannibal, *Psalm Culture and Early Modern English Literature* (Cambridge: Cambridge University Press, 2004).
Hancox, Dan, *Inner City Pressure: The Story of Grime* (London: HarperCollins, 2018).
Hankey, Wayne J. and Douglas Hedley, eds, *Deconstructing Radical Orthodoxy: Postmodern Theology, Rhetoric and Truth* (Aldershot: Ashgate, 2005).

Harrison, Carol, *On Music, Sense, Affect and Voice* (London: Bloomsbury 2019).
Hart, Kevin, *Poetry and Revelation: For a Phenomenology of Religious Poetry* (London: Bloomsbury, 2017).
Hartman, Geoffrey, 'The Poetics of Prophecy' and 'Romanticism and Anti-Selfconsciousness', in *Beyond Formalism: Literary Essays 1958–1970* (New Haven, CT: Yale University Press, 1970), 160–8.
Harvey, Carol J., 'Macaronic Techniques in Anglo-Norman Verse', *L'Esprit Createur* 18, no. 1 (Spring 1978): 70–81.
Hass, Andrew, David Jasper, and Elisabeth Jay, eds, *The Oxford Handbook of English Literature and Theology* (Oxford: Oxford University Press, 2009). Oxford Handbooks Online.
Heaney, Seamus, *North* (London: Faber & Faber, 1992).
Hedges, Paul, 'The Rhetoric and Reception of John Milbank's Radical Orthodoxy: Privileging Prejudice in Theology?', *Open Theology* 1, no. 1 (19 January 2014): 24–44.
Heffelfinger, Katie M., *I Am Large, I Contain Multitudes: Lyric Cohesion and Conflict in Second Isaiah* (Leiden: Brill, 2011).
Hegel, G. W. F., *Hegel's Aesthetics: Lectures on Fine Art*, volume 2, translated by T. M. Knox (Oxford: Clarendon, 1975).
Henderson, Andrea K., *Romantic Identities: Varieties of Subjectivity, 1774–1830* (Cambridge: Cambridge University Press, 2008).
Henderson, Mae Gwendolyn, 'Speaking in Tongues: Dialogics, Dialectics and the Black Woman Writer's Literary Tradition', in *Colonial Discourse and Post Colonial Theory: A Reader*, edited by P. Williamson and L. Crisman (New York: Columbia University Press, 1994), 257–68.
Herbert, George, *The English Poems of George Herbert*, edited by Helen Wilcox (Cambridge: Cambridge University Press, 2007).
Herbert, George, *A Priest to the Temple, or, the Country Parson* (London: T. Maxey, 1652).
Herder, Johann Gottfried, 'Essay on the Origin of Language', in *Two Essays On the Origin of Language: Jean-Jacques Rousseau and Johann Gottfried Herder*, translated by John H. Moran and Alexander Gode (Chicago: University of Chicago Press, 1966).
Hiebert, Theodore, 'The Tower of Babel and the Origin of the World's Cultures', *Journal of Biblical Literature* 126 (2007): 29–58.
Higham, Florence, *Catholic and Reformed: A Study of the Anglican Church, 1559–1662* (London: SPCK, 1962).
Hill, Geoffrey, 'The Art of Poetry No. 80', interview by Carl Phillips, *The Paris Review* 154 (Spring 2000). Online. https://www.theparisreview.org/interviews/730/the-art-of-poetry-no-80-geoffrey-hill.
Hill, Geoffrey, *Broken Hierarchies: Poems 1952–2012*, edited by Kenneth Haynes (Oxford: Oxford University Press, 2013).
Hill, Geoffrey, *Collected Critical Writings*, edited by Kenneth Haynes (Oxford: Oxford University Press, 2009).
Hill, Geoffrey, 'Poetry and "the Democracy of the Dead"' (Oxford University, 3 December 2013). Audio. http://media.podcasts.ox.ac.uk/engfac/general/mt13-hill-lecture.mp3.
Hilton, Walter, 'Of the Song of Angels', in *The Cell of Self-Knowledge: Seven Early English Mystical Treatises*, edited by Edmund G. Gardner (New York: Cooper Square Publishers, 1966), 63–77.
Hiscox, Andrew and Helen Wilcox, eds, *The Oxford Handbook of Early Modern English Literature and Religion* (Oxford: Oxford University Press, 2017).

Hodgson, Andrew, 'Clare's Lyric Impulse', *The Cambridge Quarterly* 45 (2016): 103–18.
Hopler, Jay, and Kimberly Johnson, eds, *Before the Door of God: An Anthology of Devotional Poetry* (New Haven, CT: Yale University Press, 2013).
Hošek, Chaviva, and Patricia A. Parker, eds, *Lyric Poetry: Beyond New Criticism* (Ithaca, NY: Cornell University Press, 1985).
Houghton-Walker, Sarah, *John Clare's Religion* (Farnham: Ashgate, 2009).
Howatson, M. C., editor, *The Oxford Companion to Classical Literature*, 3rd edition (Oxford: Oxford University, Press, 2011).
Hugill, Stan, *Shanties from the Seven Seas* (London: Routledge and Kegan Paul, 1961).
Hull, John, *Towards the Prophetic Church: A Study of Christian Mission* (London: SCM, 2014).
Hunter, Graham, *Discipline and Desire: Embracing Charismatic Liturgical Worship* (Cambridge: Grove Books, 2017).
Hurley, Michael D., *Faith in Poetry: Verse Style as a Mode of Religious Belief* (London: Bloomsbury, 2017).
Irigaray, Luce, 'The Age of the Breath', in *Key Writings*, edited by Luce Irigaray (London: Continuum, 2004), 165–70.
Isaacs, David, 'Unfinished to Perfection: Geoffrey Hill, Revision, and the Poetics of Stone', *Textual Practice* (13 April 2021). https://doi.org/10.1080/095023 6X.2021.1900377.
Jackson, Virginia, 'Lyric', in *The Princeton Encyclopedia of Poetry and Poetics*, edited by Roland Greene and Stephen Cushman (Princeton: Princeton University Press, 2017). https://doi.org/10.1093/acref/9780190681173.001.0001.
Jackson, Virginia, and Yopie Prins, eds, *The Lyric Theory Reader: A Critical Anthology* (Baltimore, MA: Johns Hopkins University Press, 2014).
Jagessar, Michael N., '*Dis*-Place Theologizing: Fragments of Intercultural Adventurous God-Talk, *Black Theology* 13, no. 3 (2015): 258–72.
Jakobson, Roman, *The Sound Shape of Language* (Bloomington, IN: Indiana University Press, 1979).
Jasper, David, *The Language of Liturgy: A Ritual Poetics* (London: SCM, 2018).
Jefferson, Judith and Ad Putter, eds, *Multilingualism in Medieval Britain (c. 1066–1520): Sources and Analysis* (Turnout: Brepols, 2012).
Jeffrey, David Lyle, *The Early English Lyric and Franciscan Spirituality* (Lincoln, NE: University of Nebraska Press, 1975).
Jennings, Elizabeth, editor, *The Batsford Book of Religious Verse* (London: B.T. Batsford Ltd., 1981).
Jennings, Willie James, *After Whiteness (Theological Education between the Times)* (Grand Rapids, MI: Eerdmans, 2020). Kindle.
Jennings, Willie James, *The Christian Imagination: Theology and the Origins of Race* (New Haven, CT: Yale University Press, 2010).
John of the Cross, *The Collected Works of St John of the Cross*, translated by Kieran Kavanaugh and Otilio Rodriguez, 3rd edition (Washington, DC: ICS Publications, 2017).
Johnson, Barbara, 'Apostrophe, Animation, and Abortion', *Diacritics* 16, no. 1 (Spring 1986): 28–47.
Johnson, Javon, *Killing Poetry: Blackness and the Making of Slam and Spoken Word Communities* (New Brunswick, NJ: Rutgers University Press, 2017).
Johnson, Linton Kwesi, *Dread Beat and Blood*, introduction by Andrew Salkey (London: Bogle-L'Ouverture Publications, 1975).

Johnson, Linton Kwesi, 'Jamaican Rebel Music', *Race & Class* 17, no. 4 (1976): 397–413.
Johnson, Linton Kwesi, 'Reading Bass Culture: Linton Kwesi Johnson in Conversation with Paul Gilroy', interview by Louisa Layne, Postcolonial Writing and Theory Seminar, Great Writers Inspire at Home Series (The Oxford Research Centre in the Humanities, 26 April 2018). Audio. https://www.torch.ox.ac.uk/reading-bass-culture-linton-kwesi-johnson-in-conversation-with-paul-gilroy-1.
Johnson, Linton Kwesi, *Selected Poems* (London: Penguin, 2006). Kindle.
Johnson, W. R., *The Idea of Lyric: Lyric Modes in Ancient and Modern Poetry* (Berkeley: University of California Press, 1982).
Julian of Norwich, *The Writings of Julian of Norwich*, edited by Nicholas Watson and Jacqueline Jenkins (University Park, PA: Pennsylvania State University Press, 2006).
Kabir, Ananya Jahanara, 'Affect, Body, Place: Trauma Theory in the World', in *The Future of Trauma Theory: Contemporary Literary and Cultural Criticism*, edited by Gert Buelens, Sam Durrant and Robert Eaglestone (London: Routledge, 2014), 63–76.
Keats, John, *Life, Letters, and Literary Remains, of John Keats*, edited by Richard Monckton Milnes (London: Edward Moxon, 1848).
Keller, Catherine, *The Face of the Deep: A Theology of Becoming* (London: Routledge, 2003).
Kelsey, David, *Eccentric Existence: A Theological Anthropology*, 2 volumes (Louisville, KY: Westminster John Knox Press, 2009).
Kempe, Margery, *The Book of Margery Kempe*, edited by Lynn Staley (Kalamazoo, MI: Medieval Institute Publications, 1996).
Kerr, Fergus, *Theology after Wittgenstein*, 2nd edition (London: SPCK, 1997).
Kilby, Karen, *Balthasar: A (Very) Critical Introduction* (Grand Rapids, MI: W.B. Eerdmans Pub., 2012).
Kimbrough, S. T., *The Lyrical Theology of Charles Wesley: A Reader* (Cambridge: Lutterworth, 2014).
Knowles, Beyoncé, *Lemonade* (Parkwood Entertainment, 23 April 2016). Audio-visual.
Kövesi, Simon, *John Clare: Nature, Criticism and History* (London: Palgrave Macmillan).
Kövesi, Simon and Scott McEathron, eds, *New Essays on John Clare: Poetry, Culture and Community* (Cambridge: Cambridge University Press, 2015).
Kristeva, Julia, *Revolution in Poetic Language* (New York: Columbia University Press, 1984).
Kuduk Weiner, Stephanie, *Clare's Lyric: John Clare and Three Modern Poets* (Oxford: Oxford University Press, 2014).
Kugel, James, editor, *Poetry and Prophecy: The Beginnings of a Literary Tradition* (Ithaca: Cornell University Press, 1990).
Lacoue-Labarthe, Philippe, *Poetry as Experience*, translated by Andrea Tarnowski (Stanford, CA: Stanford University Press, 1999).
Lampe, Geoffrey, *God as Spirit* (Oxford: Clarendon, 1977).
Lawson Welsh, Sarah, 'Vernacular Voices: Black British Poetry', in *The Cambridge History of Black and British Asian Writing*, edited by Susheila Nasta and Mark Stein (Cambridge: Cambridge University Press, 2020), 329–52.
Lecluyse, Chrisopher, 'Sacred Bilingualism: Code Switching in Medieval English Verse' (PhD, University of Texas, Austin, 2002).
Levertov, Denise, *The Poet in the World* (New York: New Directions, 1973).
Levi, Peter, editor, *The Penguin Book of English Christian Verse* (London: Penguin, 1984).
Lewalski, Barbara Kiefer, *Protestant Poetics and the Seventeenth-Century Religious Lyric* (Princeton: Princeton University Press, 1979).

Lewis, C. S., *English Literature in the Sixteenth Century, Excluding Drama* (London: Oxford University Press, 1954).
Linafelt, Tod, *The Hebrew Bible as Literature: A Very Short Introduction* (Oxford: Oxford University Press, 2016).
Lindbeck, George A., *The Nature of Doctrine: Religion and Theology in a Postliberal Age* (Philadelphia: Westminster Press, 1984).
Locke, Anne, 'A Meditation', in *The Collected Works of Anne Vaughan Locke*, edited by Susan M. Felch (Tempe, AZ: Arizona Center for Medieval and Renaissance Studies and Renaissance English Text Society, 1999).
Lok, Ann, *A Meditation of a Penitent Sinner*, appended to *Sermons of John Calvin, upon the Songe that Ezechias Made after He Had Been Sicke* (London: John Day, 1560).
Lowth, Robert, *Isaiah: A New Translation* (London: J. Nichols, 1778).
Lowth, Robert, *Lectures on the Sacred Poetry of the Hebrews*, edited by Calvin E. Stowe, translated by G. Gregory (New York: J. Leavitt, 1829).
Ludlow, Morwenna, *Art, Craft and Theology in Fourth-Century Christian Authors* (Oxford: Oxford University Press, 2020).
Lund, Eric, *Documents from the History of Lutheranism, 1517–1750* (Minneapolis, MN: Fortress Press, 2002).
Macleish, Archibald, *Collected Poems 1917–1952* (Boston, MA: Houghton Mifflin Harcourt, 1952).
Major, Tristan, *Undoing Babel: The Tower of Babel in Anglo-Saxon Literature* (Toronto: University of Toronto Press, 2018).
Man, Paul de, 'Lyric and Modernity', and 'Anthropomorphism and Trope in Lyric', in *The Rhetoric of Romanticism* (New York: Columbia University Press, 1984), 239–62.
Maring, Heather, *Signs That Sing: Hybrid Poetics in Old English Verse* (Gainesville: University Press of Florida, 2017), chaps 1 and 7.
Marion, Jean-Luc, *The Visible and the Revealed*, translated by Christina Gschwandtner (New York: Fordham University Press, 2008).
Marriott, D. S., *Duppies* (Oakland, CA: Commune Editions, 2019).
May, G. Lacey, editor, *English Religious Verse* (London: J.M. Dent and Sons, 1937).
McArthur, Tom, Jacqueline Lam-McArthur and Lise Fontaine, eds, *The Oxford Companion to the English Language*, 2nd edition (Oxford: Oxford University Press, 2018). Online. https://www.oxfordreference.com/view/10.1093/acref/9780199661282.001.0001/acref-9780199661282.
McDowell, John C., editor, *Philosophy and the Burden of Theological Honesty: A Donald MacKinnon Reader* (London: Bloomsbury, 2011).
McKusick, James, 'Beyond the Visionary Company: John Clare's Resistance to Romanticism', in *John Clare in Context*, edited by Geoffrey Summerfield, Hugh Haughton and Adam Phillips (Cambridge: Cambridge University Press, 1994), 221–37.
Mendelson, Sara H., 'Carey [née Jackson], Mary, Lady Carey', *Oxford Dictionary of National Biography* (Oxford: Oxford University Press, 2004). Online. https://doi.org/10.1093/ref:odnb/45811.
Mill, John Stuart, 'Thoughts on Poetry and Its Varieties', *The Crayon* 7, no. 4 (April 1860): 93–7.
Miller, Kei, *The Cartographer Tries to Map a Way to Zion* (London: Carcanet, 2014).
Miller, Kei, *There Is an Anger That Moves* (London: Carcanet, 2012).
Milovanović-Barham, Čelica, 'Gregory of Nazianzus: Ars Poetica (In Suos Versus: Carmen 2.1.39)', *Journal of Early Christian Studies* 5, no. 4 (1997): 497–510.
Milton, John, *The Reason of Church-Government* (London: John Rothwell, 1641).

Miner, Earl Roy, *Comparative Poetics: An Intercultural Essay on Theories of Literature* (Princeton, NJ: Princeton University Press, 1990).
Mirk, John, *Mirk's Festial: A Collection of Homilies*, edited by Theodor Erbe (London: Kegan Paul, 1905).
Moberly, R. W. L., *Prophecy and Discernment* (Cambridge: Cambridge University Press, 2006).
Muers, Rachel, 'The Holy Spirit, the Voices of Nature and Environmental Prophecy', *Scottish Journal of Theology* 67, no. 3 (2014): 323–39.
Muers, Rachel, *Keeping God's Silence: Towards a Theological Ethics of Communication* (Oxford: Blackwell, 2004).
Nagra, Daljit, *Look We Have Coming to Dover* (London: Faber & Faber, 2010).
Nederduitse Gereformeerde Kerk, Algemene Sinode, *Human Relations and the South African Scene in the Light of Scripture* (Cape Town: National Book Printers, 1976).
Nicholson, Mark, 'The Itinerant "I": John Clare's Lyric Defiance', *English Literary History* 82 (2015): 637–69.
Nietzsche, Friedrich, *The Birth of Tragedy* (New York: Dover Publications, 1995).
O'Brien, Bruce R., *Reversing Babel: Translation among the English during an Age of Conquests, c. 800 to c. 1200* (Newark: University of Delaware Press, 2011).
O'Donnell, Karen, *The Dark Womb: Re-Conceiving Theology Through Reproductive Loss* (London: SCM, 2022).
Okeowo, Alexis, 'Warsan Shire's Portraits of Somalis in Exile', *New Yorker* (7 February 2022). https://www.newyorker.com/magazine/2022/02/14/warsan-shires-portraits-of-somalis-in-exile.
Olson, Charles, 'Projective Verse' (1950), in *Collected Prose*, edited by Donald Allen and Benjamin Friedlander (Oakland, CA: University of California Press, 1971), 239–49.
Ong, Walter, *The Presence of the Word* (New Haven, CT: Yale University Press, 1967).
Orchard, Andy, 'Poetic Inspiration and Prosaic Translation: The Making of Cædmon's Hymn', in *'Doubt Wisely': Papers in Honour of E. G. Stanley*, edited by M. J. Toswell and E. M. Tyler (London: Routledge, 1996), 402–22.
Owen, Wilfred, *Poems* (Outlook Verlag, 2018/1918).
Palgrave, Francis Turner, *The Golden Treasury of the Best Songs and Lyrical Poems in the English Language* (London: Macmillan, 1861). http://dbooks.bodleian.ox.ac.uk/books/PDFs/590750102.pdf.
Palmer, Andrew and Sally Minogue, 'Modernism and First World War Poetry: Alternative Lines', in *The Cambridge Companion to Modernist Poetry*, edited by Alex Davis and Lee M. Jenkins (Cambridge: Cambridge University Press, 2015), 227–52.
Paterson, Don, *The Poem: Lyric, Sign, Metre* (London: Faber, 2018).
Peachum, Henry, *The Garden of Eloquence Conteyning the Most Excellent Ornaments, Exornations, Lightes, Flowers, and Formes of Speech, Commonly Called the Figures of Rhetorike* (London: Richard Field for H. Jackson, 1593).
Percy, Martin, 'Sweet Rapture: Subliminal Eroticism in Contemporary Charismatic Worship', *Theology & Sexuality: The Journal of the Institute for the Study of Christianity and Sexuality*, no. 6 (1997): 71–106.
Pickstock, Catherine, *After Writing: On the Liturgical Consummation of Philosophy* (Oxford: Blackwell, 1998).
Porta, Miquel and John M. Last, eds, *A Dictionary of Public Health*, 2nd edition (Oxford: Oxford University Press, 2018).
Pound, Ezra, 'A Few Don'ts by an Imagiste', *Poetry* (March 1913): 200–8.

Purcell, Michael, 'Rahner amid Modernity and Post-Modernity', in *The Cambridge Companion to Karl Rahner*, edited by Declan Marmion and Mary E. Hines (Cambridge: Cambridge University Press, 2005), 195–210.
Puttenham, George, *The Arte of English Poesie* (London: Richard Field, 1589).
Pryce, Mark, *Poetry, Practical Theology and Reflective Practice* (Abingdon: Routledge, 2019).
Quash, Ben, *Theology and the Drama of History* (Cambridge: Cambridge University Press, 2005).
Quash, Ben, 'Wonder-Voyaging: The Pneumatological Character of David Ford's Theology', in *The Vocation of Theology Today: A Festschrift for David Ford*, edited by Tom Greggs, Rachel Muers and Simeon Zahl (Eugene, OR: Cascade, 2013), 146–62.
Rahner, Karl, 'Poetry and the Christian', in *Theological Investigations*, volume 4 (New York: Crossroad, 1974), 357–67.
Ramazani, Jahan, 'Code-Switching, Code-Stitching: A Macaronic Poetics?', *Dibur Literary Journal* 1 (Autumn 2015): 29–41.
Ramazani, Jahan, *Poetry and Its Others: News, Prayer, Song, and the Dialogue of Genres* (Chicago, IL: Chicago University Press, 2013).
Rasheed, Kameelah Janan, 'To Be Vulnerable and Fearless: An Interview with Writer Warsan Shire' (November 2012). http://wellandoftenpress.com/reader/to-be-vulnerable-and-fearless-an-interview-with-writer-warsan-shire/.
Reddie, Anthony, Pamela Searle and Seidel Boanerges, eds, *Intercultural Preaching*, Congregational Resources, volume 1 (Regent's Park College Oxford: Centre for Baptist Studies in Oxford, 2021).
Regan, Stephen, *The Sonnet* (Oxford: Oxford University Press, 2019).
Reginald of Durham, *De Vita et Miraculis S, Godrici, Heremitæ de Finchale*, edited by J. Stevenson, Surtees Society (London: Nichols, 1847).
Ricks, Christopher, 'Geoffrey Hill and 'The Tongue's Atrocities', *The Times Literary Supplement* 3978 (30 June 1978): 743–7.
Ricoeur, Paul, *Essays on Biblical Interpretation*, edited by Lewis S. Mudge (London: SPCK, 1981).
Rienstra, Debra, '"Let Wits Contest": George Herbert and the English Sonnet Sequence', *George Herbert Journal* 35, nos. 1–2 (2011–12): 23–44.
Roberts, Andrew Michael, editor, *Strangeness and Power: Essays on the Poetry of Geoffrey Hill* (Swindon: Shearsman, 2020).
Robinson, John A. T., *Honest to God* (London: SCM, 1963).
Robinson, Roger, *A Portable Paradise* (Leeds: Peepal Tree Press, 2019). Kindle.
Rogers, Eugene F., *After the Spirit: A Constructive Pneumatology from Resources Outside the Modern West* (Grand Rapids, MI: Eerdmans, 2005). Kindle.
Rogers, W. E., *The Three Genres and the Interpretation of Lyric* (Princeton, NJ: Princeton University Press, 1983).
Rolle, Richard, *The Fire of Love or Melody of Love and The Mending of Life or The Rule of Living*, translated by Richard Misyn, edited by Frances Comper, 2nd edition (London: Methuen, 1920).
Rolle, Richard, *Richard Rolle's Melody of Love*, translated by Andrew Albin (Toronto, Canada: Pontifical Institute of Mediaeval Studies, 2018).
Romer, Stephen, 'Laus et Vituperatio: The Triumph of Love (1998); Speech! Speech! (2000); The Orchards of Syon (2002)', *Études Anglaises* 71, no. 2 (2018): 191–206.
Rowland, Christopher, *Radical Prophet: The Mystics, Subversives and Visionaries who Strove for Heaven on Earth* (London: I.B. Tauris, 2017).

Rowlands, Anna, 'The Language of the Common Good', in *Together for the Common Good: Towards a National Conversation*, edited by Nicholas Sagovsky and Peter McGrail (London: SCM, 2015).

Ruf, Frederick J., *Entangled Voices: Genre and the Religious Construction of the Self* (Oxford: Oxford University Press, 1997).

Salminen, Antti, 'On Breathroutes: Paul Celan's Poetics of Breathing', *Partial Answers: Journal of Literature and the History of Ideas* 12, no. 1 (2014): 107–26.

Sampson, Fiona, *Beyond the Lyric: A Map of Contemporary British Poetry* (London: Chatto & Windus, 2012).

Schlegel, Friedrich, *Philosophical Fragments*, translated by Peter Firchow (Minneapolis, Minnesota: University of Minnesota Press, 1991).

Schoenfeldt, Michael, *Prayer and Power: George Herbert and Renaissance Courtship* (Chicago: University of Chicago Press, 1991).

Serjeantson, Deirdre, 'The Book of Psalms and the Early Modern Sonnet', *Renaissance Studies* 29, no. 4 (September 2015): 632–49.

Shanks, Andrew, *Faith in Honesty: The Essential Nature of Theology* (Aldershot: Ashgate, 2005).

Sharpe, Jenny, 'Dub and Difference: A Conversation with Jean 'Binta' Breeze, *Callaloo* 26, no. 3 (Summer 2003): 607–13.

Shelley, Percy Bysshe, 'A Defence of Poetry' (1821), in *Essays, Letters from Abroad, Translations and Fragments*, edited by Mary Shelley, 2 volumes (London: Edward Moxon, 1840), 1:1–57.

Sherry, Vincent, *The Uncommon Tongue: The Poetry and Criticism of Geoffrey Hill* (Ann Arbor: University of Michigan Press, 1987).

Shire, Warsan, *Bless the Daughter Raised by a Voice in Her Head* (London: Chatto & Windus, 2022).

Sidney, Phillip, *The Defence of Poesie* (London: William Ponsonby, 1595).

Sidney, Phillip and Mary, *The Sidney Psalter: The Psalms of Sir Philip and Mary Sidney*, edited by Hannibal Hamlin *et al.* (Oxford: Oxford University Press, 2009).

Silkin, Jon, 'The Poetry of Geoffrey Hill', *The Iowa Review* 3, no. 3 (Summer 1972): 108–28.

Slee, Nicola, *Fragments for Fractures Times: What Feminist Practical Theology Brings to the Table* (London: SCM, 2020).

Slee, Nicola, *Praying Like a Woman* (London: SPCK, 2004).

Smith, James K. A., *Imagining the Kingdom: How Worship Works* (Grand Rapids MI: Baker Academic, 2013).

Smith, James K. A., *Thinking in Tongues: Pentecostal Contributions to Christian Philosophy* (Grand Rapids, MI: Eerdmans, 2010).

Smith, Michael, 'Mi Cyaan Believe It', *'Mi C-YaaN beLiēVe iT'* (Island LP #ILPS 9717, 1982). Audio.

Sonderegger, Katherine, *The Doctrine of God*, Systematic Theology, volume 1 (Minneapolis: Fortress Press, 2015).

Sonderegger, Katherine, *The Doctrine of the Holy Trinity: Processions and Persons*, Systematic Theology, volume 2 (Minneapolis, MN: Fortress Press, 2020).

Soskice, Janet M., *Metaphor and Religious Language* (Oxford: Clarendon, 1985).

Sperling, Matthew, *Visionary Philology: Geoffrey Hill and the Study of Words* (Oxford: Oxford University Press, 2014).

Spinks, Bryan D., *The Worship Mall: Contemporary Responses to Contemporary Culture* (London: SPCK, 2010).

Stanton, Robert, *The Culture of Translation in Anglo-Saxon England* (Cambridge: D.S. Brewer, 2002).
Steiner, George, *Language and Silence: Essays 1958–1966* (London: Faber & Faber, 2010).
Steiner, George, *Real Presences: Is There Anything in What We Say?* (London: Faber & Faber, 2010).
Steinman, Andrew E., *Genesis: An Introduction and Commentary* (Downers Grove, IL: InterVarsity Press, 2019).
Sterrett, Joseph, editor, *Prayer and Performance in Early Modern English Literature: Gesture, Word and Devotion* (Cambridge: Cambridge University Press, 2018).
Steven, James, 'The Spirit in Contemporary Charismatic Worship', in *The Spirit in Worship – Worship in the Spirit*, edited by Teresa Berger and Bryan D. Spinks (Collegeville, MN: Liturgical Press, 2009), 245–59 (248–50).
Stevenson, Debris feat Jammz, *Poet in da Corner* (London: Oberon, an imprint of Bloomsbury Publishing Plc, 2018). Book.
Stevenson, Debris feat Jammz, *Poet in da Corner* (London: Accidental Records, 2020). Audio.
Stewart, Susan, 'Letter on Sound', in *Close Listening: Poetry and the Performed Word*, edited by Charles Bernstein (Oxford: Oxford University Press, 1998), 28–52.
Stormzy, *Gang Signs & Prayer* (#Merky; Warner; ADA, 2017). Audio.
Stormzy, *Heavy Is the Head* (#Merky; Atlantic, 2019). Audio.
Strawn, B. A., 'Lyric Poetry', in *Dictionary of the Old Testament: A Compendium of Contemporary Biblical Scholarship*, edited by Tremper Longman III and Peter Enns (Westmont: InterVarsity Press, 2010), 437–46.
Strawson, Galen, *Real Materialism: And Other Essays* (Oxford: Oxford University Press, 2008).
Strong, James, *The Exhaustive Concordance of the Bible* (New York: Abingdon-Cokesbury Press, 1947).
Sugano, Douglas, editor, 'Play 40, Pentecost', in *The N-Town Plays* (Kalamazoo, MI: Medieval Institute Publications, 2007). Online edition. https://d.lib.rochester.edu/teams/text/sugano-n-town-plays-play-40-pentecost.
Swinton, John, *Dementia: Living in the Memories of God* (London: SCM, 2012).
Targoff, Ramie, *Common Prayer: The Language of Public Devotion in Early Modern England* (Chicago: University of Chicago Press, 2001).
Targoff, Ramie, 'The Poetics of Common Prayer: George Herbert and the Seventeenth-Century Devotional Lyric', *English Literary Renaissance* 29, no. 3 (1999): 468–90.
Taylor, Kevin and Giles Waller, eds, *Christian Theology and Tragedy: Theologians, Tragic Literature and Tragic Theory* (London: Routledge, 2011).
Tempest, Kae, *The Book of Traps and Lessons* (New York: Republic Records, 2019). Audio.
Tempest, Kae, *Hold Your Own* (London: Picador, 2014).
Tempest, Kae, *Let Them Eat Chaos* (London: Picador, 2016).
Tempest, Kae, *The Line Is a Curve* (New York: Republic Records, 2022). Audio.
Tempest, Kae, *On Connection* (London: Faber & Faber, 2020). Kindle.
Thompson, Anne B., editor, *The Northern Homily Cycle* (Kalamazoo, MI: Medieval Institute Publications, 2008). Online. https://d.lib.rochester.edu/teams/text/thompson-northern-homily-cycle-homily-33-pentecost.
Thompson, Edward, editor, *O World Invisible: An Anthology of Religious Poetry* (London: Ernest Benn, 1931).
Thomas, R. S., editor, *The Penguin Book of Religious Verse* (Harmondsworth: Penguin, 1963).

Tomlin, Carol, *Preach It! Understanding African-Caribbean Preaching* (London: SCM, 2019).

Townes, Emilie M., 'Women's Wisdom: On Solidarity and Differences (On Not Rescuing the Killers)', *Union Seminary Quarterly Review* 53, nos 3–4 (1999): 153–64.

Tracy, David, *Fragments: The Existential Situation of Our Time: Selected Essays*, volume I (Chicago: University of Chicago Press, 2020).

Vanhoozer, Kevin J. editor, *The Cambridge Companion to Postmodern Theology* (Cambridge: Cambridge University Press, 2003).

Vanhoozer, Kevin J. editor, *The Drama of Doctrine: A Canonical-Linguistic Approach to Christian Theology* (Louisville: Westminster John Knox Press, 2005).

Vendler, Helen, *The Art of Shakespeare's Sonnets* (Harvard: Harvard University Press, 1997).

Vendler, Helen, *The Given and the Made: Strategies of Poetic Redefinition* (Cambridge, MA: Harvard University Press, 1995).

Waal, Edmund de, *The White Road: A Pilgrimage of Sorts* (London: Chatto & Windus, 2015).

Walker, Jeffrey, 'Aristotle's Lyric: Re-Imagining the Rhetoric of Epideictic Song', *College English* 51, no. 1 (January 1989): 5–28.

Walton, Heather, 'Re-visioning the Subject in Literature and Theology', in *Self/Same/Other: Re-visioning the Subject in Literature and Theology*, edited by Heather Walton and Andrew Hass (Sheffield: Sheffield Academic Press, 2000).

Walton, Heather, *Writing Methods in Theological Reflection* (London: SCM).

Ward, Pete, *Liquid Ecclesiology: The Gospel and the Church* (Leiden: Brill, 2017).

Ward, Pete, *Selling Worship: How What We Sing Has Changed the Church* (Bletchley: Paternoster Press, 2005).

Warton, Thomas, *The History of English Poetry from the Close of the Eleventh to the Commencement of the Eighteenth Century*, 3 volumes (London: J. Dodsley, 1774–81).

Waters, William, *Poetry's Touch: On Lyric Address* (Ithaca: Cornell University Press, 2003), 1–4.

Wellek, René, *The Rise of English Literary History* (Chapel Hill: University of North Carolina Press, 1941).

Wells, Samuel, *Improvisation: The Drama of Christian Ethics*, 2nd edition (Grand Rapids, Mich: Baker Academic, 2018).

Welsh, Andrew, *Roots of Lyric: Primitive Poetry and Modern Poetics* (Princeton, NJ: Princeton University Press, 1978).

Wenzel, Siegfried, *Macaronic Sermons: Bilingualism and Preaching in Late-Medieval England* (Ann Arbor, MI: University of Michigan Press, 1994).

Wenzel, Siegfried, *Preachers, Poets, and the Early English Lyric* (Princeton, NJ: Princeton University Press, 1986).

Werker, Janet F. and Richard Tees, 'Influences on Infant Speech Processing: Toward a New Synthesis', *Annual Review of Psychology* 50 (1999): 509–35.

White, Adam, *John Clare's Romanticism* (London: Palgrave, 2017).

White, Gillian C., *Lyric Shame: The 'lyric' Subject of Contemporary American Poetry* (Cambridge, MA: Harvard University Press, 2014).

Whitehead, Christina, 'Middle English Religious Lyrics', *A Companion to the Middle English Lyric*, edited by Thomas Gibson Duncan (Cambridge: D.S. Brewer, 2005), 96–119.

Wilcox, Helen, 'When Is a Poet Not a Priest?', in *George Herbert's Pastoral: New Essays on the Poet and Priest of Bemerton*, edited by Christopher Hodgkins (Newark: University of Delaware Press, 2010), 93–102.

Wilder, Amos N., *Theopoetic: Theology and the Religious Imagination* (Eugene, OR: Wipf & Stock, 2014).

Williams, Rowan, *Anglican Identities* (Lanham, MD: Cowley Publications, 2003).

Williams, Rowan, *The Edge of Words* (London: Bloomsbury, 2014).

Williams, Rowan, *Grace and Necessity: Reflections on Art and Love* (London: Continuum, 2005).

Williams, Rowan, *On Christian Theology* (Oxford: Blackwell, 2000).

Williamson, Craig, translator, *The Complete Old English Poems* (Philadelphia, PA: University of Pennsylvania Press, 2017). Kindle.

Wolfson, Sam, 'Kate Tempest: The Performance Poet Who Can't Be Ignored', *The Guardian* (10 April 2013). https://www.theguardian.com/books/ 2013/apr/10/kate-tempest-performance-poet-cant-be-ignored.

Woolf, Rosemary, *The English Religious Lyric in the Middle Ages* (Oxford: Clarendon, 1968).

Wootten, William, *The Alvarez Generation: Thom Gunn, Geoffrey Hill, Ted Hughes, Sylvia Plath, and Peter Porter* (Liverpool: Liverpool University Press, 2020).

Zahl, Simeon, *The Holy Spirit and Christian Experience* (Oxford: Oxford University Press, 2020).

Zieman, Katherine, 'The Perils of Canor: Mystical Authority, Alliteration, and Extragrammatical Meaning in Rolle, the Cloud-Author, and Hilton', *The Yearbook of Langland Studies* 22 (2008): 131–63.

INDEX

Adorno, Theodor
  on lyric 7, 14, 17, 96, 106–7, 112, 137
  on poetry after Auschwitz 141
  on parataxis 141–2
affectivity 6–7, 89, 93–4, 114, 120, 123, 158–9. *See also* lyric/affective-expressive
alliteration 25 n.118, 26, 37–8, 41, 47, 139
Anglo-Saxon poetry 20 n.95, 25–9
apophasis 19, 60, 128–9, 134
Aristotle 5, 9, 16 n.71, 132, 140
assonance 55, 78
Augustine
  Confessions 27, 118
  jubilatio 37 n.26, 38
  on the Spirit 75–6
  von Balthasar on 10–11

babble 34–5, 38–9, 41–2, 48–9, 61
Bakhtin, Mikhail 7, 12, 56
Balthasar, Hans Urs von 9–12, 67, 121, 155
  The Glory of the Lord 11
  Theo-Drama 10, 67
Begbie, Jeremy 33
Bennett, Louise, 'Colonization in Reverse' 51–2
Bernard of Clairvaux 40
Bernard, Jay, 'Patois' 60
Bhabha, Homi. *See* hybridity
Black British Poetry 49–62, 151–3
Blake, William 119, 140
  Marriage of Heaven and Hell 101–2, 104
  'Poetic Genius' 100–1
  on poetic inspiration 20, 100
  Songs of Innocence and Experience 101–6
Boethius 10, 37 n.26, 169
Brathwaite, Edward Kamau 51
breath
  atemwende (turn-of-breath) 144–6
  exhalation and breathlessness 18, 97, 145–6, 147
  of God 20, 29, 98
  inspiration 19–20
  as invocation 129–30
  in lyric poetry 115, 126
  in prayer 18, 74, 91–2, 94
  resurrection 16, 140, 147
  Spirit as breath 17–22 (*see also* Spirit)
  umbilical 135
  and word in the act of creation 19, 97, 135, 154
Breeze, Jean 'Binta', 'Simple Tings' 55
Brueggemann, Walter 112 n.84, 122
Buber, Martin 111, 121
Byron, Lord 161

Cædmon's Hymn 20, 26–7
cæsura 25 n.118, 26, 33, 74
Carey, Mary, elegies 73–6
Celan, Paul 145–6
Certeau, Michel de 60, 63
Clare, John 106–13, 129
  'I am' / 'I Feel I Am' 111–13, 129
Coakley, Sarah 21, 80, 90–1
Coleridge, S. T. 5, 7, 99, 108
creation as speech act 19. *See also* breath/and word
Culler, Jonathan. *See also* lyric/present
  as anti-theological 6, 15–16
  on lyric address 67–8, 76, 90
  on the lyric 'I' 96
  his lyric theory 15–17

Derrida, Jacques 97–8
Donne, John 76–82
  'Batter my Heart' 78–82
  'Good Friday, 1613, Riding Westward' 87–8
drama. *See* generic taxonomy (epic, lyric, dramatic)

eala 27–8
Eliot, T. S. 8, 76, 135–7, 148
English lyric tradition(s) 2–3, 22–5, 126–7
  accentual-syllabic metre 23
  anglocentrism 23–4

hip hop 115
iambic pentameter 19, 23, 51–2, 78
MLE 56–7, 60
multilingualism 42–3, 46, 48, 53
epic. *See* generic taxonomy (epic, lyric, dramatic)
episode 148–50, 152–3

Farrer, Austin, *Glass of Vision* 101
Ford, David 11, 48, 132
fragments 29, 96, 125–7, 148–9, 154
Frye, Northrop 8–9, 34–5, 68

generic taxonomy (epic, lyric, dramatic) 1 n.3, 4, 8–10, 16 n.71, 96, 125, 155, 157
  drama 2, 10–13
Gray, Thomas, 'The Bard' 99
Gregory of Nazianzus 80, 159
Grime 56–8

Hegel, G. W. F., *Aesthetics* 9, 95–6
Heidegger, Martin 2, 5
Herbert, George 24 n.115, 68, 84–9
  'Antiphon (I)' 85
  'The Call' 90–1
  The Country Parson 88–9
  'Prayer (I)' 91, 129
  rhetorical style 76
  'Sighs and Grones' 87
  The Temple 84–5
heteroglossia 56–7, 59–60
Hill, Geoffrey 126–7, 135–47
  density 138
  difficulty 137–8
  'A Pastoral' 139
  'Poetry as "Menace" and "Atonement"' 136, 138, 141
  'September Song' 142–4
  'Two Formal Elegies' 139
Hölderlin, Friedrich 141
Hopkins, Gerard Manley 143
hybridity 60–1
hymns 14, 25 n.117, 26, 45, 71, 96

inspiration. *See* breath
interruption 9 n.36, 60, 78, 143, 146, 149
invocation 22, 65, 76, 79, 80, 83, 90, 129
Irigaray, Luce 18

John of the Cross 11, 20, 92
Johnson, Linton Kwesi 52–3, 54

Keats, John 7, 67, 108
Kempe, Margery 37, 42
Kristeva, Julia 33

Lampe, Geoffrey 21
Levertov, Denise 78, 84
Lewis, C. S. 81
Lindbeck, George 11
Lok, Ann, 'A Meditation of a Penitent Sinner' 69–73
Lowth, Robert 98, 101, 105, 109
lullaby carols 40–1, 45
lyric
  address (*see* Culler, Jonathan)
  affective-expressive 6, 27, 65
  anti-lyricism 12, 14, 127, 141
  charm 6, 32, 39, 41, 158
  elegy 27–8, 73–6, 138–40, 142–4
  liturgical connections 17, 28, 38, 72, 74–5, 76, 83–6
  macaronic 42–8, 60–2
  New Lyric Studies 7–8, 14–15
  nonsense 29, 33–4, 38–9, 41, 63
  'O' 65, 67, 70, 76–8, 82–3, 107–9. (*See also* eala)
  ode 8, 14
  orality 5, 25–6, 36, 54–5, 96–7. (*See also* spoken word)
  pastoral 99, 101, 139, 144
  performance 14, 17, 19, 51, 54, 68, 84–6, 89, 115–20, 152
  present 160–1
  ritual quality 16–17, 66–7, 72, 83
  sequence 29, 72 n.37, 84, 119
  short 8, 125
  sweetness 32, 39–41, 47–8, 58, 61, 103, 140–2
  weave 32, 154

MacKinnon, Donald M. 13, 144, 146
melopoeia 126, 139–40
melos. *See* song
metaphor
  epistemological and theological implications 5, 35, 148
  in poetry 31, 32, 52, 59, 80, 142
Mill, John Stuart 7, 65, 136

Miller, Kei 51–2, 59
Milton, John 76
modernism 5, 8, 14, 127, 137

Nagra, Daljit, 'Look We Have Coming to Dover' 50 n.79
narrative 9 n.36, 72, 75, 132 n.36, 149–50, 155, 162 n.20
New Criticism 6, 14
Nietzsche, Friedrich 33

Olson, Charles 97 n.11, 126, 132
Ong, Walter 11, 97–8
Origen 91, 94
Orpheus 31

parataxis 126, 132, 141–4
Paterson, Don, *The Poem* 32
performance poetry. *See* spoken word
Pickstock, Catherine 83
Plato 7, 9, 16, 21
Pound, Ezra 5, 126, 141
prayer. *See also* breath
   'Abba!' 73, 75, 82, 92
   as battle 80
   as dialogue between 'I' and 'Thou' 67
   as flawed 81
   as irresistible 87
   lyric as the genre of 10, 22, 65
   poetry and 92, 129
   posture of 88–9
   public and private 73, 86, 93
   sincerity of 66, 68, 75, 84
   in the Spirit 90–2
   Spirit in 78, 83
preaching 20, 36, 76, 88–9
prophecy 20, 98, 100–1
   honesty 100
   as love song 104, 119
   as lyric testimony 98–9, 102–3, 113–14, 117, 122–3
   as universal 115
   voice of the Lord 98–100
public theology 121–4
punning (paranomasia) 42, 53–4

Rahner, Karl 11 n.49, 134, 158
rhetoric 6, 16, 33, 76–82, 93, 101, 159–60

rhyme 5, 17, 33–4, 84, 101
   in discussions of particular poems 41, 44–5, 47–8, 71, 74, 86, 139
rhythm 5, 17, 34, 77–8, 156, 158
   of breath 19, 137
   four-beat 36
   heartbeat 26, 51–2
   hip hop 58, 115
   of speech 23
Ricoeur, Paul 113, 117, 150
Robinson, Roger, *Portable Paradise* 54–5
Rolle, Richard 37–8, 40
Romanticism 2, 6–8, 10, 23, 95–100, 108, 113, 148
   Jungian 114

Shelley, Percy Bysshe 67, 83, 99
Shire, Warsan 127, 151–3
Sidney, Mary
   'Psalm 51' 70
   'Psalm 150' 85–6
Sidney, Phillip 76
Silence 19, 60, 128–30, 133–5, 145
Skelton, John 42
Smith, Michael (Mikey), 'Mi Cyaan Believe It' 54
Sonderegger, Katherine 21, 58, 156
song 8, 26–9, 78. *See also* Augustine/*jubilatio*; Blake/*Songs of Innocence and Experience*; Hill/'September Song'
   canor 37 n.29, 40
   copla 141
   of heaven 36–9, 43–4
   love song 46–8, 120
   melos 35–9
   Spirit as 40
   worship songs 93
sonnet 66, 69–70, 78–9, 85, 91, 112, 129, 139, 143
   volta 66, 143
Spirit. *See also* breath/Spirit as; song/Spirit as; testimony/of the Spirit
   circumambient 98, 132
   as hurricane 50
   as mixed, mingled or melded with humanity 21–2, 30, 94, 156
   as wind 17–19, 130, 132, 135, 146, 154

spoken word 54, 115–16
Steiner, George 33, 134
Stevenson, Debris 56–8

Tempest, Kae 99, 114–24
testimony
  of Christ 103
  prophetic 113–14, 117, 121
  of the self 122–3
  of the Spirit 72–3
Tracy, David 148–9
Trinity 21, 76, 79, 90

Watts, Isaac 24 n.115, 103
Wesley, Charles 24 n.115, 25 n.117,
  103
Williams, Charles 135 n.47, 138
Williams, Rowan 12, 35 n.20, 69 n.23,
  97 n.11, 147
Wittgenstein, Ludwig 5, 10, 12
Wordsworth, William 17, 95, 106, 108,
  115, 161
Wyatt, Thomas 70

Yeats W. B. 120, 136, 141

INDEX OF BIBLE VERSES

Genesis 1.1-3	11, 19, 126, 137, 145, 154	Hosea 7.8	61
1.28	35	Joel 2.28-29	115–16, 120
2.7	17–18		
11.1-9	35, 59, 61	Matthew 6.9-13	75
		15.11	121
Exodus 3.14	98, 110	25.29	121
15.1-21	9 n.36		
		Mark 7.15	121
Numbers 11.29	100, 115		
		Luke 2.29	75
2 Samuel 12.13-18	72	4.1-4	126, 146
1 Kings 19.12	18	John 1.23	99 n.24, 113, 119 n.111
Psalm 33.3	38	3.1-8	130, 132–3
33.4-6	18	3.28	113
51	69–73	20.22	18, 97 n.9, 155
78.39	18		
150	85–6, 92	Acts 2.1-8	18, 20 n.95, 31, 40, 45–6, 50, 61–2
Isaiah 5.1-7	104–5	2.16-18	114–16
11.2	42		
30.33	18	Romans 8.15-34	92
38	69	8.15-16	72, 75, 82, 91
40.3	99, 118, 124	8.26-27	78, 81, 87, 90 n.123
40.7	18		
47.8	110		
49.15	103	1 John 4.18	115
Lamentations 3.1	110–11	Revelation 3.20	79 n.65
		19.10	103
Ezekiel 33.32-33	103	21–22	113 n.87
37.1-14	147	22.17	22, 90–1, 156

www.ingramcontent.com/pod-product-compliance
Lightning Source LLC
Chambersburg PA
CBHW051524230426
43668CB00012B/1736